HIMALAYAN QUEST

PEARL HONG CHEN

Published by
ACA Publishing Ltd.
University House
11-13 Lower Grosvenor Place
London SW1W 0EX, UK
Tel: +44 20 3289 3885
E-mail: info@alaincharlesasia.com
Web: www.alaincharlesasia.com

Beijing Office
Tel: +86 (0) 10 8472 1250

Author: Pearl Hong Chen
Translator: Jiang Lin

Published by ACA Publishing Ltd in association with the China Translation & Publishing House

Original Chinese Text © 徒步喜马拉雅极地·与你相遇 *(Tú Bù Xī Mǎ Lā Yǎ Jí Dì Yǔ Nǐ Xiāng Yù)* 2014, China Translation & Publishing House, Beijing, China

English Translation © 2020, ACA Publishing Ltd, London, UK

ALL RIGHTS RESERVED. NO PART OF THIS PUBLICATION MAY BE REPRODUCED IN MATERIAL FORM, BY ANY MEANS, WHETHER GRAPHIC, ELECTRONIC, MECHANICAL OR OTHER, INCLUDING PHOTOCOPYING OR INFORMATION STORAGE, IN WHOLE OR IN PART, AND MAY NOT BE USED TO PREPARE OTHER PUBLICATIONS WITHOUT WRITTEN PERMISSION FROM THE PUBLISHER.

The greatest care has been taken to ensure accuracy but the publisher can accept no responsibility for errors or omissions, or for any liability occasioned by relying on its content.

Paperback ISBN: 978-1-910760-92-5
eBook ISBN: 978-1-910760-93-2

A catalogue record for *Himalayan Quest* is available from the National Bibliographic Service of the British Library.

HIMALAYAN QUEST

TREKKING A THOUSAND KILOMETRES ACROSS NEPAL

PEARL HONG CHEN

ACA PUBLISHING LTD

Some people are destined to belong to the wilderness and mountains...

CONTENTS

Author's Foreword	vii
Prelude	ix

CHAPTER I
WEARING FLOWERS ON THE WAY TO POKHARA

1. A wanderer starting from Lhasa	3
2. Why hippies travel to Kathmandu	7
3. No trekking, no paradise in Pokhara	13

CHAPTER II
ANNAPURNA GODDESS

1. First day of trekking in the shadow of death	25
2. Stopping at Tolka due to food poisoning	37
3. Seeking seclusion in nature	46
4. A beautiful path gets more beautiful because of you	59
5. Himalayan flowers and vertical limits	75
6. Follow the snow light of Fish Tail and wander	91
7. Retreat in the full moon at Annapurna	107
8. Lotus flowers and snow mountains	120
9. The Zen of walking and the beauty of the body	131
10. Larger space, more freedom	142
Notes: The greatest expense is seeing a doctor	153

CHAPTER III
PILGRIMAGE TO JOMSOM

1. Arriving with my feet on a lotus	159
2. God is the lighthouse in the eclipse	169
3. Bidding farewell means eternity	175
4. A broken jar can also reflect light	184
5. Life is a deep-rooted roving	203

CHAPTER IV
EVEREST DRUMMER

1. Departure: Smells like Teen Spirit	229

2. Low altitude: the sky turns blue because of you	238
3. High altitude: his love is for you	265
4. Being at home: Come as You Are	323
Postscript	337
Acknowledgments	341

AUTHOR'S FOREWORD
NO COURAGE REQUIRED IN TAKING A SINGLE STEP

Walking is a posture, a way of self-cultivation, a deep breath and a way of life. It is a state of physical and spiritual freedom that everyone can achieve thanks to their forthright and sincere natural instincts.

I used to be a feminine, home-bound sort of girl, living an urban life to the full and at maximum speed. I would not have thought myself capable of walking a million-and-a-half steps to the roof of world, the Himalayas, covering a thousand kilometres. I am often asked how I mustered the courage to complete this great journey. After pausing for thought, I reply that I just took one step after another before eventually reaching my destination.

It is romantic to tramp over hills and dales to see the world. We go to far-off places such as the polar regions and Mount Everest not simply to reach a specific destination but also to experience different lifestyles. There are countless distant places that one cannot reach in a lifetime. But if you want to enjoy different scenery, experience another life and seek a lightness of spirit, then pack your bags and begin your journey.

No courage is required in taking a single step forward.

PRELUDE

A ONCE-IN-A-LIFETIME TREK TO THE HIMALAYAS

There are times when we all need to experience the satisfaction of reaching a peak. It involves thoroughly remoulding oneself and tasting the ultimate beauty of life, which can serve as a pilgrimage for the soul.

Before going to the Himalayas, I had no idea about where the world's deepest canyons or most beautiful snow-capped mountains were located, or where the best trekking could be found. I just knew it to be the place with the world's highest mountain range and that it had been conquered by only a small number of crazy mountaineers. I never imagined that, one day, I could touch it with my own hands and feet.

There are only fourteen mountain peaks above 8,000 metres in the world, of which ten are in the Himalayas. Sixty-five million years ago, the Indian and Eurasian tectonic plates were separated by a beautiful blue ocean – the Tethys. The Indian plate to the south and the Eurasian plate to the north frequently collided, causing giant earthquakes and landslides, until the seawater drained away and the world's highest and youngest mountain system lifted up – the Himalayas.

It is difficult to appreciate the sheer scale of this mountain range. If it could be unfolded like a magic carpet, it would span the whole of Europe, from London in the west to Moscow in the east.

Stretching 2,400 kilometres from west to east and 200-300 kilometres from north to south, the Himalayas are home to most of the highest mountains on earth. More than forty mountain peaks have an elevation above 7,000 metres. The great peaks of these mountains stand higher than all other mountain ranges, all of them above a permanent snow line. These peaks block moist air blowing from the Indian Ocean, thereby creating a mild and humid climate with abundant rainfall on the southern mountain slopes of India, Nepal and Bhutan, and a dry and cold climate with scarce rainfall in the northern slopes of the mountain range in Tibet, China.

For thousands of years, the Himalayas have had a profound impact on ethnic groups living on both sides of the mountain range. Ancient Indian pilgrims called 'snow' *hima* and 'abode' *alaya*, thus creating the Sanskrit word 'Himalayas' (Place of Snow) for this majestic mountain system. In the Tibetan language, *chomo* means 'goddess' and *lungma* means 'third', and so the word for Mount Everest used affectionately by Tibetans is Chomolungma, the 'third goddess'. In Nepali, the mountain is called Sagarmatha, which means 'sky goddess'. All these names reflect local reverence for this mountain range and for nature more generally.

The Himalayas exert a major influence on people living either side of the mountain range

Today, the Himalayas have become one of the world's most attractive destinations for mountaineers and trekkers. Ever since the New Zealand mountaineer Edmund Hillary and the Nepali-Indian Sherpa mountaineer

Tenzing Norgay first ascended Mount Everest in 1953, twenty-four people have climbed the fourteen mountain peaks above 8,000 metres, and about 7,000 have climbed at least one of them.

Nepal, which is located at the southern foot of the mid-Himalayas, is sometimes known as 'a great little country'. It is roughly rectangular in shape, 885km wide from west to east and 177km long from north to south. On the map, it looks like a long, flat pea closely attached to the arc-shaped Himalayas. In essence, Nepal is a country of high mountains and it has many candidates for the title of the world's most beautiful scenic spot. Nepal is home to almost all the highest mountain peaks on earth, containing more than 240 mountains with an elevation of more than 6,000 metres. Among the ten highest peaks on Earth, eight of them are wholly or partially located in Nepal, of which the highest, Mount Everest, is situated on the border of Nepal and China.

Due to its special terrain, mountaineering and trekking are the best ways to take in the beauty of Nepal. Just imagine waking up on a sunny morning, sipping coffee on the terrace of a mountain hut and surrounded by snow-capped peaks. What else could rival such a moment? In terms of breathtaking mountain scenery, nothing can match a trek in the Himalayas.

Mountaineering became popular in Europe in the second half of the nineteenth century. After conquering the highest Alpine peak – Mont Blanc (4,810 metres) – Europeans turned their attention to the Himalayas, where the summits are considerably higher. In 1883, the Englishman William Woodman Graham went to Nepal and climbed a 6,000-metre mountain peak. After World War II, in 1951, Nepal opened its doors to foreigners and thereby ushered in a golden age of Himalayan mountaineering. The call of the wild has always aroused the adventurous spirit of human beings and inspired modern adventurers to explore each corner of Earth.

In the 1950s, adventure travel to the Himalayas often involved hiring a large number of labourers and Sherpas to transport supplies and mountaineering equipment. A team of porters might stretch several kilometres; sometimes, it could take a whole day for people at the end of the line to arrive at the destination after those in front. During an attempted ascent of Mount Everest in 1953, a British expedition team hired more than a hundred porters, ten of whom had the sole task of transporting coins. Much like the base of a pyramid, at the foot of the mountain a large team provides support to the relatively small number actually involved in climbing.

The word 'trek' is derived from the Boer language, meaning a long, hard journey

The Himalayas are not only a paradise for mountaineers, but also for trekkers. There is no public road directly to central Nepal. Therefore, the only way to reach this area is to cross countless mountains on foot. Many paths and mountain tracks have been worn away over a period of centuries or even thousands of years. Trekking, a word coined by Europeans, was used in the 1960s to describe mountaineering in Nepal, and since then it has become prevalent.

In Nepal, trekking involves joining queues of local people, walking along mountain trails, passing through distant villages and transcending tranquil mountains one after another, until the sacred land of a snow-capped mountain is reached with a campsite at its base. Taking in the most magnificent Himalayan sunrise and sunset and enjoying its tranquillity is the experience of a lifetime, like a magnificent banquet sent from heaven.

Trekking in the Himalayas is quite different from mountaineering. Mountaineering teams walk on the same paths favoured by trekkers in order to reach the base of a particular mountain, but their objectives are different. The appeal of trekking is to take in the natural landscape, religious conventions and cultural characteristics along the way.

There are no highways in central Nepal, so the only way to cross the region is to trek

In 1983, two British brothers, Richard and Adrian Crane, crossed the Himalayas from Darjeeling to Rawalpindi. They spent a hundred days completing this journey of 3,200 kilometres, ascending 8,400 metres in altitude and scaling sixty-five mountains.

In 1996, two French mountaineers Alexander Poussin and Sylvain Tesson, after cycling around the world, started another journey and spent 174 days trekking 2,500 kilometres in traversing the entire Himalayas from east to west.

"The Himalayan trekking trail is the best long-distance hiking trail in the world," says Apa Sherpa, a 51-year-old 'Super Sherpa' who has successfully climbed Mount Everest twenty-one times. Starting in January 2012, he spent 120 days completing a 1,700-kilometre trek across the incredible spine of the Himalayas.

Visitors can discover many unique attractions while trekking in the Himalayas, such as serene villages, stone huts and houses built in distinctive styles, pristine mountain wildernesses, fascinating temples and the allure of the yeti. Locals can be seen driving packhorses and donkeys or carrying heavy loads. After two or three hours of walking, you will come across villages and wooden huts where you can get food and accommodation or tea houses and stone terraces where you can take a break. Your hired Sherpa guide or porter from the Gurung ethnic group will faithfully protect you and carry your luggage up to the temple at the foot of each snow-capped mountain.

Villages offer food and lodging every two or three hours' trekking

Even though the journey may take weeks or months, there is no need to carry your own tent, sleeping bag or food. Nowhere else can you find the perfect trekking facilities that Nepal offers. Nowadays, hundreds of people arrive each year at Mount Everest's base camp, as this climb is no longer restricted to professional mountaineers such as Hillary and Tenzing Norgay. In the surrounding villages, you can meet locals from different ethnic groups. Their simplicity, friendliness and humour, as well as their various traditions and religious holidays, only add to the experience. Walking along mountain pathways, you will meet hikers from around the world, so you will feel far from alone. You will also come across strangers who share similar interests and objectives, and who show great kindness and offer sincere friendship.

As you progress further and higher, the highland grasslands, endless forests, flowing rivers and deep canyons replace peaceful scenes such as spring planting and autumn harvesting. The breathtaking mountain views change according to season and altitude. While your courage, strength, stamina, willpower and intelligence are tested, your soul is continually purified, improved and transcended.

The Himalayas give us such a broad, beautiful field of vision. They enable us to see our past, present and future. Every peak is like a book. In turning each exquisite page, I need to read those magnificent and poetic articles with my footsteps just like those pilgrims and monks of former times.

The spirit of the Himalayas smiles on us. Trekking touches our inner joy and energy every minute and second. Although there are countless beautiful scenes on Earth, nothing is more alluring than the high mountains against the backdrop of an azure sky.

CHAPTER I

WEARING FLOWERS ON THE WAY TO POKHARA

"You always lead a wandering life. But it is also your mental pursuit for freedom and fantasy." No matter what we have, lose, imagine or chant in the starry sky and dark night along the blue Lhasa River, the Himalayas in my mind is not in Lhasa, Barkhor Street, the Potala Palace or Ngari Prefecture.

It is on the way!

Nepal used to be the fairyland of hippies. Is it a paradise? No one knows. The sweet sound of bells and the happy smiles generate the deepest love in the heart. Such smiles can influence people's mood and status and even the entire world. I do indeed live there.

DAY ONE

A WANDERER STARTING FROM LHASA

IF A PLACE EXISTS that is worth a thousand return visits, it must be the Himalayas in Nepal.

I got my visa in Lhasa at 2pm, when the sun was strong and dazzling. I made a long-distance call to Basanta, my friend in the central Nepalese city of Pokhara. He was the boss of Annapurna Trekking Company, located on the southern side of the Himalayas.

I was born and raised in southern China, where the Pearl River fans out into a delta. I'm a daughter of this river, where oyster shells grow slowly and quietly, and sometimes host crazy grains of sand that will later be turned into shining pearls. This is why I was named Pearl. Buddha once compared the cosmos to a vast net or river composed of innumerable bright, clean pearls. Each tiny pearl has a multitude of invisible facets and each Mani stone can reflect other pearls in the net or in the river and contain the secret images of other pearls.

Now I feel that my body is flowing upstream like a small drop of water or like thousands of freshwater fish swimming upriver and returning to lay eggs in the place of their birth. The end of the flowing water is the source of all rivers. It is the pure, sacred snow mountain. The ancient Hindu poets held the view that glaciers and snow-capped ranges were created by the thunderous laughs of Shiva, the God of Creation and Destruction. The laughs were crystal white and the river, like shining silk clothes, flowed naturally from the head of Shiva. When I looked up, I saw Kathmandu, Pokhara, Nepal and the Himalayas.

A traveller with temporary residence in the body

I have visited Lhasa plenty of times in order to get a visa or make flight connections. Lhasa is the destination of numerous travellers and the spiritual centre for Tibetan Buddhists. It is extraordinarily crowded, bustling and prosperous.

The word 'body' is vividly described as 'I' in Tibetan, meaning 'the stuff left behind', just like luggage. The word 'I' in English refers to 'self'. When I say 'I' in Lhasa, I seem to remind myself that I am only a passer-by, a temporary resident, a wanderer on foot, a dream catcher weaving a net of dreams or a knight flying on a sheepskin drum. Lhasa seems to be the transfer station of my soul and the graveyard for my reincarnation. The temporary tranquillity in my body is like the first stage of my life, but my soul will go on a long, distant journey. I will continuously trek through this life and into a future world.

The flight from Lhasa to Kathmandu passed over the undulant Himalayas at ten o'clock on that sunny morning. The ten world-class snow peaks above 8,000 metres would be the destination of my journey in search of mental cultivation. The stretching, enormous Kanchenjunga is 8,586 metres above sea level. It is the world's third highest peak. Ten minutes later, we flew over Lhotse, 8,516 metres high, the world's fourth highest peak, followed by Makalu, 8,463 metres high and Cho Oyu, 8,201 metres high. They were like proud princes clustering around the Third Goddess, Mount Everest, at 8,848 metres, towering into the sky.

Thinking of those mountaineers who had scaled Mount Everest at almost the same altitude as many passenger planes crossing the sky, I was amazed at the daring and whimsical nature of mankind.

Through the plane window, I stared at the ramparts of the peaks of more than 7,000 metres, known as the roof of the world. Only then could I appreciate the courage and ambition of those trekkers and mountaineers.

No matter whether remnants of the ark built by Noah can actually be found on Mount Ararat in Turkey or whether the Himalayan range is home to gods, the peaks are still the most fascinating places.

Bringing the heart home

The philosophy in the Himalayas that has prevailed for more than 2,000 years is that this is a home for everyone, a place of purity and peacefulness. I can picture the Buddha sitting serenely, solemnly in meditation beside a banyan tree at the foot of a snow-covered mountain with a clear, blue sky above. Everything seems to be in perfect harmony, transparent and unobstructed.

When I sit as still as a mountain, my heart, like the sky, rises, leaps, soars and unfolds itself. The pearl and the river, the running water and the mountain, the sky and the earth, the mortal world and the paradise give me the wings to fly like a bird. I am bestowed with a determination to keep on living in this world under a boundless sky.

A number of trekkers, backpackers and wanderers eager to cross the border at Zhangmu from the northern slope of the desolate Himalayas in

Tibet to its southern side covered by dense forests were gathered together on Xianzu Island in the Lhasa River. Many travellers from Tibet and Lhasa congregate in this place where, according to legend, celestial beings reside. They jokingly refer to it as a 'honeymoon nest after a romantic encounter'. The natives of Lhasa are not interested in making romantic encounters like foolish travellers but bask in the sun, listen to Buddhist music, drink beer and cook barbecues on the banks of the slow-moving Lhasa River.

The livestock walking leisurely on the mountainsides enshrouded by variegated shadows in the closing light sound like Sanskrit from heaven. Travellers hang out, wander, conduct romantic affairs and then form groups to travel further in this paradisal land.

In a small bar near Lhamo Latso Lake, sitting on a bed used for meditation, a large group of young people were singing along to a number by the itinerant singer, Nan Liu: "We were born lonely, we were born lonely." I listened to Nan Liu's singing accompanied by guitar right up until daybreak.

The Lhasa River at the misty dawn was devoid of everything but golden sand, fish and the sweet melancholy of departure.

It reminded me of a verse by the ascetic monk Milarepa: "You always lead a wandering life. But it is also your mental pursuit for freedom and fantasy." No matter what we have, lose, imagine or chant under the starry sky and on dark nights along the blue Lhasa River, the Himalayas in my mind do not reside in a particular location, in Lhasa, on Barkhor Street, the Potala Palace or Ngari Prefecture.

They lie in the journey.

Even the smallest, least significant thing can enjoy the spring. The wild lily also has its own spring. My best time is always while travelling.

DAY TWO

WHY HIPPIES TRAVEL TO KATHMANDU

IF I HAVE NO ONE to turn to when I get old, I'd like to live in a quiet environment. When it is time for me to depart, I'd like to melt in the snowy Himalayas.

Arriving at Tribhuvan international airport in Kathmandu, I told myself that I would either live a leisurely, sunny life or trek for adventure.

Kathmandu, with a population of one million, has more than 2,700 temples, one for every 370 people. There are as many pictures or statues of a god or of the Buddha as there are citizens. The famous poet Laxmi Prasad Devkota could not help chanting: "You are a temple in my high admiration."

All sorts of religions and beliefs are gathered here, including Hinduism, Buddhism, Christianity, Islam and Shamanism. Kathmandu is variously known as 'City of Light', 'City of Temples' and 'Paradise of the Himalayas'. Air passing over the warm current of the Indian Ocean blows across the vast Indo-Gangetic and Terai plains, rising gracefully as it approaches the magnificent Himalayas and Kathmandu Valley, presenting a picturesque scene of bright sun and blooming flowers.

The hippies sang 'K-K-K-Kathmandu' on their way to Kathmandu

Hippies and flower children

During the 'Summer of Love' gathering in 1967 in San Francisco, hippies and flower children beamed with smiles and pledged to 'make love, not war'. They did as they liked and dressed how they liked. Many walked bare foot and wore cheap bead necklaces, embroidered gowns, ripped jeans and flowing long dresses. Lilac garlands were draped around their necks and some of their faces were painted. They held incense sticks while humming the famous Scott McKenzie song, *San Francisco*, or chanted the Bob Seger number *Going to K-K-K-Kathmandu*. Making the long journey to this land of their dreams, they would fly to Istanbul and from there travel overland via Pakistan and Afghanistan or take the sea route to Goa or Bombay. Like a breeze drifting over a warm current, they arrived in Kathmandu and Pokhara at the foot of the Himalayas, in the hope of finding tranquillity.

The rolling peaks give birth to a pure terrestrial land and isolate the turmoil in this world. Singers, travelling musicians, recluses, ascetic monks and spiritualists have all come here, enjoying simple pleasures and pursuing the search for a more complete and meaningful life. The British singer Cat Stevens spent three months in Kathmandu's central market square, Asan Tole, writing *Katmandu* in a smoky tea room: "Katmandu I'll soon be seeing you, and your strange bewildering time will hold me down." During this time, his wife eloped with another man and he developed tuberculosis and indulged in alcohol and drugs. Despite these problems, however, he managed to achieve spiritual tranquillity and release in the religion and snowy peaks of Nepal.

Danny Ben-Israel, the Israeli musician who joined the army and fought to protect his homeland, wrote a song as he started his own journey to Kathmandu. "We heard many rumours that marijuana was readily available on the streets and in the drugstores of Kathmandu. So we sat in Tel Aviv and dreamed of flying there one day." His whimsical song *Take a Trip to Kathmandu* was a call for hippies to make the long journey to the City of Light.

Flowers, yaks, pagodas and yetis

More than five decades later, Kathmandu remains an intoxicating 'back garden' for Western travellers and a 'fairyland on Earth' for European and American hippies and those young Asians who are dissatisfied with what life back home has to offer. This is a country of flowers, yaks, pagodas, yetis and Sherpas.

Kathmandu is a worldly paradise of overlapping and mutually-influencing time, cultures, races and beliefs. The air seems to contain the breath of Hindu's living goddess, Kumari, the vitality and energy of Shiva, the God of Love, the spirit of European and American hippies from the 1960s, the fragrance of Indian curries and Nepalese sandalwood, the florid cashmere shawls of the Kashmiris and their mournful, olivaceous eyes...

Kathmandu is actually a hotchpotch of influences from the previous millennium, and it is both ancient and modern at the same time. The scenes of dreamers and drifters, like those in *A Tale of Two Cities*, are displayed here every day. In the minds of all travellers eager for love, freedom and enjoyment, Kathmandu has two overriding characteristics. The first is a chaotic metropolis bustling with sacred cows, monkeys, ascetic monks, slum dwellings and car fumes. You can get lost in the dazzling beauty of its exquisite lanes. It requires both creativity and patience to forge a path through the winding, narrow streets that are often without signs.

Kathmandu is a melting pot of past and present, antiquity and modernity

The other chief element is religion, featuring all sorts of spice, incense, tinkling bells, chants and marigold garlands, where the red-brick temples with towering pinnacles are set amid omnipresent blue water, azure skies and magnificent snowy peaks. These sights, sounds and smells purify the mind and help eradicate desire, self-indulgence and psychological trauma.

In Kathmandu, you can be a naked monk, a hedonistic hippie, a Beatle dreaming of eternal youth, a peacenik looking for mixed marriage, Eastern worship or environmental harmony, or a mountaineer, an adventurer, backpacker or trekker. You may even become a ray of clean sunshine, a glittering silver coin or an exotic Xi Shi (one of the renowned four beauties of ancient China) in the eyes of your lover.

Walking along Freak Street in Basantapur Square in Kathmandu, it is easy to imagine the time when this was once a famous hippie street that resonated with the rhythms and melodies of *Katmandu* by Bob Seger and The Silver Bullet Band.

Originally called Jhochhen Tole, this ordinary-looking street close to Hunuman Dhoka and Shiva-Parvati Temple embraced Western travellers who rebelled against society and was renamed 'Freak Street' because of the numerous hippies who gathered there. 'Freak', meaning bizarre, weird and unconventional, is also the antithesis of 'square', a word used to describe conservative groups who conform to social conventions. 'Flower children' found a paradise on Earth. They spoke different languages, wore their long hair down loosely, deftly ate spicy rice dishes with their right hand, donned white Hindu robes or bright yellow Buddhist cassocks and devoutly revered these Eastern religions. Their licentious behaviour forced the Nepalese government to rigorously restrict the entry of hippies into the country.

Visited by singers, painters, dancers, writers, travellers, occultists and rave artists from all over the world, Thamel in northern Kathmandu became a new base camp for travellers. It remains a magnet for young people, drawn by old editions of the *Kama Sutra* left by hippies in the second-hand bookshops in Freak Street, along with the trumpets of shuttling tricycles, the call of vendors hawking fresh juice and the cheap inns, bars and tea rooms that resonate with mystery and decadence.

In those years, the hippies chose a freedom that ignored society. And today, a new generation of hippies still reject what they regard as the detestable, materialistic adult world. The carnal world, with its narrow lives, mortgage slaves, mistresses and sex scandals, is vulnerable. We yearn for the innocent Garden of Eden and the Utopian dream and turn to the infinite power of individual wishes and the magical power of belief. Although the hopes and dreams that prevailed in the era of Martin Luther King and the specific objective of an ideal human community and brotherhood may be out of date, hippies still exist in popular culture across the world, have become classic and revolutionary idols. The lifestyle of hippies is still fresh and alive.

Nepal used to be a fairyland of hippies. Is it a paradise? No one knows.

The sounds of many different bells, the sight of so many smiles can generate a feeling of love and influence people's moods.

I do indeed live there.

DAY THREE

NO TREKKING, NO PARADISE IN POKHARA

THE WARM SEPTEMBER wind stirred the long, loose hair of the flower children. The loud, enchanting music, together with the river and the rising incense smoke, lingered in the azure sky. Thousands of flower children were sitting on temple terraces in the old towns of Patan and Pathi and in seating areas for pilgrims, enjoying the last feast of the hippy era, while I, the next morning, left the boisterous Thamel in Kathmandu and took a colourful tourist bus that bumped, rocked and rolled its way to Pokhara at the foot of Fish Tail Peak.

The bumpy King's Highway

Kathmandu is surrounded by valleys, but only two main highways exist beyond the capital: one is the Arniko Highway that runs northeast to Tibet and the other is the Prithvi Highway that runs west along the roaring Trisuli River to Pokhara. These two thrilling highways that wind into and out of the valley remind me of the merciless valley floor as described by Jin Yong, the martial arts writer. In one of his books, *Little Dragon Maiden*, the head of the Ancient Tomb Sect finds a way out of the valley by carving characters on the wings of bees.

In olden times, it took ten days to travel from Kathmandu to Pokhara on horseback. The journey involved fording numerous freezing rivers, and many died in the process. Elephants and packhorses were used for labour and transportation. An imported car bought by King Tribhuvan was actually carried into the capital by groups of people. Packhorses were used on the Prithvi Highway until it was paved with cobblestones and opened to vehicles in 1970.

Sitting in a car being driven on the 206km-long highway named after King Shah, I experienced what it was like to travel on the crazy 'Hippy Highway'.

It may be one of the busiest roads in Nepal, but it's quite unlike what most people would think of as a national highway. It is more like a country trail, with innumerable craters and potholes. The mountain road that snakes for tens of kilometres is crowded with Tata vans, large and small, along with shabby little buses, Indian-made Bolero SUVs, a multitude of Chinese-made motorbikes, tractors, sacred cows, sheep, dogs, chickens and wandering children, all moving in different directions and at different speeds. Every few yards, the car would jerk in a kind of spasm, and the passengers inside would shriek.

Preparing to set off on the crazy, 206km-long 'Hippy Highway'

Rocks situated along the highway are painted with red warning signs: 'Slow driving brings happiness, speeding leads to hell!', 'Better late than dead!', 'Peace, love and care!' The mottled handwriting has been eroded by the weather, and the drivers seemed to ignore the messages, frantically trying to find gaps in the traffic. It was then that I finally understood why walking is one of the most popular modes of transport in this hilly landscape. It is simply the most relaxing and comfortable way to get around.

Though my body was being jolted, my eyes were flying in heaven. The scenery along the way was quite beautiful as the road passed through one deep valley after another, winding along an emerald green river, passing by ancient stone houses and golden paddy terraces. The locals drove their livestock over narrow, teetering bridges that spanned canyons, with bamboo baskets of fresh grass on their backs, walking with great ease.

Tucked amid the rolling hills are some of Nepal's most important religious shrines. The Manakamana Mandir on the Mugling Mountain Road is not only one of central Nepal's oldest temples, but also an important Hindu pilgrimage site. During festivals, it is almost overwhelmed with worshippers and animals. The Hindu goddess Parvati, wife of Shiva, one of the three main gods in Hinduism, is reputed to make wishes come true, so young couples flock here in cars, praying that they can have a boy, a bit like what happens in rural China. Several of the vehicles going up the mountain have special compartments for keeping pigeons and goats. Worshippers sacrifice them on a bloody altar beside the temple. Witnessing the blood sacrifice, foreigners will often leave the scene open-mouthed and with their hands covering their eyes.

The bouncing vehicle continued its journey westwards, passing Bandipur, the ancient Gurkha capital during the Shah dynasty. In its early days, Gorkha was a tiny country that pledged allegiance to the capital city, Kathmandu. However, Prithvi Narayan Shah was born there and became the new conqueror of the Kathmandu Valley and the founder of modern Nepal. He established a kingdom bordering India and China's Tibet in 1769. Gurkha warriors holding the famous *kukri*, the national sword of Nepal, would later serve in Britain's boldest and most powerful regiment during the two world wars. They could instantly cut off a head with their *kukris*. So if you park your car in order to take a break in dusty Bandipur, be sure to smile at the Gurkha man in his tea stall and make friends with him rather than complain about the muddy-looking Nepalese milk tea he is selling. It is never a good idea to make an enemy of these men from the mountains with their hook noses and dark complexions.

Gurkha warriors, armed with kukris, carry oxen and sheep to offer sacrifices in the temple

It also makes sense to be careful. Travellers should always be prepared to be kind to others, as the Chinese saying goes. I smiled to myself as I drank the spiced milk tea.

Sitting next to me in the car were a mother and daughter who had just returned from a trip to Kathmandu to see her husband. Young Nepalese women are as slim as princesses, but once they get married and give birth, their waists become as thick as buckets. To save money, the mother hadn't bought a ticket for her daughter. During the entire hot journey of seven hours, we three sat like fried dumplings, squeezed on two narrow seats. The back of the seat of a Chinese traveller in front of us was broken and this cramped us further. I had to repeatedly ask her to move her seat forward a little, saying we had a child with us.

I told the nine-year-old Salona: "Shall we rename the King's Road as 'Jumping Road' or 'Monkey Road'?" She nodded her head softly, then threw up. Later, when I saw her in deep sleep, leaning on her mother's arms and with her long eyelashes and small nose ring trembling slightly, I felt a kind of wordless, maternal love gushing inside me.

Salona sitting on the narrow seat next to me

When I was a child in China, my mother carried me like that and we travelled in all sorts of shabby vehicles. She was a regional table tennis champion and an important art designer in her work unit. She often took part in table tennis competitions and travelling art exhibitions held in state-owned coal companies. When she played table tennis, she asked me to read by myself in the guest house where we were staying; when she was preparing an exhibition, she entrusted me to the waiters and asked them to feed me. Without doubt, my natural instincts for travelling were inherited from my mother.

My leg-numbing journey in Nepal reminded me of reading *The Adventures of Tintin* when I was a child. I dreamed of travelling around the world with a cute wire fox terrier like Snowy and leaving my footprints in the Congo, Egypt, China, the Red Sea and even on the Moon, like Tintin, a young journalist with a blond quiff... Adventure, long journeys, bonfires, camping, nightingales, unicorns and happy encounters all sprang into my mind. The little Nepalese girl made me think of my own childhood and rekindled my dream of becoming a knight in a distant land.

When we were thirty kilometres from Pokhara, the 'Monkey Road' entered the vast alluvial plain of the Seti River and the imposing Fish Tail Peak appeared clearly like a beacon under a clear and distant sky. The local Nepalese I met liked to sit on the bus roof and thereby pay only half fare. They would expose their bodies to the sun and wind, and enjoy looking up at the peaks that were calling to them.

The scene reminded me of my dog Xiaoban (Little Spot), which always stuck its head out of the car window with its hair and ears flapping in the wind when we drove to Miyaluo in Tibet. How cool that was!

If you ever get the chance, you too would enjoy the excited, elated expressions of others taking the same journey.

Pokhara trekking base camp

When the Swiss explorer Toni Hagen visited in 1952, Pokhara was just a small rural town where Newars and Gurungs lived. The only vehicles were buffalo carts being pulled along streets dotted with Newari-style red brick houses. There were no proper roads.

In the footsteps of this lonely, brave explorer to Pokhara came a large crowd of Western hippies via the King's Highway. The gorgeous scenery of the area, along with its slow pace of life and abundant marijuana, provided the perfect destination for the flower children on the South Asian land route. The hippies pitched large tents or stayed in rundown inns around Phewa Lake in Pokhara. They smoked weed, listened to psychedelic music and absorbed the intoxicating scenery before them – the snowy peaks and bright blue lakes. They were happy to trade the conventional society and vulgar bourgeois life of the West for a true highland civilisation and indigenous tribal totemism in Pokhara.

As a Mecca for hippies, Pokhara witnessed a special, brilliant period in its history. Today, however, travellers come for the trekking, rafting, mountaineering, flying, cycling or exploring. They are equipped with backpacks, pickaxes, ankle boots, spiked shoes, paddles, inflatable dinghies, parachutes and mountain tyres, and listen to John Lennon's *Imagine* – "Imagine all the people, living for today / Imagine all the people, living life in peace." They also come with new reasons to visit the Himalayas. They pursue the essence of power, self-confidence, courage and fearlessness, and the unrestrained, vehement and ethereal realm of love.

Three of the ten highest mountains above 8,000 metres are situated in Pokhara. Among them, Annapurna I, at a height of 8,091 metres, was the first of the ten to be scaled and Dhaulagiri, at a height of 8,167 metres, was the last, hence it is known as 'Devil's Peak' or 'Killer Mountain'. Another one of the ten, the magnificent Manaslu, stands at a height of 8,163 metres and is known as 'Holy Mountain'.

Picture the scene: an inverted image of snowy mountains in the tranquil Phewa Lake and Begnas Lake, like blue eyes reflecting the green of Pokhara, lush with plant life.

Most of the travellers come here for the Himalayas but Pokhara is the best place to appreciate the six peaks: Hiunchuli (6,441 metres) and the five majestic Annapurna Peaks of Annapurna I, Fish Tail Peak (6,997 metres), Annapurna II (7,937 metres), Annapurna III (7,555 metres) and Annapurna IV (7,525 metres) tower above the city and the lakes. If you raise your head a little, you can see at least one or two snow-covered mountains. There are two charming images of each mountain: one in the sky, the other reflected in the lake.

Nepal was the birthplace of Sakyamuni Buddha, and it contains the world's highest peaks, deepest valleys and best places for rafting, trekking and paragliding. Many young people are fanatical about outdoor exploration and extreme sports, and Nepal is among the top destinations for these activities.

The Himalayas offer great opportunities for mountaineering and trekking and challenging routes for mountain biking. Pokhara is regarded as a leading venue for rafting and canoeing, with its many rivers tumbling down the mountains and along the valleys. If you don't actually go rafting or canoeing in the Himalayan rivers, you won't know how thrilling and exciting life can be. Or try bungee jumping from a height of 160 metres above the floor of a Himalayan valley, or flying into the blue sky and the snow-covered Annapurna Peaks in a paraglider. Pokhara has become one of the world's best places for paragliding. Moreover, the cost of extreme sports, whether it be mountaineering, trekking, rafting, mountain biking, paragliding or bungee jumping, is only about half of that in the United States, New Zealand, Kenya or Argentina.

Pokhara is a city noted for its dramatic landscapes and is sometimes known as the 'Switzerland of the East'. The strong aroma of incense floats in the air. The noise made by independent travellers penetrates the quiet, clear air of the mountains and plains. The Hindu chants and the Sanskrit mantra 'Aum, mani, padme, hum' linger in the hundreds of cafés, bars, internet shops and stores selling CDs, drums, prayer flags, carpets, perfume and outdoor goods. Hundreds of riverside family inns, flophouses and hotels accommodate the backpackers and trekkers of different complexions and speaking different languages, all anticipating their journey to the high mountains and lakes.

No one can accurately sum up what Pokhara is really like. Pokhara is at the end of the Annapurna circuit trail and also the starting point of several trekking routes in the Annapurna Peaks, including treks to Annapurna Base Camp and Upper Mustang, pilgrimages to the village of Jomsom and panoramic trekking tours. Trekking in the Annapurna Peaks has become extremely popular. A series of mountain trekking routes of various degrees of difficulty and at altitudes ranging from 2,000 to 5,000 metres offer trekkers panoramic views of the magnificent Himalayas. While challenging, trekking is less difficult than climbing and offers superior facilities in terms of inns and campsites along the way. The snow mountains around Pokhara have long been an important base for preparation and training for international mountaineers to climb the snowy Himalayan peaks at an altitude of more than 8,000 metres. Each year, more than 100,000 mountaineering enthusiasts travel to Pokhara, which has become known as a 'trekking paradise' to travellers across the world.

For most travellers, Pokhara is the last comfortable place on their journey, where they can enjoy lamb rogan josh, Sichuan cuisine, grilled lake fish and cold beer before setting out on their journey of exploration. On returning from the mountains where the only dishes on offer are hyacinth bean soup and other vegetarian options, you can taste the delights of pan-fried beef steak with black pepper or Chongqing spicy hot pot.

The imposing mountains, gorgeous lakes and soul-stirring majesty of nature arouse the heartfelt reverence of travellers. It made me devoutly set out alone, act modestly, think calmly and experience the secret of a perfect life.

Although we do not have wings, we are always soaring.

ITINERARY

Chongqing-Lhasa, flight time

2.5 hours; land distance: 2,145km, seven days; altitude: Chongqing 400 metres, Lhasa 3,650 metres

Lhasa-Kathmandu, flight time

1 hour 12 minutes; land distance: 900km, 20 hours; altitude: Lhasa 3,650m, Kathmandu 1,337m

Kathmandu-Pokhara, flight time

30 minutes; land distance: 206km, 7hr.; altitude: 884m at Pokhara

Running lines

Kathmandu to Malekhu to Mugling to Dumre to Bandipur to Pokhara

CHAPTER II

ANNAPURNA GODDESS

"Why climb Mount Everest?"

"Because it is there."

I like to wander, following in the footsteps of Mallory, feeling his presence on my back or beneath my feet. People's facial appearance, skin tone, body shape, stamina and posture all change over time and in different environments, but only the colour of their eyes remains the same. I feel that trekking fully reflects some peculiar, unchangeable idiosyncrasies in my character. They are immutable, just like the colour of my eyes.

Between spring, when the ice and snow melt, and winter, when the mountains are covered in heavy snow, the shepherds take their families up to the high mountains. When I rummaged through my pockets and took out my last two 'Alps' sweets, a little shepherdess with a round, brown face asked me: "Madam, which valley do you live in?" Her innocent question made me reconsider the mystery and beauty of the valley and the poetic quality and essence of the world.

DAY ONE

FIRST DAY OF TREKKING IN THE SHADOW OF DEATH

It was three in the afternoon when the bus arrived in Pokhara. Having fetched my large backpack from the storage area, I found that it was wet. It wasn't hard to work out how it had happened. Just like me, the bag had been jolted during the seven-hour journey and was exposed to the wind and rain. I couldn't worry over such trifles and straight away hired a compact Suzuki taxi at a cost of 150 rupees to take me to the Himalayan Hotel. After washing my dirty, wet clothes, I rented a bicycle with a basket from a bike shop near the hotel and cycled all the way to Basanta, boss of the Annapurna Trekking and Paragliding Company.

I was to return there three years later and immediately recalled the familiar scene: the streets, the stores, the throngs of people, the sacred cows, the sunshine, the dust and smell. I asked myself: Have I been away so long? Am I really here once more?

Basanta, weighing ninety kilograms and wearing a T-shirt and jeans, hugged me passionately. "Didi, you're still in good shape!" he said, calling me by the name the Nepalese give their sisters.

Yes, time, like a butcher's knife, ages people, but one's outlook can remain unchanged. To prepare for my visit to the Himalayas, I had spent an hour every evening in August climbing the mountains in Chongqing. After giving Basanta a small box of Chinese green tea, I said: "Bai, please bring me the map. Where's my guide? I plan to set out tomorrow."

Then my guide came in. He was called Chebat, twenty-eight years old and from the Gurung ethnic group, one of the main Gurkha tribes. He had very dark skin, and he was slightly taller than me and not particularly handsome. This left me somewhat disappointed, but to his credit he was well built, agile, spoke good English and had worked as a guide for ten years. We drew a route that would take about ten days to complete. We agreed on a fee of eighteen dollars a day for his guiding services, and then he took me to the hotel on his motorbike, checked out my backpack and clothing, and promised to pick me up at half-past six the next morning.

However, by 8am Chebat had still not shown up and his mobile phone was switched off. I became anxious so I called Basanta, but he couldn't reach him either. Basanta asked me whether he should send another guide. But I thought that, since I'd established a connection with Chebat, I'd wait a little longer and give him the chance to earn some money.

That morning, when I came down for breakfast in the hotel's dining room, I read the English edition of the Nepalese newspaper *Himalayan Trekking*. It was then that I saw the news that a mountaineering team from France and Russia had got caught up in a snow slide while climbing Manaslu, the world's eighth highest peak. Nine of them died and six were missing, including the Nepalese guide and porter. The Manaslu Circuit is one of the best treks in Nepal (*manaslu* means 'soul' in Sanskrit). Maybe part of the appeal of mountaineering lies in its difficulty and unpredictability, and the inherent dangers that come with them.

Wearing a garland of flowers and leaves, a typical Nepali way of welcoming guests

At 4pm Basanta sent another guide called Bikram to the hotel. They had received news that Chebat's family were missing and he had returned to his home village in Gurung. My heart went out to him. These dangers now felt so close.

I unpacked my backpack again so that Bikram could check my clothes and supplies. I would be trekking in the mountains for about ten days, so I decided to leave behind all unnecessary items since they would be a burden for the guide who would be carrying the load. I wore clothes like an onion, one layer on top of another to keep me warm when it was cold, and easy to take off down to my T-shirt when it got hot. I even left out some everyday drugs and instead only took some remedies for colds and altitude sickness. That decision nearly cost me my life.

My backpack now weighed only twelve kilograms, minus Bikram's satchel which he put into my big bag. The distant snow mountains and wilderness were summoning me. I thought of what the American activist Martin Luther King once said: "You don't need to see the whole staircase, just take the first step."

I started my journey early the next morning.

Why go trekking?

Phedi, the starting point of the journey to the long-anticipated Annapurna Base Camp, was actually just the entrance to a mountain path with a few prayer flags draped alongside. There was little around but a few thatched shops and some small buses parked up. It was barely even a village. I asked Bikram to put my backpack on a stone pedestal under a banyan tree and we had our photo taken together.

Everyone was elated to be stepping onto the mountain path. We were now in a position to leave our past lives behind and begin the march towards the unknown. Asked why they trek, a thousand trekkers might give you a thousand answers. They might cite the gorgeous scenery or the desire to lose weight, improve their body shape or kick a drug habit. It might simply be the adventure, the challenge, fervent devotion, or to escape from pollution and enjoy a greener lifestyle. Others seek some relief from the stresses of their busy lives, to purify their soul or go on a pilgrimage and transcend the bondage of life and death... I trek for all of these reasons.

Before I set out on my journey, my mother was unexpectedly diagnosed with advanced lung cancer. As a Christian and volunteer worker, I made it a habit each Christmas Eve to stay with sick friends in hospital. But that year I spent Christmas Eve with my mother in hospital. Since I left home to study at the age of fourteen, I hadn't lived with her for any length of time. I didn't even know that she had produced so many great works of art, including scrolls that were so long that they could only be painted by lying on the floor.

Phedi, the starting point of the journey to Annapurna Base Camp

It was the first time that I had been at her bedside in hospital. I brought my favourite gladioli and plum blossom to the ward, helped her take a bath, cleaned her body, washed her hair, scrubbed he underclothes by hand, wrung her towel dry, took her for a walk, cooked, cut what hair remained after chemotherapy so that she looked like a handsome boy, wrapped a scarf around her neck, put a hat on her, catalogued her paintings and organised a solo painting and calligraphy exhibition for her. My mother's name was Silver Pearl, just like her silvery, shining, innocent heart.

For the first time, we talked about life and death in a frank manner. As someone who had left home early, I'd been thinking that our mutual affection was rather fragile. But I still felt pain when she ached. It was not until she went into hospital that I knew our hearts were bound together and how much I loved her.

. . .

My mother became ill at the age of forty-two and underwent a thoracotomy. She divorced at fifty-one, realising that she had a different temperament, interests and hobbies to her husband. She loved her painting, while my father was a businessman. She was fifty-six when my brother was killed in a struggle with two criminals who were trying to steal his car. At sixty-nine, she was diagnosed with cancer. Many times, I could not help questioning why God had made my mother suffer so much pain and hardship. But when I unpacked her Buddhist paintings, I suddenly understood that we were born to suffer and only though suffering could we get purified.

I stopped writing, having nearly finished my book *Across Paradisal Xinjiang*. That was because, as an only child following the death of my brother, I was my mother's spiritual prop. Holding her hands in mine, I accompanied her during that eight-month struggle in hospital, wandering in the cold, clinical environment of that building, with her so close to death, and helplessly watching her undergo six rounds of chemotherapy that overwhelmed her with sorrow. She survived chemotherapy due to her extraordinary willpower. Her bone marrow results showed that the cancer cells were now under control.

We returned home in midsummer, a time of growth and resurrection. My mother was strong enough to spend an hour or two each day on her exquisite brush paintings of flowers and birds, and of the Buddha and Avalokitesvara. We brewed her traditional Chinese medicine, which we stored in a large bamboo basket. We went to a mountainside well behind the university, filled a pot of refreshing water and slowly walked home together with my dog Little Spot. At that time my husband was starting to establish our Hong Chen International Writing Camp. I continued with the manuscript of *Across Paradisal Xinjiang*, which had been interrupted four times. In July and August, I suffered for sixty days in the furnace of Chongqing until I got piles and my right arm became calloused. But thanks to the inspiration of my mother, I managed to complete the whole manuscript of 300,000 words. I dedicated the book to her, in recognition of her courage, resilience and devotion to me.

When I submitted the draft manuscript and images to the publishing house in September, my mother's health seemed stable and her medical reports showed that her cancer was in remission. I then made a bold decision, to return to Nepal to finish my thousand-kilometre Himalayan trek. In 2007 and 2008, in the capacity of journalist, backpacker and volunteer, I went to that small mountainous country and left my footprints on the towns, gardens, temples and cultural relics and on some of the paths and snowy Himalayan mountains. I managed to blend in with local life and wrote my first travel book on the country, entitled *Fragrance of Nepal*. I now wanted to write a new book on the Himalayas in recognition of Sakyamuni, Bodhidharma (Master of Zen) and Padma Sambhava, which my mother painted every day, to pray for my mother and all other mothers afflicted by cancer, and to challenge my life and the unknown realm in my life.

Feeling guilty, I asked my mother whether she would feel sad and lonely if I were to leave her for three months.

My mum sewed elastic into the hem of my tracksuit bottoms to protect my shoes and socks from the rain and snow. She then reinforced the stitching on my bag straps lest they should break or fall apart during the journey. My mum, my husband (I affectionately call him 'Elder Brother'), Little Spot and my mum's carer Xiao Qin gave me wordless support and strength. I strapped on my backpack weighing twenty-five kilograms and set out without hesitation.

Later on, I heard that my mum endured the three months I was away with great difficulty. She sewed her love in the stitches of the trouser legs and in my heavy backpack, suffering in pain all by herself and melting away in the 5,119-word *Diamond Sutra* that she was transcribing She was too weak to eat anything, only coughing, spitting and suffering endless pain every second. But she gave me the freedom to travel for the 129,600 minutes of those ninety days. As a matter of fact, she endowed me with the power to soar.

A vertical climb to Dhampus

During our lifetimes, we have to face and experience many 'first times'. When my guide Bikram told me that I would climb thousands of steeply rising stone steps, I didn't realise the physical and mental torment it would involve.

In Nepali, Phedi, at an altitude of 1,130 metres, refers to low-lying land at the foot of a mountain while Deurali, at an altitude of 2,100 metres, is manifestly the mountaintop, the summit, with an altitude difference of some 1,000 metres. All mountaineers and trekkers know how exhausting it is to climb steps.

Out of breath after climbing no more than a flight of a dozen steps, I had to shout 'Bassnu' in Nepali to stop for a breather. My knees and Achilles tendons were stretched to breaking point. Trekkers prefer to call their guide 'Gai', an abbreviation of 'Guide' in English. My 'Gai' instructed me to move ahead with my backpack and he would follow behind, step by step. Every now and then he stopped to check my progress.

By noon, I had climbed at a snail's pace to Dhampus at an altitude of 1,650 metres, and I struggled for four hours on a mountain path that would normally be completed by a local or a guide in only ninety minutes. I was climbing at less than half their speed. The sunlight dried the sweat on my hair, face and body. I yearned to reach Dhampus and eat lunch before falling into a bamboo chair.

On arriving in Dhampus, most short-haul trekkers stay the night in a log cabin where flowers and plants grow and then return to Pokhara the next morning along the same route having watched the sun rise over Machhapuchhre Mountain, otherwise known as Fish Tail Mountain. Dhampus is a large village that has been home for generations of Brahmin, Chhetri and Gurung ethnic groups. About six thousand villagers live in places scattered around the mountain. The rolling terraces of golden, fragrant paddies and the buffaloes lumbering along a raised path through the fields formed a poetic, pastoral scene, while the murmuring brooks and chirping crickets were the only sounds to disturb the silence of the mountains and plains.

In Pokhara, I could only make out the pyramidal face of Fish Tail Mountain. I wondered why the locals gave it this name. If it looked like a fish, it should have a scissor-shaped fish tail. However, Dhampus offered the best view of the two perfect faces of Fish Tail. Mountaineers refer to unclimbed peaks as virgin peaks, and many of them long to conquer virgin peaks. But Fish Tail Mountain, shining at sunrise like a mermaid, stands as a holy mountain in the minds of locals. The Nepalese government prohibits climbing this snowy peak, so Fish Tail remains a dignified, holy and pure virgin peak.

. . .

There's a rural bus station in Dhampus. A narrow road zigzags along the ridge to Pokhara. Once the bus arrives in Dhampus, it returns to Pokhara at five in the afternoon. In 2007, my husband and I drove a jeep, traversed the north slope of the Himalayas, went across Zhangmu on the Tibetan border and drove to Kathmandu, Pokhara and finally Dhampus. It also marks the end of the rural highway. No roads go beyond here, only paths for passing pack horses and trekkers. So when I climbed to Dhampus, the pain of the experience was unforgettable.

My guide pointed to a snow peak glittering on the horizon. It was five days later that we arrived at Machhapuchhre Base Camp. I stretched out my arms in a gesture of embracing the sky. I could see and hear things in the far distance, but the prospect of walking there, step by step, made me feel faint.

Greeting every stone

On a roadside in Dhampus, there is a small log cabin and a striking signboard with information about the Trekkers' Information Management System and the Annapurna Conservation Area Project. An inspector with pitch-dark skin issued the permits and signed and dated them. The blue and green sheets of paper would give us permission us to continue trekking in the coming days. Two young Chinese women had duped the long-faced inspector. To save money, they hired a porter at a restaurant in Pokhara for eight dollars a day and ventured into the mountain without a permit. There was only a single mountain path and it was impossible to avoid paying the fee. They were fined sixty dollars, twice the cost of the permits. I tried my best to put in a good word for them by saying that they had long wanted to climb this region thousands of kilometres from home out of a shared love for the holy mountains. The Nepalese man was kind-hearted and asked the two girls to pay the original fee. They went on their way, and everyone was happy.

I found that Western trekkers liked to walk slowly and independently in order to fully appreciate the splendid mountain scenery; by contrast, some Chinese trekkers did not appear constrained by any code of conduct, and they often ignored the feelings of others. Whenever they fell into the company of three or four others, they would invariably make a racket at the campsite.

. . .

My guide walked beside me the whole way, a man of few words and innermost tranquillity. In appearance, he wore a red and black T-shirt, and was brown-skinned, 1.75 metres tall, as thin as a bamboo pole and hook-nosed. I asked myself why Basanta had sent me a cold 'Al Qaeda warrior'? But when he grinned at me and showed his clean, white teeth, I was drawn to his calm temperament, as cordial as sunshine. I knew that we would get along fine for the next ten days or more. If he was rude or impatient with me or lacked care, that would plunge me into a dark hell.

The checkpoint in Dhampus at an altitude of 1,650 metres

I asked Bikram whether I was his slowest client during his ten-year career as a guide. He gently nodded 'yes' but then added pleasantly: "I took this job as a vacation." He had once guided a German group that was so fit and strong that they completed the whole 220-kilometre journey to Annapurna Base Camp, with their guide and porter carrying all their luggage, in just six days. I progressed at a rate of a little over ten kilometres a day, which in his eyes was tantamount to being paid for a holiday.

A guide usually makes twenty trips to Annapurna Base Camp during the six-month-long high season. I asked Bikram whether he ever got tired. He gave me an unexpectedly poetic answer: "Each stone and leaf along the way greets me."

Carrying luggage for clients is the only means of earning a living for the majority of Nepalese men in these mountainous areas. They live from what the land can provide. This interdependence gives rise to a very warm emotion. They love and revere the mountains that they climb and the paths they walk. There's no lack of beautiful scenery in this world but we rarely give it our proper attention or gratitude. This ordinary mountain farmer Bikram enabled me to have a taste of the wonderful mountain life and gave me the sense that the people, plants, animals, rivers, fields and sky along the way were in the embrace of the mountains. It was the harmonious beauty of an interdependent life and death in this mortal world.

There was another checkpoint when we arrived at Pothana at an altitude of 1,890 metres, overlooking the verdant valley of the twisting Mardi Khola River. My guide said there was a shortcut to his village that took only half an hour and where I could visit this Brahmin village. His parents had nine children, and when he was a boy he travelled three hours to and from Dhampus every day until he graduated from senior high school. He worked as a porter in Pokhara at the age of eighteen, obtained a guide permit, settled down, got married and now had a four-year-old daughter.

Though thirty-one years old, Bikram looked like a boy, partly because so many Nepalese are lean and carry little fat. I wisely declined the invitation to go to his village because I knew that a journey of 'half an hour' would take me at least ninety minutes. I was too tired to make the detour.

At a quarter past five, we arrived in Deurali at an altitude of 2,100 metres. There were three inns set into precipitous cliffs. The villagers living along the trekking routes turn their houses into family inns to receive trekkers. We stayed in Nice View Lodge whose fat hostess had lived there for twenty-six years. Her sixteen-year-old daughter was called Ful Maga, meaning 'flower of love' in Nepali. Lit up by the glow of a fire, the rosy-cheeked girl cooked chicken curry with rice for me in the kitchen. What rare, delicious food! I wolfed it down, the meal reminding me of spinach and beancurd soup, the food for the immortals in heaven, what the exiled king had eaten.

I stayed in a low-ceilinged room and had to duck my head on entering. There was no separate bathroom but it was quite clean. The landlord put two plastic buckets outside to sort the rubbish, one for plastic and the other for cans. There was also a giant black bucket called the 'tank', under which a small switch enabled us to gargle and wash in front of the snow mountain.

That night I began to cough bitterly and my nose was blocked. I thought I must have got cold during the day as a result of sweating. I rose to take medicine three times during the night, an infusion of Radix Isatidis, Vitamin C tablets and antibiotics. But I hadn't brought any cough medicine. It was difficult enough to access water and power in this mountainous region, let alone find a clinic or medicine. As a result, I coughed heavily during my first night on the cliff, listening to the strong wind outside.

DAY TWO

STOPPING AT TOLKA DUE TO FOOD POISONING

ALTHOUGH I SUFFERED torment throughout the night and felt painful all over every time I turned over in bed, I went out to brave the cold wind outside the log cabin, holding my camera when the sun rose resplendently at six o'clock.

On the cliff at Deurali, I looked northwards towards Annapurna South (7,219 metres) and Hiunchuli (6,441 metres). Two young men and a young woman from Hamburg stood beside me. We had met the day before and stayed in the same log cabin in Deurali. Hamburg is a cosmopolitan port city and ocean liners from all over the world berth there. It is therefore regarded by locals as a gateway between Germany and the rest of the world. For this reason, the three of them had set out from beautiful Hamburg in the north and were determined to finish the trek to Annapurna Base Camp, carrying their own backpacks rather than hiring a guide like I had.

On their first day of the trek, each of them carrying packs weighing ten kilograms, the young Germans were soon out of breath and trudged at the same pace as me. On many occasions we took a break on the same *chautara*, close to the point of collapse. However, after a night's rest and recuperation, they showed their high spirits and became more bold. Cold and shivering, while holding a cup of Nepalese milk tea to warm their hands, they looked in the same direction as me. Martin Heidegger, the eminent German philosopher, once said: "Humans have to work hard but they should live poetically." At that time I had to give in to my ever-growing obsession with sunrise derived from a desire to find poetic beauty from the aesthetic.

I love watching the sun rise, in the same way that we all strive to live a glorious, resplendent life. I have so many memories of the sunrise when I travel; all trekkers are crazy about watching the sun rise and set at different stages of their journey. Travelling day and night, crossing mountains and rivers, and being subjected to physical pain, all the suffering turns to dust when the gloriously radiant sun rises and sets.

I closed my hands, uttering the Nepali word for 'hello', '*namaste*', to the flying gods in the sky. I then set off in the radiant daylight.

The wild can be fatal

Pointing to the plunging stone stairs, my guide said that we would walk down to the Modi Khola Valley, pass over a wooden bridge and climb up to the village of Bheri Kharka opposite Annapurna.

Looking at the distant Annapurna South from my three-room lodge in Deurali

Although the mountain top was clearly visible, the six-kilometre-long mountain path winding through the V-shaped valley was daunting for an urban writer like me who is not an accomplished trekker. The purple petunias growing either side on the mountain slopes were like a butterfly's wings, while oak leaves were scattered on the deserted path like old bookmarks and the stream at the bottom of the valley rippled. A ravine stream or a tributary of a river in Nepal is called '*khola*' and the source of Modi Khola was Annapurna Base Camp surrounded by snow peaks.

Bheri Kharka is a small village comprising about ten Gurung households and is situated at about the same altitude as Deurali. Despite a lack of resources, the villagers make good use of waste materials, creatively cutting the discarded drinks bottles of trekkers and using them to plant marigolds and dahlias that would later bloom on window ledges in the wind and sunshine.

The landlady of one of the inns knew Bikram, and she enthusiastically served him a cup of black tea while cutting two large pieces of cucumber for me. We put down our bags and rested a while. This was the first time I had seen such a large cucumber, as thick as a wax gourd. I wondered whether it was wild. I never had unboiled water or raw food on the mountain path. However, seeing the locals chomp away on these crisp and thirst-quenching cucumbers, I peeled mine with a Swiss Army knife and ate two small pieces. I watched the dogs chase after some chickens on the path. Moving on only fifty metres ahead with my camera, I felt a searing pain in my belly and started to sweat all over. I beckoned Bikram to help me to the toilet where I vomited and suffered diarrhoea for twenty minutes. Then I collapsed.

Bikram had never encountered such a case, and the kind-hearted landlord of another inn let me lie on her bed. I soon lost consciousness. An hour later, I opened my eyes and found it was already noon. Bikram was perched on the edge of another bed and nervously kept watch over me. I saw flowers in the discarded bottles in bloom against the backdrop of the snow mountains. I quickly came to my senses.

'Being-towards-death' was a pet phrase of Martin Heidegger but it is one of the most difficult to comprehend. Even so, it sprang into my mind at that moment. I didn't expect that gluttony could nearly kill me. Different people respond differently in cases of phytotoxicity. For some, micro toxicity might be highly dangerous. In the developed world, our bodies have long been accustomed to vegetables grown in greenhouses and sprayed with pesticide, but we are unaccustomed to wild, natural food, and sometimes allergic to it.

In order to reduce their load, Himalayan porters and guides never carry a water bottle or food with them. They drink mountain spring water when thirsty and wash themselves in bitingly cold melted snow. They eat a rice and lentil dish known as *dal bhat*, wild fruit and whatever else they can find, cooked or raw. But we urban dwellers live in container-like spaces and cannot survive in the wilderness like them. Therefore, along the route to the base camp, the Annapurna Conservation Area Project distributed water-purifying devices for international trekkers.

In our eyes, the forest is free, magnanimous and vigorous, but also dangerous, strange and forbidding. You may encounter various unexpected issues and disasters or get infections and suffer from toxic reactions, allergies, bruising and diarrhoea. The law of nature is the survival of the fittest, and the survivors are those who adjust best to the environment. I was determined to be cautious, not eat indiscriminately, accustom myself slowly and emerge from the forest alive.

Later I was told that the original, yellow-skinned cucumbers were brought back from the tropical rain forest at the southern foot of the Himalayas by Zhang Qian after returning from his diplomatic mission in the Western Regions about two thousand years ago. The long, crisp and delicious green-skinned cucumbers that we buy in supermarkets today are the result of many years of selected cultivation in order to improve yields and develop resistance to disease.

A frightening encounter with leeches

My guide pulled out a trekking pole and put it in my left hand. I gave two sweets to the landlady for her kindness in giving me a soft bed to lie on when I collapsed. But before I managed to get to my feet, I screamed in terror at the sight of a leech attached to my right ankle. My guide squeezed it and blood spilled out onto the clean bed sheet. Bikram said we would pass through an infamous leech forest track on the way to Annapurna Base Camp. He asked me to quicken my pace as we went across the grass and to walk on the outside of the path rather than close to the rocks on the other side, near a dank turf slope.

There's a Nepalese legend that describes a battle in which a giant devil is killed and cut into pieces by the deity Indra lest it should recover one day. However, Indra made a blunder, because the bloody fragments of the devil turned into blood-sucking worms, leeches, mosquitoes, fleas and lice. Their presence means it is impossible to hold outdoor sports events in the rainy season from June to August. Apart from the incidence of natural calamities such as floods, landslides and road blocks, the ubiquitous leeches are one of the major reasons for the impossibility of staging outdoor events.

Nepalese leeches are as small as rice grains. Even though it was late September, Nepal was still under the influence of the warm air flow of the Indian Ocean. Below an altitude of 3,000 metres, especially in sunshine following rainfall, the slippery invertebrates turn out in full force.

Like ghosts, they usually hide themselves on leaves, in grass and on cattle, horses and dogs. They are highly sensitive to the surrounding sounds and smells. They can hear the footsteps of trekkers, smell their sweat and instinctively jump onto them when they pass by unaware.

Their sucking disc is round and situated on either side of a thin, delicate body. Even if you cut them in half, they can live on. They will latch onto a human body and release an anaesthetic which means that the person doesn't feel its bite and they secrete an anti-clotting enzyme so that the blood flows freely. They are found everywhere, in people's shoes and on their trouser legs, trekking poles, neck, hands and back. My guide bent down to help me tighten my trouser legs. I was wearing white lace gloves and covered my head with a scarf, making me look like an Arabian Bedouin. When I saw a troop of monkeys frolic and jump among the trees overhead, I stopped, held my breath and took some photos, only to find a leech on top of my shoe sucking blood through my thick sock.

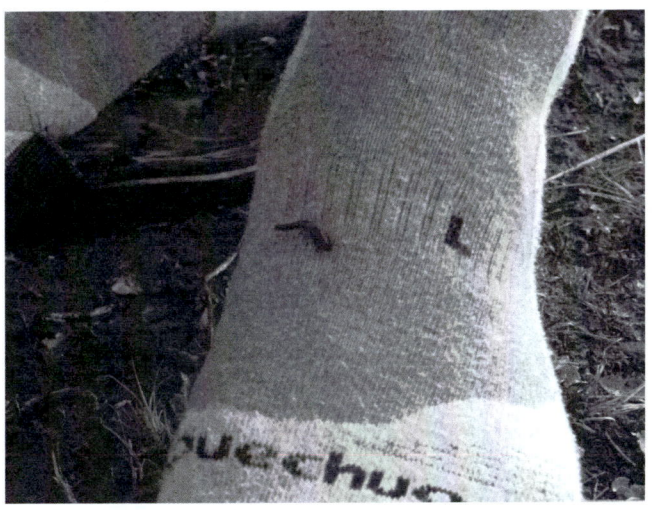

Leeches can worm their way through thick socks to suck blood

I shrieked. My guide told me to burn the leech so that it would relax its bite and fall off in pain. But the problem was that, since coughing the day before, I had pledged to give up smoking on the way and put my cigarettes and matches in the deepest recess of my backpack for fear that I would lose my willpower. Instead, my guide had to nip it with his fingers. The leech's body was as swollen as an earthworm so that blood flowed all down my leg. The wound stung and the bleeding continued more than an hour later. I could not help thinking what the leeches would live on if we hadn't been there. Air? Rain and dew? Magic breath? A leech that has not gorged on blood is almost invisible to the human eye.

The answer, like objects washed away by a river, could not be found again. European doctors used to recommended the therapy of bloodletting and refreshing by leeches. If such a doctor ever walked into a Nepalese forest, he would no longer think that way.

. . .

Tolka, at an altitude of 1,700 metres, is a serene village comprising eleven Marga households. The Marga are Buddhists, and they are as yellow-skinned as the Chinese. Most of them live in two-storey stone buildings whose roofs are covered with dry thatch or tiles. The Maachathite, as the ethnic Marga people are known, are honest, brave, disciplined and cheerful in disposition. All these traits are appropriate for a military life. This is why Marga are the largest group in both the Gurkha Brigade and the Nepalese Army. Many young men from Marga villages serve in the army and regularly remit money back home. This gives them a decent living and helps the country in terms of foreign currency earnings.

The Marga women of Tolka mostly work outdoors, drying beans in the sun and cleaning bronzeware and coffee sets. Trekkers pass occasionally but the inns do not openly tout for business, which is something I admire. It was such a serene, quiet environment that I could clearly hear the munching of cattle eating grass and the sucking sound made by leeches.

Bikram noticed my ashen face and said we should not press on but instead stay in Tolka. I felt hugely relieved. There is an iron donation box next to the primary school at the entrance to the village where passers-by can make donations. The children were playing a game of 'hawk-and-chicken' on a small patch of flat ground. The game is no longer played in the cities but I have happy memories of it from my childhood. I put two hundred rupees in the box and felt a swelling of pleasure inside.

We stayed in Mommy Rupa's place. The moment we entered, my guide asked me to take off my clothes to check my wounds. I was wearing a loose, sun-proof royal blue *kurta*, traditional everyday clothing worn by Nepalese women. The garment comes down to the knee, has long sleeves and is often hand embroidered with beautiful flowers and leaves. I took off my *kurta* as quickly as possible and saw my belly bleeding. Before I even spotted the leech, I started to scream.

It is said that leeches can taste the blood type of humans, and those with the O blood group are affected most seriously. Luckily, I have the much rarer type AB blood, which is usually shunned by leeches. So I could count myself lucky.

I carried my sweat- and blood-stained clothes to the outdoor laundry. Bikram went to help me by squatting on the ground, kneading my clothes by hand, rinsing them under running water and then stamping on them. It is the same washing method used by all Nepalese mountain dwellers. I now truly appreciated the value of my guide. If I were Don Quixote, that ridiculous knight riding a thin horse and carrying lance in hand, fighting windmills that he imagines are giants and challenging flocks of sheep and mountains, then my guide must be Sancho Panza, the simple, amusing and wise retinue.

A beaming Mommy Rupa

Mommy Rupa's inn has a small satellite antenna to receive TV programmes. With a solar water pot glittering on its roof, I took a hot bath straight away. The establishment had been open for twelve years. She has two sons and two daughters. She cooked potato curry and rice over the firewood, the fragrance of which filled the clean air. The potatoes are carried from Chhomrong by porter and sell for two hundred rupees per kilogram, very expensive. I later found out that potatoes are sold for only fifty rupees per kilogram in Pokhara.

I sat in a thatched shed opposite Annapurna South and wrote my diary for the previous two days while a group of men watched an Indian talent show in a sitting room filled with sunshine and decorated with a poster of Li Yuchun, the Chinese singer and actress, hanging on the wall. Bikram was lying on a stone table covered by a straw mat, sleeping with his hands shielding him from the bright sun. To him, my slow progress was like a God-given holiday. I thought that God blessed his subjects in the Himalayas. Although there are no abundant crops, and leeches crawl all around and food is in short supply, the people are bestowed with sunshine, trees, valleys, snowy mountains, plentiful power and simple contentment.

It is the only place on the route to Annapurna Base Camp that provides free phone and camera recharging. Only when I lay under the thatched shed watching the sky, clouds, houses and facial expressions of the locals did I recognise the trivial nature of a traveller's daily concerns, their aches and pains, tiredness or sleeping problems. As long as you carry your simple luggage, sit there with your mind rested, lay down your burdens and take a deep breath, you will see claret-red dahlias rising from the stone-tiled roof, amazingly pretty in full bloom.

DAY THREE

SEEKING SECLUSION IN NATURE

THE SUNRISE REFLECTED on the glass window of my room. It was a new day. The fragrance of grass and trees coming from the mountains and plains comforted my nostrils. I quickly packed away my scattered belongings and decided to walk on in the wilderness even though my cough had not improved. The free, simple beauty was difficult to resist.

At the age of sixteen, I fell in love with Jack London's *The Call of the Wild* along with his other stories about the polar wilderness in North Alaska. It captured a young person's innermost yearning for a carefree existence, leaving home, embracing the wilderness, working as an 'oyster pirate' or sailor, going to South America, Africa and other far-off places and discarding my boring, repetitive, dreadful exam-oriented life!

It was not until years after I had grown up that I realised that my idol Jack London himself lived in the north for only a single winter. After achieving fame at twenty-seven, he openly declared that writing was nothing but a commercial enterprise for him. He thought he was entitled to a life of luxury. He poured a great sum of money into building a yacht called *Snark* and then spent a hundred thousand dollars, an astonishing sum at that time, on building a villa called Wolf House only for the property to burn down before he and his wife Charmian got to live there.

The celebrated writer was an alcoholic, obese and poor, and he spent most of his time indoors, which was quite the opposite of the popular image of him rebelling against the bourgeoisie and the young man travelling in search of freedom. After making a name for himself, he did not obtain happiness but emptiness instead. At the age of forty, he shot himself on his luxury ranch. Nothing could do more to suppress a person's spirit of adventure than inertia and a hedonistic lifestyle. He could not rekindle the passion of his youth, nor return to the wilderness.

People who have too many strong desires are often unable to be happy or contented. They resign themselves to a monotonous, routine life for years and do not have the courage to change their circumstances or the pace or direction of their lives. Instead, they confine themselves to a safe, comfortable and repetitive existence that goes on in circles. I wanted to change today, enjoy my life and go on an unrestrained journey. Even if I were to get lost on the journey of solitary adventure, I will still move on towards the extraordinary wilderness at the bottom of my heart.

The happiness of each individual usually comes from the discovery of a new life and a new horizon, and the indefatigable curiosity and spirit of adventure are the core of the vigour of life. What could be more relaxing than embracing the different horizons of different places every day!

Fantasy valley of Landruk

I call the valley along the gentle slope from Tolka down to Landruk, the Valley of Phantoms.

Goats, donkeys and buffaloes walked slowly from the rice terrace and basked in the dawn light. A clear stream has run here for a thousand years and is now spanned by a drawbridge. I asked my guide what 'Landruk' meant and he told me that, a century ago, the people of the Annapurna Peaks were not well educated and some of the place names were meaningful while others were not. 'Landruk' has no meaning in Nepali, but it sounds good. But I still called it my Valley of Phantoms.

Nearly two thirds of Nepal's territorial area is covered by mountains, and the range in altitudes is astonishing: from the Terai Plains at an altitude of a hundred metres to the 'Top of the World' at 8,848 metres. The different, changing altitudes form the landscape at different levels, which is quite amazing. The people are surrounded by mountains, meaning that nearly all the country's fields have to be terraces. The houses are scattered among the terraces that spiral up. Under strong sunlight, the tower houses reflect faint rays of turquoise, looking like the celestial cottages of hermits.

The US magazine *Travel + Leisure* identified seven of the world's finest terraces: Banaue in Ifugao, the Philippines, Yuanyang in Yunnan, China, Ubud in Bali, Indonesia, Annapurna in Pokhara, Nepal, Mae Rim in Chiang Mai, Thailand, Sabah in Lao Cai, Vietnam and Dragon Ridge in Guilin, China. In the Annapurna Peaks, the wonderful terraces look like escalators extending to heaven, while the mountains roll in layers. I felt my body climbing step by step on these escalators into the white clouds.

I met some Gurung men on my travels in the mountain area. They wore wide suspenders made from coarse cloth, which I called 'pocket clothes' like those worn by the beggar gangs headed by Hong Qigong in a famous Chinese kung fu novel. The suspenders contained pockets to hold things such as sickles, food and water for the labourers working in the fields. They don't plant rice or wheat here but a special strain of millet that is able to grow in this harsh environment. Those ethnic groups that have been living in the mountainous area since ancient times regard millet as the holiest crop granted by God. Set off by the snow mountain, the millet looked like wild green foxtail grass swaying in the wind.

Initially, I mistakenly thought that the area was inundated with green foxtail and wondered how the mountain farmers could survive without sufficient food. I didn't know that millet was an essential foodstuff for the Nepalese tribal people, nor that they also used it to brew *raksi*, a kind of rice wine with an intoxicating flavour and strength similar to arrack or China's *erguotou*. They believe that the white spirit boasts miraculous properties and refer to it as nectar. Whenever I reached campsite in the evening, I would take a sip of *raksi*, just like the tribal people. Drinking it gave me an extraordinarily comfortable sensation in the throat. My aches and general fatigue from the day's walking seemed to disappear. The drink started to affect my vision, making the mountains appear shrouded in clouds and mist, looking like a 3D animation.

In China, my friends often asked me what I did on my trips to Nepal.

"Nothing but trekking and existing in a trance," I would always answer.

This rarely visited mountainous country on one side of the Himalayas can make people fully appreciate the merits of a simple life. Here, there are few temptations to shop and no one urging you to hurry up. There are few stores or supermarkets, artificial scenic spots or man-made entertainment facilities to wring money out of you. No one will set you a time limit, disturb your solitude or start a quarrel. All I did, each day, was to walk slowly in solitude, enjoying this unrestrained and vast landscape.

The beauty of a simple life

The path took a fork as we passed through Landruk. The path to the left led to Ghandruk, the largest Gurung village in the Annapurna Peaks which I would visit on my return trip, while Chhomrong was to the right.

We took the right fork and came to the New Bridge at the bottom of the valley floor next to a terrace. New Bridge is actually a long, tall, shabby bridge over the limpid Modi Khola. An old Gurung woman was picking the delicate and charming leaves of a wild plant. The plant is dried and then pickled and made it into a most delicious pickle to accompany *dal bhat*. I didn't know that some of the pickles I was eating every day were made from wild mountain plants.

Turn left to Ghandruk and right to Chhomrong

A huge number of plant species grown at different altitudes are eaten for their fibre content. A kind of Himalayan nettle with lacerated leaves called '*nilgiri*' will give you a piercing pain if eaten as a mature plant. However, the young plant can be consumed pickled. The stems of mature *nilgiri* contain poisonous plant fibre. The women skin the nettle with their teeth, soak, beat and boil the fibre and spin it into a coarse and strong white cloth to make *kurta*-style gowns. The farmers believe that eating *nilgiri* gives them strength, while wearing the gowns protects them on their travels. Like them, I think my body cannot exist without *dal bhat* or the *kurta*.

We decided to have lunch in Himchuli Lodge on the banks of the Modi Khola. It usually took about forty minutes to make steamed rice, chicken and potato curry, and lentil soup, which they served with fresh, hot *dal bhat*. The food helped replenish our depleted energy levels. I lay on the bench to rest, with the sound of a nearby waterfall and the cool, poetic wind touching my face. Suddenly, a glass mantis landed on my body in perfect silence.

The trees by my side glistened. Their fat leaves, resembling the palms of a giant, are used in traditional herbal medicine to treat cows, buffaloes and goats. I was coughing continuously and wondered whether it could cure my own illness. In a country with limited modern medical facilities, the locals have a good knowledge of herbal medicine. Nepal has six hundred different types of herbal medicine whose beneficial effects have been confirmed. That's why Medicine Buddha, holding a lotus and medicine bowl and wearing a wise countenance, is one of the most beautiful and revered Buddhas worshiped by the Nepalese.

A Gurung woman making pickles from wild plants

The landlady's two-year-old son was quietly climbing naked onto the table and was about to take my hat. His mother picked him up and dipped a cotton swab into water boiled with parmelia lichen to bathe him under the sun. Parmelia is also used as a seasoning and in making incense for rituals in India and Nepal. Additionally, it used to extract and purify perfume and acts as a natural cleansing agent thanks to its antibiotic properties. The naked child, like the Christ Child held in the hands of a goddess, glittered in the transparent sunlight above the Himalayas. It made me want to take a celestial bath with parmelia so that the strongly radiating Himalayan sunlight could disinfect me.

The naked child glitters in the sunlight

Thinking of the things I had seen and encountered each day, like the grains of millet and rice, the rocks, trees, leaves, paths, insects, tribal people and children, and feeling the sweat rolling down my skin and the wind on my face, I found I had rediscovered the significance of the simple life – we were born into this world to appreciate the beauty of nature.

How can human beings who know the name of everything discover the splendour of everything and inhale the smell of sweet dew and flowers? How can people live detached from the land?

I really appreciated the opportunity given me by the God of Himalayas to come here and experience these things.

Wild chrysanthemums on bamboo poles

Traversing the river at the bottom of the valley, I knew that I had to climb another mountain. When I took off my lace gloves to apply suncream, a leech jumped onto the gloves. Cold-blooded animals are always bloodthirsty.

On the path that spiralled up, I met a young woman from Hong Kong called Kowai. She was the only solitary female Chinese backpacker I encountered on the way to Annapurna Base Camp. She hadn't even hired a porter, and she carried her own eight kilogram pack all by herself. I was filled with admiration for this extraordinary woman. While I was also a Chinese woman travelling alone to the same destination, I had hired a superb guide to help me.

I asked her why she didn't hire a porter.

She said that she was thirty years old and hoped to challenge herself by trekking alone to Annapurna Base Camp. If successful, she would trek solo to Everest Base Camp next year.

She walked slowly, taking measured breaths and short strides, with sweat soaking her sunburnt face and green, quick-dry clothes. Her solitary figure looked like a silent stone; she seemed to have existed on the path for a millennium. My guide mischievously whispered to me: "The upper part of her body looks like that of a woman but the lower part is as strong as that of a man."

I burst out laughing because this Brahmin was speaking from a male perspective. Until then, I hadn't really thought of him as a man, but instead as just a guide.

I asked Bikram jokingly why he grinned on first seeing me and then agreed to my offer without bargaining. "Pearl," he responded, "your feminine smile instantly won me over."

I regarded Kowai as a wanderer in the true sense of the word rather than simply a trekker. For a while, I didn't see her on the winding path, and I asked my guide whether she had perhaps taken the wrong route and become disoriented in the thick bush. My guide headed back quickly, found Kowai and led her back to the correct path. Seeing me panting and coughing on the stone steps and sipping tea from a stainless steel cup, Kowai immediately gave me some throat lozenges she had pulled from her pocket. This timely help soothed my throat and alleviated the coughing.

At three o'clock, when it was still scorching, I met a group of ten Americans who had hired a guide and six porters. The porters, like pack horses, carried an array of items including tents, sleeping bags, tables, chairs, picnic baskets, food and oil lamps. I was only carrying a small bag but still found myself out of breath while these short, bow-legged mountain men wearing plastic sandals, thin clothes and straps over the heads trekked for six to seven hours every day carrying a load of forty to fifty kilograms. Like Himalayan elves bestowed with extraordinary power, they forged ahead and delivered all the supplies in advance before the trekking team arrived at their destination. For all this heavy work, a porter received a mere eight dollars a day, out of which he had to pay for his own board and lodging.

I really felt for the porters when I saw them plod by my side. We are all humans, but their ability to endure all kinds of hardship was animal-like. Usually, a trekker can provide work for six or seven Nepalese. In the peak six-month season, each porter can make about 70,000 rupees and each guide about double that, which provides their entire income for the whole year. Due to poverty, arduous working conditions and a shortage of medical facilities, a Nepalese man has a life expectancy of only sixty-eight years, much lower than the average of seventy-six years for Chinese men and eighty years for Japanese men, let alone the eighty-one years for Swiss men who live at the foot of the Alps.

Taking a breather with the old porter

I didn't expect the old porter who was taking a breather with me on a *chautara* to be so cheerful. The pack basket he was carrying weighed forty kilograms. His clothes and the basket straps were dark with sweat. He fashioned two simple bamboo poles into two load-bearing trekking poles and arranged several wild chrysanthemum flowers on top. The romantic, yet simple flowers cheered him up on the long, arduous trip and warmed my steps.

I invited him to take a photo with me before we went our separate ways. He immediately put away his clothing that was drying in the chilly wind and made a devout blessing gesture of 'Namaste'. With this blessing, I felt calm and reassured. As you know, after Tenzing Norgay, the Nepalese man who helped Sir Edmund Hillary climb Mount Everest for the first time in 1953, the Nepalese are no longer regarded as just porters or labourers. They are greatly valued not just because of their inborn mountaineering ability but also for their strong build, honest virtues, simplicity, loyalty, kindness and their friendly, brave and enthusiastic outlook. The porters are the firmest 'rocks' in the great Himalayas.

Hot spring in the wilderness

At 4.30pm, we arrived at Jhinu Danda on a hillside where many trekkers stop and bask in the sun wearing only a bath towel. My guide said to me: "Pearl, we'll stay here tonight and there's a surprise waiting for you later."

In this remote place at an altitude of 1,750 metres, a bottle of cola was on sale for 175 rupees, which was too expensive for me. Was there an alternative? Was there a high-altitude honey that could soothe my chest and make me more comfortable?

The ginger-lemon tea I sipped helped refresh me from the fatigue of the trek, and I heard the tinkling sound of water from below the cliffs and saw the heat moving up from the deep valley as thin and light as the clothes of a fairy in the sunshine. Wow, a hot spring hidden in the valley!

Fish Tail Mountain looking silver in the moonlight

Thanks to its special geologic structure and conditions, the Annapurna Peaks contain a number of hot springs, large and small. Many sections of the Modi Khola were formed along major fault lines. The running water gashes the earth's crust like sharp tongues, flowing like blood and giving off sulphur and heat. Hot springs were formed near the rocks.

My guide sat on a straw mattress in the courtyard, with a cup of ginger-lemon tea I had prepared for him. Blowing the steaming tea with his mouth, he told me that a Gurung prince had once caught measles, and when he was out riding one day he discovered holy water near these hot springs, and his measles miraculously disappeared.

The ancestors did not understand the magical effect of natural sulphur minerals contained in hot springs in terms of oxidation resistance and making the skin shinier, so they reckoned it must be the work of a 'deity'. The sense of relief it gave me, a dog-tired trekker, was no less than that experienced by the Gurung prince.

The hot spring situated at the bottom of the valley had a sunny exposure. It took us a little over twenty minutes to clamber down the steep ridge but probably more than an hour to climb back up after the bath.

My stripped-down luggage didn't contain any life-saving medicine, let alone a bathing suit, and my guide didn't have one with him either. I thought to myself: That's all right. I'll take a bath in this place closest to the sky, even with my clothes on.

As we neared the raging river along the cliffs, the sight of the verdant ponds with steam curling upwards emboldened me. Some of the trekkers there were naked, while two Australian girls who hadn't brought bathing suits either were in their bra and pants. I quickly took off my *kurta* and followed suit. With great excitement, I looked down at my sweat- and mud-caked legs being cleansed in these healing waters. Once again I was able to appreciate my smooth, clean body.

My guide ran to the flowing water, took off his clothes down to his underpants and washed himself, at last free of the responsibility of taking care of me. It was the first time I had seen the muscular body of a Himalayan man, like a wild mountain animal. He had a thin red thread hanging over his right shoulder. It was the sacred thread that adult Hindu men must wear on their body and should not remove, even when taking a bath. I came to realise that the lives of the people here are closely entwined with the mountains and rivers.

An emperor during the Tang dynasty wrote a fine inscription commemorating a hot spring, entitled *Wenquan Ming*: "Its quality doesn't change and the temperature is the same in both winter and summer. It runs day and night like the sun and moon but is neither full nor empty, making the world around complete, relieving drought and benefiting this region forever." The emperor was Li Shimin, wise founder of the Tang dynasty. Li Shimin and his beautiful concubine Lady Yang loved bathing in the Huaqingchi hot springs, "washing delicate skin with the smooth hot spring water" and spending beautiful moments together. He also made hot springs a vital part of royal culture. He not only bathed and exercised there, but also handled court affairs and conducted foreign diplomacy. Many foreign envoys were given gifts by the Tang emperors while bathing in the hot spring in Lishan Mountain in the ancient capital of Xi'an.

The Himalayan hot spring is at one with nature, where partially-dressed men, bare-chested women and naked children use it to rebalance their bodies in the 'warmth' of a dense water mist and reconcile their yin and yang. An older porter who was drying off told me that there are particular requirements about the best time, days and seasons to bathe in a hot spring.

The hot spring in Jhinu Danda receives only a limited water flow while the mineral content is highest in the spring and autumn. It is the place where villagers, young and old, enjoy themselves together. There's no discrimination between nobles and the lower strata of society as they feel the warmth under the pure white snow mountain. I believe it is the unadorned simplicity and liberty that attract people to return to their innocent state and fill the village at the foot of the snow mountain with a simple, joyful atmosphere.

We left satisfied and our bones softened, with the quiet, clear crescent overhead bringing an unforgettable tranquillity to the scene. However, my guide was unusually remiss in failing to tell me to bring along a head lamp and a windproof coat. It is easy to cut oneself in the bush or trip over in wet clothes and beach sandals, as we staggered upwards in the dark, dense woods in the bone-biting coldness. My guide held my hand and walked close to the inner side of the turf slope to protect me from the leeches. After a short while, I saw him pinch the 'vampires' that clung to his feet and body. His white T-shirt was already smeared with blood.

Being short-sighted and suffering from astigmatism, I could make out little on that dark night. Sensing my difficulty, an Australian girl following us removed the lamp she was wearing and fastened it round my head.

She said she could share a lamp with her boyfriend, who had taken off his shoes and was walking barefooted. They had just finished three months of overseas volunteer work at a primary school in a mountain village in Pokhara organised by the Ford Foundation. They were now on their way home after trekking in the Annapurna Peaks. Anyone would be moved by the moral character of these volunteers and their willingness to help others. Their good deeds, like the light penetrating the dark night in that dense forest, reflected their tender feelings. As it happened, I was being supported by an experienced guide while the volunteers were walking with greater difficulty and in some danger on an unfamiliar cliff path.

Suddenly, a barking deer flashed by, its body shining like silver in the moonlight. An animal can give out extraordinary scent in the Himalayan moonlight. The musk deer is nearly extinct in the Annapurna Peaks and few can now be seen. The small, barking deer lives in the Himalayan forest. It quickly forded the warm, flowing stream and then disappeared into the bush.

I was so touched by the sight of this deer that I couldn't find appropriate words to express my emotions. All I could do was move my long, sturdy legs, look up and sigh with emotion.

Our small group moved on silently for fear of disturbing the serenity of the Temple of God in the wilderness. Having moved on, our souls, like the barking deer, will return to live a quiet life, far away from the noisy world.

DAY FOUR

A BEAUTIFUL PATH GETS MORE BEAUTIFUL BECAUSE OF YOU

THERE'S NO END TO TRAVEL; trekkers are always on the move.

It was the fourth day of our trek in the mountains. How long we walked each day depended on the sun. We set out before sunrise and stopped to rest before sunset. We did not walk during the night for the sake of safety.

The Himalayan mountain paths are all on ridges that link the mountains at an altitude of above 7,000 metres. Nowadays, people can 'travel' the world by scanning maps or looking at images on the internet. But few people bother to consider the fact that the places marked on a map or viewed on a mobile phone actually present innumerable challenges in the real world. On a map of the Annapurna Peaks with a scale of 1:125,000, our daily route covered only a few centimetres. But those few centimetres involved a long, hard trudge.

The cool morning breeze in Jhinu Danda blew on my face. Two porters were helping an American girl tie up her giant bags.

Two porters helped the American girl tie up her bags

I glanced at my Protrek watch. The altitude gauge showed we were at 1,750 metres, meaning our journey that day would involve a testing climb. The normal stride of an adult is about sixty-five centimetres, so a distance of one kilometres can be completed in 1,538 strides. In the stories of Conan Doyle, the detective Sherlock Holmes can calculate the stature and habits of a person through his stride and, from that, identify a criminal suspect. I thought it would take more than 330,000 of my steps to cover the 220km-long journey to Annapurna Base Camp. What a distance! I wondered whether Sherlock Holmes could judge me, a trekker not particularly good at trekking, and find out what kind of person I am or evaluate the significance of each of my small steps!

In campsites, it is common to meet trekkers of different ages and from different countries. Since their stamina, physical power and walking speeds differ, trekkers setting out at the same time in the morning are unlikely to meet again in the evening. Therefore, whether it is Buddhist pilgrims on a journey of enlightenment, travellers in search of the exotic, spiritualists wanting to experience life in the developing world, porters working for clients or tribal people going about their normal business, they all walk along the same routes and sometimes accompany each other for a little while. We all value the God-given opportunity to walk together. Walking on crumbling paths where wild flowers bloom abundantly, we continue our way while writing our unfinished stories.

I find that life is sometimes like a trek that physically and mentally trains us and unconsciously cultivates our outlook and behaviour. If the process is enjoyable, the length and difficulty of the journey is irrelevant.

In praise of paths

Leaving Jhinu Danda, I walked up a long, steep slope with an altitude difference of 500 metres. Fish Tail Mountain, with two perfect faces in the shape of a cut feather, seemed to be within reach. However, it was quite difficult to get there. I could only look up at the azure sky and move step by step, panting heavily.

After walking about two kilometres, I saw stone terraces piled up with dry stones in the shape of a rectangle, about one metre high and covering an area of about three square metres. These stone terraces, known as *chautara*, were made up of two layers, with the first layer standing at a height that was convenient for trekkers to place knapsacks and baskets for a short break or to lean against or lie on for a longer rest. The second layer was larger, allowing trekkers to stack bulky goods or have a picnic. Bikram told me that some of these *chautaras*, meaning 'resting-place' in ancient Nepal, had been in use for up to a thousand years.

The winding paths in Nepal are uneven and pose great difficulties to trekkers. As an act of kindness, the Nepalese villagers have built thousands of *chautaras* for trekkers to unload their luggage and take a rest. Some are located in the shade of banyan trees or on the pass of precipitous ridges, while many are located amid the ruins of ancient Indian temples. However, the one positioned at the entrance to each village is the focus of rural life.

Banyans usually stand between stone terraces, with their roots stretching under the stones and weeds. They have a special religious importance because the Buddha attained enlightenment while sitting under a banyan. Hence they are usually planted around a temple or on a stone terrace. People often stop by, enjoy the cool, take a breather, sleep or make a simple lunch in the shade. It is the place where villagers like to congregate, chat, conduct business or hold religious ceremonies. Porters ask for news of their hometown, while trekkers ask questions about the conditions ahead.

On one occasion, several women drying potatoes on a stone terrace looked at me and shouted: "Sherpani, Sherpani!" They had mistaken me for a Sherpani, who are known for their almond-shaped eyes, high cheekbones and brown skin. They are the typical facial features of local Tibetans in the high altitude regions of Nepal. I was quite happy to be misidentified because it meant that I, a woman of a quarter Mongolian descent, resembled an indigenous woman after a couple of days' exposure to the blazing sun.

Each *chautara* seemed to be home to a lively rural club or a place to drink coffee. Buddhism and Hinduism advocate the law of retributive justice. So the tribal people, rich and poor alike, walking on mountain paths all their life, devote their entire property and efforts to building a stone terrace. They regard it as a way to change a predestined relationship, enshrine and worship the god of mountains, and do good deeds for public benefit – an extraordinarily lovely 'station of happiness'.

Trekking in the mountains, I would occasionally see a small white stone Buddhist pagoda with a certain name inscribed on the base and covered in moss and with a bunch of wild flowers on its tip. At first, I thought they were shrines for the mountain god. However, having walked on many smooth paths paved with flagstones, I came to realise that they were graves in honour of those who had funded the building of these paths. Hindus are cremated after death and their ashes are thrown into a sacred river or mountain stream, leaving no trace. The locals erect a tombstone in the centre of the path facing the snow mountain in reverence for the deceased person who has funded the construction of a long stone staircase or opened up a long mountain path.

Walking on a beautiful mountain path covered with blue stones and bathed in light sunshine and the scent of flowers, I could not fail to appreciate the tribal people who trudge here throughout their lives. The towering, steep ranges of the Himalayas make for an extraordinarily harsh environment, but the Nepalese have great respect for all the mountains, rivers, ridges and peaks. Even though they are mortal, they will eventually become pavement stones or shady stone terraces. They devote unwavering loyalty to the rugged paths to show a lifetime of gratitude.

The significance of a sweet

It was 10am when we climbed to the village of Chhomrong, at an altitude of 2,210 metres. We bought a potful of hot water, sat on a stone terrace and ate some Oreo biscuits. Chhomrong is the highest major permanent settlement in the Annapurna Peaks and is home to more than eight hundred Gurung villagers. It has fifteen inns and offers gorgeous views. The terrace of each household faces three snow mountains, Annapurna South, Hiunchuli and Fish Tail. I yearned to spend the rest of my days here and live a romantic life. But my guide told me that we had still not covered half of the whole distance to Annapurna Base Camp.

We met two Chinese girls on the stone terrace. It was pleasant to hear that they'd read *Fragrance of Nepal*, my first book on the country. That was such a happy moment for me, a travel writer whose face was recognised on a Himalayan path. There are hundreds of millions of roads in the world, just like the innumerable stars, but travellers encounter each other in faraway places and this can light up their souls and warm them on their journey. My best times always involve travel.

I left Chhomrong and moved on. The location of campsites and the number of inns is decided by the Annapurna Conservation Area Project, as are the specific places where trekkers can pitch tents. Wood burning is not allowed above an altitude of 2,000 metres, so we had to cook with kerosene or liquefied natural gas tanks. The sale of meat and the slaughtering of animals on holy mountains and on land higher than Chhomrong is also prohibited. Hence, Chhomrong was the last place where I could enjoy fried chicken or steak.

The gravestones of road donors always face the snow mountains

Although Chhomrong is the highest place of human habitation in the valley, in the summer months shepherds drive their flocks of sheep and goats to graze on higher ground. After descending a long flight of stone steps, we arrived at Chhomrong Khola where we could hear a roaring torrent. Carefully walking across a suspension bridge with a drop of 1,860 metres, we continued to climb through a dense forest of bamboo, azalea trees and oaks.

At noon, in a small hillside inn, I ate some *dal bhat*. The lunch was as light as the surrounding air. It seemed as if I had barely eaten anything and I was still hungry and feeling deprived of oxygen. On raising my head, I saw a little boy dart towards me, having emerged from a distant shepherd's tent.

When he saw me, he handed over a small leaf and said softly: "Sweet!" Villages and signs of human habitation are rare above an altitude of 2,000 metres. It turned out that the little shepherd boy had run to me in the hope of getting a sweet.

I shook my hands and responded: "No sweet, no sweet!"

At that moment, I was only trying to protect myself. In the bag being carried by my guide, there were a small number of chocolate creams. Since we would be trudging for several days in the mountains, the sweets and biscuits were there to restore our strength and perhaps even save our lives if we got short of food and were suffering an oxygen deficit. So I instinctively replied that I had no sweets.

Placing the leaf in my hand, the little boy stood in deep disappointment. I sensed the light fading from his eyes.

We continued to trek towards Sinuva. My guide said that he hadn't worn decent clothes or been to Pokhara until he was eight years old. But on one occasion a trekker had given him a sweet and he tied it to some string and played with it for three days before reluctantly deciding to eat it.

A single sweet can bring great happiness to a child

On hearing this childhood story, I was filled with shame. I now appreciated how significant a sweet might be for a child in the Himalayas. When the little boy approached me, he didn't specifically ask for a sweet, but instead used a more formal word that conveyed the sweet, fragrant, pleasant flavour of candy.

Some guides advise travellers not to give sweets or money to impoverished children because it encourages a habit of begging. I thought this was ossified thinking brewed in the modern civilisation. In urban life today, where all kinds of delicacies are available, you rarely appreciate tasty food. But if a sweet can give a child such pleasure and a wonderful memory, how could I be so selfish? How could I begrudge giving away a tiny sweet?

About two thousand years ago, the Buddha said: "What you give will eventually be paid back." When I entered the main peaks of the Himalayas eleven days later, I ditched my colourful clothes, spare camera lens and mountaineering equipment and replaced them with plenty of sweets. It would give me great pleasure to sit on a rock in the sun and share my sweets with the shepherd children I met on the way or to the girl living alone in the log cabin at the pass. The children and I thought that sweets were the most delicious food in the world. Their glistening smiles would linger in my mind forever.

When I saw the sun rise over the eight Himalayan mountains above 8,000 metres, I thought that few trekkers would be able to complete their great journey to the Himalayas without the help of guides and porters. Similarly, the local children, with their sweets, pleasant dispositions and sense of loyalty, would grow into the most helpful, reliable guides and porters for generations to come.

The arrival and departure of a life

When the temperature was at its most scorching, between two and three in the afternoon, I felt the most tired. I sat on a path to the 2,340-metre-high Sinuva, totally exhausted. My guide poured some hot tea into a stainless steel folding cup and handed it to me.

Suffering from alienation, pressure, anxiety, fatigue and physical exhaustion, people can develop all kinds of phobia, related to a wide variety of things such as examinations, marriage, flights, social interaction, sexual intercourse, urban life or pets. When I arrived in Dhampus on the first day, I met two fashionably dressed and well-equipped women from New York. They had given up after covering a distance of just eight kilometres, complaining that the trekking paths were not what they had expected.

"Should they be like the pavements on Fifth Avenue," I asked, "or perhaps you envisaged being whisked up thirty-three storeys of the Empire State Building in a lift?"

"Who knows?" they grunted. "There are only endless mountains, ridges, stones, steps and leeches here."

At that time, I was suffering from a phobia of hills. Every day I was repeatedly climbing up and down. I seemed to be following in the footsteps of poor Sisyphus in Greek mythology, who was forced to push a stone uphill, only for the stone to roll down the hill as he neared the summit. He repeated this miserable task for eternity. But maybe it was just the persistent spirit of 'a foolish old man' that encouraged me to traverse the mountains.

The Japanese drink tea and sleep on tatami mats while the ancient Chinese smoked opium, sipped tea and napped on an opium bed. I felt most comfortable on Nepal's own tatami-style mats, calling them 'stone roadbeds'. When I leaned on my 'roadbed', I had my first formal conversation with Bikram.

I wondered how much the trekking company was paying him, whether customers should tip him after the journey and, if so, what the proper amount should be. During the journey, I had become ill and feeble, struggling and feeling discomfort, and his care and concern for me far exceeded my attention to him. Every day, he read the menu, ordered some dishes for me in the kitchen and then disappeared for a while. I didn't even know whether he had actually eaten anything himself.

Bikram told me that a guide would usually work for several trekking companies that would receive a commission of two or three dollars as an agency fee out of the eighteen dollars paid by the customers each day. This meant he would make only fifteen dollars a day. Most nights, the guides slept on cushions in the living room of an inn. Good inns would provide them with a free bed in a passageway. Every morning, the kitchen would dole out free cups of black tea to each guide and porter but did not give them any food. As a result, in order to save some money, they often went without food and only had *dal bhat* for lunch. They were charged about half price for the *dal bhat*, while other food was charged at the same price paid by all customers.

The food and drinks on the mountains were too expensive even for me, let alone for the porters and guides. So all they ate was *dal bhat*, every day. After the journey ended, some customers would tip them ten or fifty dollars; some would give them their windproof jackets or shoes; an American woman once paid a year's school fees for Bikram's daughter. That was the greatest amount, a hundred dollars, he'd ever received.

"Whether they give me tips or not, I'll take good care of them because it is our responsibility." Bikram smiled, sat beside the stone terrace and said these words like a loyal mountain dweller.

The United States Military Academy at West Point, New York, has twenty-two military regulations. Just like them, the mountaineers have their own rules. For guides, loyalty is an obligation and they must act like warriors to fulfil their obligations. At that point I made a decision. I told my guide: "I won't tip you but I will buy you breakfast every day. I don't want you to carry that bag on an empty stomach. And I'll treat you to whatever I eat for supper, OK?"

I was struck by a phobia of hills, just like poor Sisyphus in Greek mythology

As a matter of fact, most trekkers have a tight budget and I was no exception. I tried to save all the pennies I could. If I treated Bikram to breakfast and supper, my expenditure would increase by half. But I thought the Chinese are a sympathetic race, which has something to do with our ethnic characteristics and willingness to act charitably and our preference to live a sociable life.

Western trekkers tend to be more independent. They seldom invite a guide or porter to meals or have drinks with them. Instead, they tip them to express their gratitude. But it is more difficult for a Chinese person to enjoy meals without friends and to consume food and drinks alone. Sharing a meal is more harmonious and enjoyable. And the Chinese are less conscious of social class discrimination. The wandering beggar Zhu Yuanzhang was a lifelong friend of Guo Zixing, leader of the Red Turban Rebellion in the fourteenth century; General Qin Qiong used to share meals with Li Shimin, who would become the second emperor of the Tang dynasty, in conquering new lands together. I found that Bikram was the only Nepalese person to be treated to a meal by a foreigner.

If you ask a porter or a guide which country their favourite trekkers come from, most will tell you they like the Chinese most because they are friendly and generous and like to eat together in a large group. When they buy water, they will invariably give a bottle to their companion. Every Nepalese knows Chairman Mao. Two leaders of the Nepalese Maoists, Pushpa Kamal Dahal and Baburam Bhattarai, were intellectuals. After ten years of guerrilla warfare in poor rural areas, they finally won positions in government. Dahal was elected prime minister since the 'Maoists' were regarded as saviours of the poor children and peasants, and the two leaders advocated the ideal of social and wealth equality.

We talked about the subject of payment without embarrassment. Afterwards, Bikram made a small request. He hoped that I would be able to quicken my pace. Usually a trekker would spend eight or nine days on completing the whole journey but I originally planned to finish it in twelve to fifteen days. However, he hoped I would be able to cut that to ten days.

I asked him why. He told me that his wife was expecting to give birth in a couple of days, and he was worried about her and wanted to return soon to take care of them.

"Why didn't you tell me that earlier?" I cried out. "I could have found a different guide."

Bikram looked in my eyes and replied in embarrassment: "Pearl, I really wanted to work for you in order to make some money. I thought we would finish our trek in ten days!"

What is more exciting than a new life? I rose to my feet and felt a warm torrent surging through me.

A bank of cloud was passing overhead and covered the peak. A rainstorm started unexpectedly and I then promised Bikram that I would quicken my pace.

Bikram opens up with me for the first time as we rest alongside a mountain path

Bikram then made another misjudgment. Before we set out, I asked him whether I should bring a raincoat. He said there was no need because the rainy season had passed. But it was now pouring and there were no large trees to provide shelter from the storm. I asked him to take out the waterproof camera bag from the upper part of my backpack, and then I tightly wrapped the camera in the bag. We had no option but to move on in the heavy rain. With our feet in the mud and the lightning flashing around us, we trudged on in the biting wind towards the village of Sinuva. Only on arrival could we find an inn to shelter from the storm.

Sinuva was worthy of the name because it is a place where the wind roars and the misty rain curls upwards all day long. That is why three inns had been set up there. It was really a refuge on the road to paradise. All those trekkers who had set out that day were sheltering there from the rain. We were the last trekkers to arrive. I saw wet dresses, trousers, shoes, hats and knapsacks hanging on ropes in front of the gate. I'd become drenched from spending forty minutes in the rain. Even my underwear had become wet and my hair was soaked through.

Sinuva, a refuge on the road to paradise

Bikram asked for two cups of hot ginger tea. I took a shower heated by water from a liquid gas storage tank. It was the last place I would be able to take a free shower. A group of youths from four different countries who had met each other in Kathmandu were in the sitting room discussing their journey the next day with their guide. A bespectacled girl from Holland shouted: "I don't trust you. Every time you said it would take five minutes to climb, it turned out that the slope went on forever!"

I laughed to myself. Actually my guide had been urging me to hurry every day of our journey. The hardships and dangers of trekking were far greater than I originally imagined. Sometimes, accidents and fear make people lose their way and they become suspicious and indecisive. Terrified people or animals can sometimes cause their own death. Only when you have confidence and stand firm can you keep a sober, flexible mind and your fears will recede. Only then will you become fearless.

Sinuva was the last place in the valley where mobile phone signals could be received. I asked my guide to call his wife so that she would feel assured that we would be back before the start of her confinement. Nothing is more important than the advent of a new life. If we failed to make good progress, I would stop trekking rather than insist Bikram accompanied me.

I took up temporary residence in a room of no more than five square metres and opened the camera to check my photos. It rained for much of the night, as if weeping in sorrow.

Eighty days later, having taken two flights to return to China, I met my husband at the airport and got into his Jeep. Not seeing my dog Xiaoban, I asked where it was. Normally, whenever my husband picked me up at the airport, it would always sit on the back seat and wait for me in excitement. Out of the blue, my husband said: "Our Xiaoban has died."

I wailed and asked him what had happened. It was the morning of 28 September, two days before the Chinese Mid-Autumn festival, when my guide and I left Jhinu Danda, that Xiaoban, who had lived with me for twelve years, left me forever and peacefully went to heaven. It died of old age in its kennel, with its head resting on its legs, curled up, as if sleeping a permanent sleep.

Not wanting to upset me in a foreign country, my husband decided to keep the news to himself. Each time I sent him a text message, he told me everything was fine, including Xiaoban and my mum, and that I should finish my pilgrimage and not be worried about the family.

Xiaoban was born on 30 June 2000, the day on which another Tibetan dog called Sisi died. Xiaoban was born in the house of a friend living far away while Sisi, who had lived with us for fourteen years, died a natural death. Before that I didn't believe in metempsychosis or the afterlife because I held no religious beliefs.

Two months later, I met with my friend who kept dogs. She had taken two spotted puppies for sale in the dog market. When I bent down, the dog named Xiaoban bit my long plait and pulled it playfully as if I were its toy or friend. Its beautiful smoky eyes watched me innocently and licked my face endlessly as if we'd known each other for ages. Meanwhile, the other dog ignored me as if I didn't exist, just licking its paws and playing with itself.

We paid 1,700 yuan for Xiaoban and took it home immediately. From then on it became the bane of our lives. It was naughty and hyperactive. It broke our belongings and got fleas. When we took it to the vet to treat a skin disease, I met the friend who sold me Xiaoban. She had taken her own dog to the vet for treatment. As we chatted, I realised that Xiaoban's birthday was the same day that Sisi died. I was astonished.

If we say Sisi was a gentleman, Xiaoban was a nuisance. It was a crazy 'hippie', following us to Yunnan, Tibet and other remote places and in the process became a dog fond of travelling. At the height of the SARS epidemic, the university where I taught was closed and dog walking was forbidden. Xiaoban was confined indoors for a month. Some students told me they often saw Xiaoban stand in front of the window on the sixth floor and greet them with its long, flat nose pressed against the glass. When I saw the messy wet nose prints on the glass, my tears welled up. It was only a dog, but it also longed for esteem and freedom.

Seeing me pack for my travels, it would leave sharp bite marks on any articles that carried my scent, such as my comb or bra. When I took out my press card at customs, I found it covered with bite marks. I was embarrassed telling the military police checking the card that the damage was caused by my dog. The young policeman smiled softly and I passed through into Tibet and Xinjiang safe and sound with my travel permit punctured with bite marks that I felt would surely bring me good luck.

Although it caused me endless trouble and made us despair, we still loved Xiaoban just as he crazily loved us. Sitting behind me while I worked, he accompanied me during each lonely day and night until I finished the book I was working on. Age eventually caught up with Xiaoban, and he could no longer get excited, rise to meet me, give me a playful bump, bite my plait, lick my face or wake me up in the morning.

Before I could wipe away my tears, my husband told me: "Your mother has been hospitalised for two weeks." We drove the Jeep directly to the hospital with all the luggage still in the back. My mother asked my husband not to tell me about her serious condition and that the cancer cells were causing her great pain. She was so strong and kind that she didn't want her suffering to spoil her daughter's journey.

I opened the door to the ward, stood in front of my mother's bed and held her frail hand lightly. Mum, I've come back. I will never leave you again in such a condition. Although we cannot predict the day of our birth or death, or the hardships that we might encounter, I will hold my mother's hands and accompany her journey into the dark night.

One rainy night in remote Sinuva, in the unseen world, I experienced the transmigration of one soul into the body of another and the baptism of innumerable lives in different time and space and the arrival and departure of different states of life. I thought that there was no adventure without torrents and no ascent without conquering adversity, and, similarly, no transcendence without true love and no rebirth without death, and finally, no sacrifice or devotion without great love and kind-heartedness. The mountain paths are circuitous, fate is full of ups and downs, and life comes and goes, but all paths lead to the peaks, having been in existence for tens of thousands of years.

We trek in order to live, and we live for trekking. The mountain paths of the Himalayas are 2,400 kilometres long and each of our steps was filled with brilliant expectations, encounters, purity and challenges. The mountains are the sons of the earth and the mountain paths are their daughters. Each mountain and each path will more grand and magnificent when you trek on them.

DAY FIVE

HIMALAYAN FLOWERS AND VERTICAL LIMITS

NATURE IS INDEED BEAUTIFUL, but it is also cruel and frightening at the same time. Nepal is not always a paradise for trekkers and mountaineers.

When I pushed open my window in the early morning of the fifth day, I was greeted with the sight of the mysterious Fish Tail Mountain. The sun was shining on the white mountains. I gargled while looking at the face of the snow mountain and listening to Nepalese sitar music on the lodge radio. Then, a young man from Hong Kong from the mixed team of four told me that a small Dornier aircraft heading for the base camp of Mount Everest had crashed following a collision with a bird at six in the morning on the previous day. All sixteen passengers, of whom five were Chinese, died in the crash along with three crew members.

I felt sorry for the victims. A similar accident happened the previous May. An aircraft carrying Indian pilgrims crashed near Jomsom Airport in northwest Nepal, killing fifteen. In another incident on 25 September last year, a plane crash killed all nineteen passengers and crew.

People from across the globe yearn for snow-capped mountains. An area covering no more than 150,000 square kilometres is home to eight of the fourteen highest mountains in the world. This tiny country, famed for it fine trekking and mountaineering, continues to attract travellers from all over the world. Nepal seems to have become a 'Garden of Eden' for those wanting to escape industrial pollution and urban life. Nevertheless, the fragile, backward transport infrastructure in this beautiful yet poor area tells you that it is not just a paradise but also sometimes a hell. A total of ninety-five souls were lost in six air crashes in Nepal over the last two years.

Trekking, horse-riding, travelling by bus, mountain biking, rafting, parachuting, off-roading or taking a light aircraft... among this wide range of options, airplanes are the fastest and most convenient form of transport but it can be a dangerous activity in this part of the world.

The challenging geographical conditions and the fast-changing temperatures in the Himalayas make the peaks penetrating the clouds loom like mighty deities or ethereal fairies. The deities are not an abstract concept or simply names muttered in prayer. The deities exist in different objects and can directly influence people's daily lives. Therefore, tribal folk often say that aircraft should not fly in the clouds above the Himalayas because the area is full of stones. It feels like there are stone giants standing high above the clouds. For decades, Nepal's tranquil valleys and small airports nestled in the steepest ridges pose the greatest dangers. Single-engine airplanes penetrate the clouds as thick as snow and follow a narrow route between two cliffs and then soar over mountains and ridges. No flight is more exciting or magnificent. For this reason, and despite the risks involved, there is always a high demand to fly above the Nepalese mountains.

In order to save time and energy, travellers often prefer to fly rather than take a slower form of transport. Nonetheless, it must be known that everything develops slowly. The mountains are forged over thousands of years. Only when we trek step by step can we take in the imposing scenery and experience its subtle beauty and sheer magnificence. Trekking is the most informative, most beautiful and safest means of travelling in Nepal.

A young Chinese woman who died in a plane crash wrote her last words on a social media site before the accident: "I don't want to sleep in a room without stars. I don't want to lie on a big bed without the sound of flowing water. I want to go to K2 because it is steep and beautiful."

Only by trekking step by step can we take in the imposing scenery

Some people are destined to belong to the polar regions. We 'trekkers' know that the snow mountains will be proud of our impending arrival, whether we actually get there or not. We revere the land under our feet and experience the happiness, temptations and lust for exploration, the laws of nature and a desire to understand how the great mountains, their forms and charms, are forged.

The mountains are holy because of our visions and because we trek.

Bewitching flowers and walking birds

I promised Bikram that I would quicken my pace. But I wasn't to know that I would experience my strangest and toughest day of travelling.

From Sinuva, we continued climbing, from a forest abundant with pink azaleas and to the 2,470-metre Kuldi on top of which the hidden villages of Bamboo and Doban came into view. The path stretched from the Chhomrong Valley to the Upper Modi Valley. Sometimes, the distance between two ridges was just a few kilometres, separated by mountains with precipitous drops that we planned to traverse in a single day.

Before setting off that morning, we stood on a mountain top and pointed to the place where we were due to arrive in the evening. It looked well within reach but was actually a long way. It usually took several hours for us to walk from the top to the foot of a mountain, cross a river, walk on a smooth gravel path and then climb for a long stretch. Sometimes, the elevation range of our trek in a single day could be thousands of metres.

The forest was lush with blooming azaleas along the sun-bathed slope of Kuldi, with lavender orchids, pink lilacs and dark green ferns under the trees. Nepal has up to thirty types of azalea, one of which, the red 'tree-shaped azalea', is the national flower. Standing more than fifteen metres tall, the azaleas change colour with altitude, from pink to pale white and then to pure white above 2,500 metres. When the snow melts in spring, the azaleas start to bloom and a gorgeous florescence persists until the rainy season in June and July.

The greatest difference between the southern slope of the Himalayas in Nepal and the northern slope of the same mountain range in Tibet, is in the abundance of azalea trees that cover the mountains and fields of Nepal. Like the romantic Sura, they bring pleasure to all the Himalayan deities. It is a miraculous integration of tenderness and power. The petals of azaleas exposed to wind and rain are both beautiful and massive, like the florid faces of women. They are utterly different from their delicate counterparts found in cities. Wild azaleas are like flowers in classical Chinese scroll paintings, neither chaotic nor complex. Trees are a favourite subject of painters. A flower can be casually inserted into one's hair, like a beautiful girl going to a feast of the deities.

The Nepalese use azaleas in incense or they soak them in saline water with the nectar that contains a natural hallucinogen similar to cannabis. Trekkers walking on paths lined with azalea petals are often reluctant to leave. They love the sensation of petals in riotous profusion falling softly on their faces and bodies. The petals rest on their bellies like fairies. The flowers at the root of the trees give off a fragrance in the white light and generate a feeling of sweet intoxication.

When the Japanese writer Yasunari Kawabata wrote his speech for winning the Nobel Prize for Literature, he began by quoting a Japanese song by the Zen Master Dogen: "Spring flowers, autumn moon, azaleas in summer bloom, pure white winter snow adds much cold." Intoxicated, dizzy in deep meditation, we traversed the ridges in Kuldi. We then walked a long section of the wet, slippery downward slope and stumbled to the bottom of Bamboo Valley where the sun cannot penetrate.

Bikram grabbed my hand and urged me to stop, pointing out an odd-shaped little bird standing on a distant rock. It wore a shining sapphire and blue skirt, with billowing sleeves, fire-red stripes around its neck and a bandana on its head, looking like a Marvel Comics bank robber. It stared at us quietly and stood motionless, taking in our unexpected presence. Then it bent its beautiful neck as if giving us a graceful curtsy, dragged its golden underskirt slowly, flapped its wings and flew away.

Bikram whispered to me that it was a Himalayan monal, a bird in the pheasant family known as '*danphe*' in Nepali, its name being derived from its metallic feathers of iridescent lustre. Ah, I remembered that it was the national bird of Nepal.

Nepal accounts for merely a tenth of one per cent of the world's total area. But it is home to ten per cent of all known birds, 850 of them in total, including seventy-two endangered species. For this reason, the imposing Himalayas are not just worshipped by mountaineers, trekkers and pilgrims but also by bird watchers from across the world. Male monals have gorgeous blue annular feathers like those of a peacock; the females are similar to grey-brown pheasants, but without the brilliant feathers. Neither the male nor the female can fly. Instead, they walk up and down the mountains on foot like us.

The rare monal pheasants are worshiped as divine birds in the Himalayas and it is highly auspicious to see one. Trekkers can spend years in the mountains and not see a single one. So Bikram told me that those trekkers fortunate enough to have seen a monal pheasant would have good luck thereafter because the Himalayan deities had smiled on them.

Yes, since I started walking in the Himalayas, I began smiling to myself all the time. It reminded me of a verse written by the Chilean poet Pablo Neruda: "Take bread away from me, if you wish, / take the air away, / but do not take from me your laughter." As I took long strides with a smile on my face, my body was able to withstand exile, torture and revolution.

Bamboo's miracle

Bamboo is a damp, recently formed valley, where the Modi Khola roars and tall bamboo blocks out all the sky. Most trekkers like to stop over in the valley so they can 'walk on high ground and sleep on low ground'. Since the altitude of the lodge where they spend the night is lower than what they reach during the day, they can adapt themselves gradually to the alpine environment and have the sense of seclusion experienced by 'birds perching in trees beside the pond and monks knocking on the door in the moonlight' in the words of a poem by Jia Dao that inspired a traditional Chinese ink painting.

A sign stating '150 rupees for hot bath' was hung on the bathroom wall, showing how expensive it is for trekkers to use water. If you want to take a hot bath, you should pay about ten yuan.

The famous Song dynasty poet Su Tungpo once wrote: "Man can live without meat but not without bamboo." These words reflected the refined pleasures enjoyed by China's literati. I now realised that the Himalayan tribal people also revere bamboo.

Nepal has twenty types of bamboo, where it is indispensable in the lives of many ethnic minorities. Bamboo is particularly valued by the Rai people, whose legend holds that it was one of the first living things to be bred in the womb of the Goddess of Creation. A typical Rai house contains more than fifty kinds of handicrafts made of bamboo. Bamboo is used to make walls and houses, mats, chairs, benches and cribs, as well as more exotic items, such as bows and arrows for hunting, mousetraps, water butts and a brush used in Shamanic séances.

They do not tend to use umbrellas but instead wear bamboo hats that are foldable and convenient for carrying. Like a giant mushroom when opened, a bamboo hat not only frees both hands for work but also covers all the items in a pack basket. Their hollowed-out pack baskets are diamond-shaped, like a potbellied arhat, being narrow at the bottom and wide at the top. A pack basket can carry loads of more than thirty kilograms. Porters fasten a cotton-knitted band through the pack basket and around their head, rather than letting their shoulders carry the burden. Their foreheads must be as strong as iron and capable of moving mountains like the Foolish Old Man tried to do in Chinese mythology.

Mountaineering is impossible without porters and bamboo baskets

In Himalayan regions at an altitude between 1,000 and 2,000 metres, tribal people mostly plant draught-tolerant crops such as barley, potatoes, millet and lentils, but few vegetables; however, above 2,000 metres, very few crops are planted at all because there are no permanent villages here. So all the food eaten by trekkers is carried by the tribal people in their pack baskets.

Goods are delivered by donkey to Chhomrong, which serves as the largest transfer station in the Annapurna Peaks. Thereafter, as the altitude rises, the mountain paths become steeper and narrower. So donkeys are replaced by porters, who carry all the materials on their backs until they reach Annapurna Base Camp. Given the heavy loads that they carry, the porters work tirelessly and take small strides, traversing mountains and delivering a constant supply of daily necessities to the remotest peaks and valleys.

Nepal is one of the poorest countries in the world and the daily income of those in their twenties averages merely two dollars a day. Those porters carrying heavy loads to the lodges and campsites also earn two dollars a day. Their pack baskets are large, light and strong but the items they carry can be bulky and dangerous, such as liquefied natural gas storage tanks and oxygen canisters, along with small items such as salt, rice, beer and Coca-Cola. They also like to cultivate small plots of land next to the campsites, somehow managing to grow Chinese cabbages and cauliflowers. A woven bamboo mat is commonly placed over a pigpen used to store vegetables to protect them from frost and the attention of livestock. Life in high-altitude mountain areas is very hard but it does lend itself to great invention.

A bamboo basket can bear a load of forty kilograms

Haunted by the yeti

Moving upwards alongside a stream flowing in the Modi Valley for about ninety minutes, we came across another place to stay in the village of

Doban. One of the main problems while trekking is hunger. I often used to dream of eating a barbecue of local delicacies and wild game.

In Doban, at an altitude of 2,500 metres, I enjoyed morning refreshments in the sun, spending seventy rupees on a cup of ginger-lemon tea and 110 rupees on a potful of hot water. I came across four young Chinese women who had met up online and an old couple from the Netherlands. The man and his wife were doctors and they hadn't hired any porters. Instead, they each carried their own twenty-litre backpacks. Jokingly referring to themselves as 'snails', they said they walked for no more than three hours every day to travel from one site to the next. When I took a photo of them, the lady smiled like a sunflower, kept on asking her white-haired husband whether she looked OK and requested me to hide her eyebags in the photo.

The Dutch couple carried their own packs

All the trekkers we encountered, whatever their age, looked young in both mind and body. A youthful outlook is not exclusive to the young. It is actually a state of mind, a kind of a joyful emotional spirit. We can stay young by overcoming cowardice and material desire and willingly giving up a cosy family life to travel in nature. A sixty-five-year-old woman can have the courage and disposition of a person forty years younger.

I walked on with the couple and clambered over snowslides, which are common between Doban and Fish Tail Mountain. Here, tons of ice and snow collect and block the paths. Some trekkers have died from becoming trapped in snowslides for days. For this reason, whenever we met trekkers coming in the opposite direction, my guide inquired about the conditions ahead. Mountaineers set up a simple shrine in a stone house along the path to consecrate mountain flowers and leaves and hung up small prayer flags, following the instructions of the God of the Mountains, and made sure not to bring eggs or meat to the mountain lest he should be enraged and inflict snowslides as punishment.

The Gurung people say that, before trekkers first came to the Himalayas, Annapurna was the best place for nurturing the soul and no animal there should be slaughtered for food. According to ancient Chinese geomancy, *ahimsa* is a cardinal virtue that is based on the premise that all living beings contain the spark of divine spiritual energy. The so-called geomantic treasure land is the most vibrant place. Therefore, hurting another being is akin to hurting oneself. For this reason, after the mountaineer Jimmy Roberts failed to ascend Fish Tail in 1956, he travelled all the way to the holy Annapurna to receive spiritual blessing there.

It was one o'clock when we arrived at the Himalayan Hotel at an altitude of 2,900 metres, where we ordered potato curry and *dal bhat*. Nothing else was on the menu. There were no shallow-fried crab eggs or delicious meat, just potatoes that tasted like the earth we trod on every day. I hoped that there was goodness in each delicate potato skin, just like the abundant treasures that exist under the earth's surface. I ate so many potatoes during my travels that I imagined their skins could be made into a beautiful Chanel skirt, reminding me of that fashion show in which the models wore clothes made with the *Southern Urban Daily* newspaper.

Outside the Himalaya Hotel, which stands at an altitude of more than 3,000 metres, is a signpost stating that two-thirds of the journey to Annapurna Base Camp had been covered.

Trekkers like to stay in the Himalaya Hotel because of its beautiful location above a bottomless valley and below the Annapurna mountains. Mist often swirls around, creating the illusion that the legendary yeti of the Himalayas would appear like King Kong in a Hollywood blockbuster. Several porters were packed into a chilly sitting room, vividly describing the legend of the snowmen to their clients. Trekkers to the Himalayas are always keen to unravel the truth about the yeti.

It is said that mysterious creatures that are both large and quick often appear in the wind and snow in the alpine regions of the Himalayas. Those porters who claim to have seen a yeti say it has red hair and moves fast, and that its feet are able to turn 180 degrees while their body remains immobile so as to facilitate their ability to climb and escape. They are said to carry heavy, black stones under their armpits to hit buffaloes, snow leopards, lynxes or even women. Having thrown a stone, the yeti would retrieve it and put it back under its armpit for future use. Male yetis are regarded as lascivious and they would frequently pursue women. So in order to ensure the safety of women in mountain areas, some villages leave open wine jars outdoors for the yeti to drink their fill. The idea is that drunken yetis would forget their lust and stagger back to their cave to sleep.

Reaching the Himalaya Hotel after five days of trekking

Although the number of trekkers and mountaineers in the Himalayas has increased over the years, and many of them are equipped with high-powered telescopes and cameras, no one has yet captured an image of the yeti. Therefore, this creature, just like the fictional Shangri-La, remains a mysterious source of attraction to foreigners.

I also wanted to spend the entire day resting in the Himalaya Hotel at high altitude, to light an oil lamp for the yeti and drink *raksi* with it. Only those who believe in the existence of the yeti and have never seen one are happy because the pleasure is derived from the pursuit and their imagination.

However, my physical condition was worsening as we climbed higher. My cough had become quite serious and I had no medicine to take. I asked a Chinese team resting there for some medicine, but they didn't have any either. My guide thought it was still early and we could reach Deorali before sunset if we moved on.

'Gay-Neck' pigeon in the storm

It was cloudy and the temperature had plunged when I left the Himalaya Hotel, so I put on my army-green Gore-Tex waterproof windcheater. As we started out, huge thunder clouds were gathering above the cliffs, while lightning illuminated the sky ahead and the trees were swaying in the whistling wind. We were ill-prepared to walk in a thunderstorm. There was only a solitary mountain path ahead and, with the rain pouring down, there was no alternative but to press on.

As a matter of fact, thundershowers in high-altitude mountain areas above 3,000 metres occur most afternoons. Usually, it is sunny in the morning as trekkers set out in high spirits. However, colder temperatures at higher elevations often lead to precipitation, since cold air can't hold as much moisture as warm air. The beautiful clouds we saw in the sky became thicker, and cumulonimbus clouds started to form. Soon afterwards, we were caught in a rainstorm.

Rainstorms pose a significant threat to trekkers. A brook can quickly be transformed into a raging torrent, and a mountain path cut into a cliff side can be inundated with falling stones. With visibility reduced to just a few metres, I found it hard to breathe when I tried to climb a single step and my lungs ached as if they were about to explode. I trekked in that state for more than three hours as the rain poured down. It felt like the toughest experience of my life.

In cities, you can always ask someone to carry your bags or give you a lift somewhere. But in nature, when you get caught in the rain or if you fall ill, there is often no one around to help. All you can do is grit your teeth, shake off the rainwater like a dog and move forward mechanically, step by step.

It is said that the yeti, while often accused of attacking people, can also save them. When Captain d'Auvergue, curator of the Victoria Memorial in Calcutta, travelled to the Himalayas alone in 1938, he encountered a fierce snowstorm. The strong light reflecting off the snow made it impossible for him to open his eyes, and he found himself with no option but to wait there and turn into a stiff corpse. On approaching death, he felt his body being covered by an animal three metres tall and his life was saved. When he slowly regained consciousness, the huge animal had mysteriously disappeared, leaving only its odour. As I recalled this story, I too hoped that a yeti would come to my rescue and clasp me under its smelly armpit like a stone before moving on into the boundless wilderness.

When I climbed to the cliff ridge at 3,100 metres, I saw a group of seven or eight trekkers taking shelter from the rain in a cave. I believed that the cave high up in the air was a blessing from God because it provided a natural shelter, like a Noah's Ark for mountaineers battered by the wind and rain. Hinku Cave provided the only natural shelter from the thunderstorm. Outside the cave, I had a commanding view of a path that ran along the Hinku Glacier that was covered with pebbles and boulders of all sizes. It was the path to Deurali.

We encountered a foreign woman who, like me, had brought hardly any rain gear. After inquiring about the route from Bikram, she leaped like a swift into the heavy rain that blurred her image as she made her way along the stone ripraps. If we decided to wait there, we would have to sleep out in Hinku Cave. I recognised one of the Chinese girls from the time when I had my morning tea and respite in Doban. Seeing my black lips and shivering form, and hearing the difficulties I had in breathing, she placed a spare piece of plastic cloth over my head.

We dashed into the rain again, and I was thinking how the leaping foreign girl reminded me of Gay-Neck, a fictional carrier pigeon that was trained to fly across the Himalayas and was later taken to Europe to serve as a messenger pigeon in World War I. Only Gay-Neck, with iridescent feathers around its neck would stay on course in a storm and become the king of messenger pigeons that can bravely fly across the Himalayas. During the two world wars, Indians and Nepalese, whatever their class, were busy training carrier pigeons for the British Army. These pigeons flew in the azure sky like floating clouds, taking their music and beautiful posture to all corners of the world. Around their colourful eyes, there is a film as thin as tissue paper that protects them from sand and dust, and from storms and strong sunshine, as they endeavoured to carry out the vital tasks of delivering messages in time of war.

I longed to be like Gay-Neck, able to fly over mountains during a storm.

Trekkers take shelter from the rain in a cave

Tears in the night

At an altitude of 3,200 metres, Deurali, meaning precipice in Nepali, faces massive snow mountains of more than 6,000 metres. Between them is an almost sheer ravine, down which granite rocks and boulders tumble noisily and mingle with the roaring sound of flowing water. This is the gateway to Annapurna Base Camp, where the Annapurna Conservation Area Project has set up two lodges. I felt unwell the moment I entered Room Four of the Dream Lodge. I thought the 300-metre climb would be the death of me.

Tearing open my windcheater, Bikram found my clothes were as soaked as if I had spent an hour in a sauna, and my body was wet and cold all over. He immediately ran to the kitchen and brought a small bowl of hot water that was provided for porters and guides so that my hands could warm up. I asked how much a basin of water cost. He told me a hundred rupees. I asked him to buy some straight away because I urgently needed to bathe my feet in hot water.

I was suffering from altitude sickness, coughing rapidly and breathing with severe difficulty. I was unable to lie on my back and my body temperature dropped, despite the fact that I'd been walking for so long. With the steady increase in altitude, I felt like Gay-Neck crossing the Himalayas and didn't pay proper attention to the overwhelming altitude stress.

When trekkers climb above 3,000 metres, they can find themselves suddenly stricken with acute mountain sickness. I had been walking in the rain for a long time and got hypothermia. With a fall in temperature, my body's natural reaction was to become numb and insensitive. I began to shiver and spasm beyond control as my body tried to warm itself. Seemingly under a magic spell, I could breathe only weakly and was unable to resist any longer. My sense of time and distance disappeared and I was lost in a trance.

When my guide came back with a small half bucket of hot water that cost 500 rupees, I leaned against the bedside and lost consciousness. He put my feet in the water, crouched and began to wash them. Scalding tears fell from my eyes and into the bucket.

My parents used to wash the feet of my brother and me when we were young. But in adulthood, a mixture of social and cultural factors along with religious conventions mean that not even the spouse of a Chinese person would wash their feet. And yet here, despite the fact that we'd been trekking together for only five days, my guide was reaching out his hands and squatting on the floor like a servant in order to try to expel the cold from my body and save my life.

The trust, care and friendship he showed by rubbing my feet are imprinted on my mind. From the tips of my toes, my whole body started to warm up. Although no words were spoken, we started to develop a strong respect for each other. Various philanthropic acts are mentioned in *The Bible*, including 'give without sparing', 'trust without wavering', 'promise without forgetting' and 'pray without ceasing'... Sometimes, I wonder whether I put myself in danger just to discover the things I had been missing, such as friendship, courage, perseverance, profundity, gratitude and fearlessness.

Sincerity and trust are crucial factors in mountain trekking. Led by my guide, I had total confidence in being able to ascend the mountain top and reach Annapurna Base Camp. The path is not narrow, insular, quiet, lonely or isolated from the modern society we come from, but is closely connected with our heart, nature, life and the entire cosmos. Your efforts will eventually be rewarded and your love will gain sincere and true respect. You, in your best light, will meet the best in others.

While listening to a Himalayan river roaring like an obstinate and unruly beast in the night, I seemed to hear an anthem sung by my guide in Sanskrit:

"I wish the Himalayan monsoon will take away your sorrows, terror and misgivings; your body will be filled with boundless courage; when it is quiet, peace and power will become your wings; courage will shine in your eyes and fill your heart with permanent power, peace and harmony..."

DAY SIX

FOLLOW THE SNOW LIGHT OF FISH TAIL AND WANDER

People's facial appearance, skin, body shape, stamina and posture all change over time and in different environments. But the colour of one's eyes never varies. Just like the colour of my eyes, trekking is an essential part of me and cannot be changed.

In a weekend edition of the *New York Times* on 18 March 1923, a journalist once asked the eminent British mountaineer George Mallory: "Why climb Mount Everest?"

"Because it is there," he famously replied.

More than half a century later, in 1999, an American expedition discovered the remains of Mallory, who had died while attempting to climb Everest in 1924. Miraculously, his body had remained intact and he was still wearing his graceful tweed suit. These early mountaineering expeditions were quite different from those of today, with their technologically advanced equipment. In those days, mountaineers wore tweed coats and took the simplest cameras to the campsite. There was no means of communication between the mountaineering team and the campsite. It meant that you had to depend on yourself from the moment you entered the mountain area. Mallory's remains were found just 678 metres away from the 8,848-metre summit, and his blue eyes were staring infinitely into the sky.

The disappearance of George Mallory and his partner Andrew 'Sandy' Comyn Irvine after their second attempt to climb Mount Everest was one of the most perplexing mysteries of the twentieth century. The public was left unsure whether he had become the first to climb the world's highest peak. The expedition team were not able to find his Kodak camera, so no proof existed of him having reached the summit. It is believed that the camera was taken by Irvine, whose remains were not discovered until recently. But their courage to overcome adversity is not disputed and is still a source of encouragement for all explorers.

"I regard Mallory as a hero. It was he who brought Mount Everest into public awareness. If only one person can reach the peak, it must be him," said Sir Edmund Hillary, who was the first to climb Mount Everest twenty-nine years later.

The thirty-eight-year-old Mallory was once a teacher at Charterhouse School in the UK, and he was also a talented writer. Handsome and with a fine physique, he was charming but also somewhat aloof. He was a romantic aesthete and an idealist, and in a tent on Mount Everest, he and his companion read *Hamlet* and *King Lear* to each other. He integrated himself with nature through mountaineering. He refused to use the word 'conquer' because, in his words: "The only enemies we need to conquer are ourselves." He was an artist and mountaineer, and future generations would come to regard him as a follower of Eastern philosophy. It was as if he was less interested in reaching the summit than in getting close to the sky.

Since his death, "Because it is there" has become a famous quotation. I like to carry it on my back and under the soles of my feet and wander seeing things through Mallory's eyes.

My luggage comprised only a camera, a laptop, a colourful bracelet, a straw hat, a windcheater and two spare pairs of pants. Without any sleeping bag, raincoat, heater or lamp, my luggage weighed only twelve kilograms. So far, I had managed to trek from Pokhara at an altitude of 884 metres to Deurali at 3,200 metres. Although the noise of the Himalayan storms shook the earth and trees and I seemed to have fallen into a thundery washing machine, after rising following a sleepless night, my altitude sickness had miraculously disappeared.

Many trekkers were caught in the rainstorm in Deurali the night before. The rows of wet clothes and bags that were hanging outside the log cabins presented a heroic scene the next morning. Should I now redouble my efforts and trek onwards to Annapurna Base Camp?

Stone signposts

The mountains in Deurali looked like rows of bizarre guards, frostily greeting the first rays of dawn and crossing the deep ravines. When I squatted on the wet earth to take a low-angle photo, I saw a Korean woman wandering alone. So I reached out my hand to shelter her from the rain and took two photos of her and the mountain. Hearing me cough as I stood up, she opened her bag and took out six cough sweets for me. Throughout the journey, I was filled with emotion on seeing solitary trekkers offer help to others.

From Deurali, we took the mountain path against the flow of the river, with stones all around. The ground was hard on the feet and there was a high risk of spraining an ankle. The clear Modi Khola meandered and darted along the valley floor. It was alternately calm then stormy, like a dark goddess losing her temper. I was careful to mind my step as I walked over the stones, fearful I might fall over. My guide joked that it was imperative to steer clear of injury since no one can crawl to Annapurna Base Camp on their hands and knees.

We set out early, only to encounter some other early birds in the form of tribal people carrying heavy boulders on their backs. We stopped to make way for them. They weren't wearing pack baskets but wooden buckets instead. Capable of bearing such a heavy weight, they were as tough as the rocks they were carrying.

Stones are used for building materials and tools in the Himalayas

There is no brick, cement, bamboo or thatch available in the high Himalayas, where stones are used for building materials and tools. Houses, roofs and sills are all made of stone, keeping the buildings warm during snowstorms. However, it is difficult to build small stone lodges for trekkers on a barren mountain between 3,000 metres and 4,000 metres high. The mountain paths are quite dangerous, especially for those trudging over piles of loose rubble with stones on their backs. They would surely perish if they fell down the mountainside.

The British army maintains a camp in Pokhara. Each year, hundreds of young men join the Gurkha regiment having passed a gruelling selection process that involves a stamina test of walking five kilometres on a mountain path with a basket on their backs containing twenty-five kilograms of stones. Only the physically and mentally strongest can finish the task. Men born from the mountainous areas of Nepal have a stronger physique and more stamina than people from almost any other part of the world. They are attracted by the prospect of earning more than a thousand pounds a month after being selected to be a Gurkha soldier, with a service period of sixteen years. In contrast, the average income of other young men from the mountainous areas of Nepal is no more than a pound a day.

Gurkha soldiers are renowned for their effectiveness in close combat. It takes them only half a second to lie on the ground, aim their gun and prepare to shoot. Some have worked in a peacekeeping capacity in Afghanistan, Bosnia and Sierra Leone or as elite bodyguards in India, Singapore, Brunei and Sudan. The foundation of their physical strength are their bones, which are as indestructible as the Himalayan mountain rocks.

As we climbed higher, I started to see rocks of various size piled up at desolate junctions, crossings and peaks. These piles might be among the oldest signposts in the world, and similar ones can be seen in many different countries. When walking in the desert, ancient Arabs would use stone piles to show a route of exploration, while two piles indicate a fork in the path ahead; a circle of small stones around two piles of stones mean that danger lies ahead and caution should be taken. Mongolians create sacred stone heaps known as *obo*, which serve mainly as sites for worshipping gods.

Ancient stone piles are now used to give directions to trekkers in the vast, desolate regions of the Himalayas. Year after year, tribal people trudge up the mountains to pile up rocks, one after another, in places where a path has become invisible. In a country like Nepal where numerous deities are worshipped, people live and prosper in the rolling snow-capped mountains. They cherish the ever-changing physical world and think that every mountain, wood and stone houses the gods of destruction and salvation.

For this reason, they carve scriptures and all sorts of figures of the Buddha and auspicious patterns in gorgeous colours on these ordinary stones at path intersections so that they are turned into sacred Mani stones.

They believe that Mani stones have a supernatural spirituality that will bring them good luck and protect them against disaster. So the tribal people, young and old, male and female, on foot or riding a horse, will add a small stone to the pile while saying a prayer and taking off their hats, bowing with their palms together devoutly and turning clockwise whenever they pass a pile of Mani stones. Adding a stone is similar to chanting scriptures. If there is no stone around, they will throw a bone, a piece of cloth or hide, or a handful of wool or hair. During a memorial ceremony, they will shout loudly: "Lasolo, the deities will win! Demons will lose! Whir, whir!" They pour out their hearts to the Mani stones, praying for everyone who passes by. The face of a deity is painted underneath each stone. This is the intersection between the mortal world and heaven and the deities.

My guide reminded me to pay special attention to the stone signposts among the ripraps. Sometimes, I saw small piles of stones. My guide told me they were signposts used by specific groups of people, for instance, hunters, mountaineers or caving experts. When I put down a small stone facing Fish Tail Mountain overhead, I yearned to become a stone in a future life to serve as a tiny, simple guidepost in the enduring texture of the Himalayas, one half in the dust in serenity and the other flying in the sky.

Monarch of the sky

A vast expanse of valleys and hills came into view, and the mountain path leading to the base camp of Fish Tail Mountain became flatter and less steep after we climbed over the ridge in Deurali.

For days we struggled on the ridge, with its precipitous slopes, valleys and rugged paths. Most of the time, we walked like ants in the shadow of high mountains. Now, the valleys unfolded before us, full of beautiful wild flowers and streams flowing serenely. Goats and sheep were basking in the sun. We were drawn into a dreamland. The valley stretched like the lines on my palm, lifelines of different lengths, rising and falling, lines of emotion and fortune. I decided to walk ahead along the smooth line of fortune.

. . .

Our route took us from subtropical, low-altitude mountain land to the snowy peaks where the air is dry, cold and clear. The path was surrounded by thick grass, giving off the rich, soft and refreshing smell of chlorophyll. A myriad of wild flowers competed for space in the thick, fertile valley soil, including many rare species, such as St. John's wort, gentian and magnolia, while giant mushroom-shaped banyan trees, orange-leaved maples, golden-flowered oaks, wattles and eucalyptus stood freely in the dry, sunny climate under a pure, clean sky.

Just as he knew all the local villages, rivers and temples, my guide was also familiar with its plants and animals. Eagles, black kites, sunbirds, sparrow hawks, wapitis, musk deer, guenon monkeys, gorals, wild boars and rabbits flourish in the plant-rich forests, along with the animals that prey on them such as Himalayan snow leopards, vultures and black bears. That is why birds and beasts could be seen at high altitude. Himalayan vultures, which have a wingspan up to three metres, build their nests in places where thermals and updrafts can assist their flight.

Why do they do it? Because of the natural instincts of a vulture!

They stand on a precipice at the entrance to a cave buffeted by the wind or soar in the sky. Their feathers are tan with streaks of white and golden yellow. When I looked up at the blue sky and saw vultures soaring among the mountains, I felt the perfect combination of strength and beauty between sky and earth.

I once interviewed Scott Mason, a trekker from London, who had become famous in Nepal because he had trained to work with falcons.

Tribal people had accidentally injured two black kite chicks that had fallen to the ground when they chopped down some trees in the Madikula forest in the Annapurna Peaks. The birds were less than a week old and would soon die without the care of their parents. When the tribal people took the little birds to Scott for treatment, he took them in and named them Sapana and Shidoko, meaning 'dream' and 'road' in Nepali.

The ancient Chinese used to train falcons to go hunting with kings and nobles. Having read ancient Chinese books, Scott had a brilliant idea: to train black kites to fly alongside paragliders.

Occasionally, the tribal people would send injured birds to Scott for treatment and he became a kind of vet for birds. In total, he took in eight birds of prey including vultures and black kites. These kings of the air with wingspans measuring at least one metre, chiefly preyed on small animals or other birds and can live up to twelve years in the wild. Scott regarded them as his own babies and began the long process of training them.

About a year later, Sapana realised Scott's dream and became the first bird of the Himalayan Bird Salvation Programme to survive to adulthood and also the first bird to successfully accompany a paraglider in flight. Later, a female black kite named Brad, only four weeks old, learned to excel in flying after eighteen months of training and Scott founded the sport of 'parahawking', in which aviators and their customers fly with vultures in the sky. The birds are able to lead paragliders to find the best thermal currents. The customers are able to feed the eagles in flight and allow them to sit on their shoulders, arms and heads.

Scott said that all the Himalayan vultures he'd taken in would sit facing the wind, from birth to the moment they could fly. They can soar in the sky nearly a kilometre above rabbits and marmots running on the grass, with their tails controlling the direction of flight. With their leg feathers blowing in the wind, they can rapidly descend to capture the prey in their claws. It is truly exhilarating to be able to fly freely with these kings of the sky.

Sapana was Scott's first chick to survive to adulthood

Shidoko means 'road' in Nepali

Brad, king of the sky

Scott training his hawk Sapana

Trekkers can fly together with Scott and his hawk

If trekkers are like snails on a mountain path and mountaineers are like elves on a cliff face, the eagles are the Aero Kings of the Himalayas. It is said that only two kinds of animal can reach the top of a mountain; one is the eagle that can soar into the sky and the other is the snail that moves upward inch by inch and can spend a month, a year or even a whole lifetime in climbing from low to high. People have been able to detect the trail of snails at the top of mountains. I thought of myself as a Himalayan vulture, climbing at a snail-like pace while my guide seemed to be the hand directing me.

I sweated, panted and climbed forward little by little. Oh, my God! Why did you make me, like a snail, climb the mountains? But when I finally stood at the base camp of the 3,700-metre Fish Tail Mountain, I couldn't help crying. I was able to view the perfect, pyramid-shaped peak just like an eagle.

My outdoor jacket and headscarf seemed to be endowed with life and flickered on me like wings.

Story of a hiker's tea house

As long as you continue climbing, you can enjoy the most moving moments of life. The sea doesn't explain its depth, but it cannot prevent all the rivers from running into it; the earth does not explain its thickness, but it still holds all the living things on earth; the mountains do not explain their height, but nothing can replace their position high in the clouds. What's the significance of hiking in the Himalayas? All of a sudden, an altitude of four thousand metres no longer seemed so high. I could stroll comfortably and then rest, and only when I climbed upwards was I conscious of the rarefied air.

After we ate a meal of instant noodles and soup at Machhapuchhre Base Camp, I saw a wooden signpost for Annapurna Base Camp, and in the distance I could make out our destination at 4,130 metres. But my guide unpacked my bag and insisted that we should stay where we were overnight because I needed to adjust to the altitude and see whether I had any adverse reaction. Usually, the last five hundred metres of an ascent are the most dangerous. At my pace, it would take at least four hours to arrive at Annapurna Base Camp, by which time it would be approaching evening. There might be no accommodation by then, since the camp only had 120 beds in service.

I tamely agreed to his suggestion and saw several ghost-men wave to me in the distance. They turned out to be the three young people from Hamburg we had met on the first day of our journey. They had already reached Annapurna Base Camp two days previously and they were now on their way back. They encamped in the snow mountain, slept in sleeping bags, bathed in the snow light at Fish Tail Mountain, sipped coffee and basked in the sunshine. What gave them the most pleasure?

"Soaking up the sun," they replied. The Chinese characters '沐浴', composed of 'three dots and wood' and 'three dots and valley', mean that life should be filled with mountains, rivers, trees, grain, delicacies, gorgeous scenery and abundant sunshine. Being unable to step into the sunshine is a great sadness, no matter how wealthy you are or what goals you have achieved. I regard innermost pleasure, composure and serenity to be the true source of happiness.

Machhapuchhre Base Camp on Fish Tail Mountain

Machhapuchhre Base Camp was built in the style of an Alpine cabin. Foreigners call it Fish Tail simply because of its shape. In Nepali it is called Machhapuchhre, meaning pure white holy virgin peak. In modern times, as travellers shifted their attention to the boundless outdoors, the Himalayas, one of the world's greatest natural landscapes, remained isolated.

Revived by a cup of coffee, I watch the sun set slowly behind Fish Tail

Nepal didn't relax its restrictions on foreign travellers until 1949, so those mountaineers who had conquered the most challenging European mountains were frustrated in being able to test their mountaineering skills in the Himalayan peaks. Without roads or modern modes of transportation, the first explorers willingly withstood the challenging environment and hired porters and packhorses, took their own supplies, ate the local food and stayed in basic tents for months at a time.

Lieutenant Colonel Jimmy Roberts of Britain's Gurkha regiment left the army and became the first businessman to become involved in trekking tourism. He climbed a number of peaks in Nepal and Pakistan, and in 1964 he set up the first hiking travel agency in Nepal to provide a full range of services, including the provision of maps, porters, guides and campsites for trekkers. At this time, trekking tourism was starting to take off in Nepal.

Rural tea houses and lodges were built by the villagers at both ends of each popular trekking route. Hence, a new English phrase 'tea house trekking' was coined. Similar to Alpine huts, these tea houses or lodges were made of wood or stone with internal dividers splitting the area into a dining zone, sitting rooms, private rooms, public toilets and garden-style corridors and courtyards. The tea houses made it possible for solitary trekkers or trekking teams to travel without having to carry heavy camping equipment. A sleeping bag may be required, but there's no need to bring a tent, cooker or food. Trekking from one tea house to another or from one lodge to another can also enable trekkers to experience Nepalese family life and appreciate their values: family strength, unity, respect, love, a pure mind, geniality and friendship, as well as the pleasant sense of humour of tribal people.

Nepal has set the standard for high-quality international trekking. If trekkers are unwilling to stay in a tea house or lodge, a tent-pitching team can be employed. An expedition of six trekkers might be accompanied by a back-up team of twelve, including porters, a guide, cook, handyman and a supervisor known as a sirdar. A sirdar, meaning tribal chief or commander, ensures the safety and comfort of the trekkers. He is able to speak fluent English and is responsible for supervising the deployment and dismissal of back-up team members and resolve any disagreements should they arise. The guide usually accompanies and assists the trekkers on mountain paths, while the porters carry all the food and camping equipment including the tents, chairs and personal articles of the trekkers.

Every evening, the tents are put up near a stream or another source of water, usually at the foot of the Himalayas or overlooking glistening green paddy fields, where the trekkers can return to nature and enjoy the idyllic tranquillity. The cook and handymen prepare all sorts of Western or Asian food, while the trekkers listen to music, drink Nepalese brown tea or fresh milk coffee and bask in the sun.

In Machhapuchhre Base Camp, the air is clean and dry, and the sky is dark blue. Without any pollution, and surrounded by white, boundless mountains, the clean air at high altitude is a major attraction. The best campsite in the area offers a panoramic view of Annapurna Peaks, including Hiunchuli (6,441 metres), Annapurna South (7,219 metres), Annapurna I (8,091 metres), Annapurna III (7,555 metres), Gangapurna (7,455 metres) and the ever-changing Fish Tail (6,997 metres). Experienced trekkers rarely suffer from altitude sickness here and, more important, it is the best place for them to enjoy a cup of cappuccino with fresh ewe's or cow's milk provided by the mountain shepherds.

The cappuccino was invented in Italy in the early years of the twentieth century. Strong coffee was brewed in a machine driven by steam pressure, to which frothing milk was added, thereby creating a drink that looks like a snow-white handkerchief sitting on the dark brown robes worn by the Capuchin friars of Vienna. The cappuccino was born, with it irresistible, unique charm and sweet smell. With your first sip, you can sense the sweetness and softness of the foam. With the second, you can taste the bitterness and richness of the coffee beans. After your final sip, the fragrance still lingers... Different flavours can be tasted from different kinds of coffee bean. Isn't that magical? It is similar to trekking, the hardships and joys of climbing, the freshness and serenity of the valley and the intoxication on the snow peaks.

All kinds of trekkers from different parts of the world are drawn to Machhapuchhre Base Camp and they enjoy cups of hot, snow-capped cappuccino. Here, coffee is cheaper than a pot of boiled water. Some trekkers lie on the grass in a daze, tending to the blisters on their feet, airing their damp boots, clothes and socks or playing poker with the porters and guide. Although there are often linguistic barriers, friendships form between the group members who share the same day-to-day experiences and relax over a coffee. Trekking is a mixture of sweet and bitter, just like coffee. We always value loyalty on the journey, and we expect a successful outcome.

The sun sank slowly below both faces of Fish Tail Mountain. The air was vibrantly clean and cool. As the Nepalese say, this is the time when the gods bring darkness for us to rest and soothe our exhausted bodies. Amid the silence of the night dotted with gems, tents are warm nests, ewes give us ewe's milk, and shepherds and trekkers are companions for friendship and conversation. I lay in my sleeping bag, watching the stars. The young man from Hamburg managed to create a lovely picture of mountains, bears, birds, leaves, flowers and a soft heart on the milky surface of the coffee.

"Pearl," he said. "Have you finished that cup? Do you want another?"

At that time, I suddenly wanted to fall in love at the foot of the snow mountains because the pure feelings were so good. My body was free but my eye had wandered to the remote snow mountains.

DAY SEVEN

RETREAT IN THE FULL MOON AT ANNAPURNA

YOU NEVER KNOW what sights will unfold around the next corner.

The 6,997-metre Fish Tail Mountain is by no means the highest of the Annapurna range, but it is the symbol of Nepal. When dawn lights up the needle-shaped snow peak of Fish Tail, its mystery, steepness, dignity and holiness give it a romantic charm unlike other peaks. It is an insurmountable and overwhelming architectural beauty.

The mountains of Nepal pose a great challenge for all mountaineers. In June 1950, Maurice Herzog led a brave French mountaineering team to Annapurna I (8,091 metres). They encountered a terrible snowstorm but still succeeded in becoming was the first mountaineers in history to climb a peak of 8,000 metres. It was the rainy season when they went down the mountains and they experienced great difficulties. The team doctor had to amputate the frostbitten fingers and toes of several team members, including most of Herzog's fingers. Despite these difficulties, the team's overall success was the start of a golden decade of climbing Nepal's highest mountains.

Annapurna I became the first 8,000-metre mountain to be climbed. But it was by no means an easy ascent. Due to a high incidence of avalanches, it is regarded by mountaineers as one of the world's most difficult mountains to scale. For twenty years following the first successful ascent in 1950, no other team succeeded in scaling its peak. Mountaineers have analysed the climbing mortality rates on fourteen mountains. The one with the highest mortality rate was not the 8,848-metre Mount Everest, nor the world's second highest mountain Qogir (K2), but Annapurna I in north central Nepal. With a mortality rate of more than 50 per cent, it is the deadliest of all peaks above 8,000 metres. Altogether, 106 mountaineers have reached its peak but fifty-four of them did not return alive. In contrast, the mortality rate of those reaching the summit of Mount Everest was 14 per cent.

Although the weather in Annapurna Peaks is just as complicated and changeable as that on Mount Everest, it is increasingly popular among explorers. In this country of mountains, the government permits the climbing of 263 mountains, 245 of which have been categorised as 'expedition peaks'. Those trekkers wanting to scale mountains above 6,500 metres need to acquire a government permit. There are different routes of varying degrees of difficulty in Annapurna. Whatever your mountaineering or expeditionary skills, there is a route for everyone, each of which offers amazing scenery. Every year, more than 100,000 people trek on Annapurna, treble the number of those hiking on Mount Everest.

It is interesting that the name Annapurna does not mean 'killer' or 'demon' but 'Giver of Grain' and 'Goddess of Fertility' in Nepali. The river that flows from it is known as the source of life, it is the provider of monsoon rain that irrigates farmland, and the mountain ice and snow that melt in spring supplies water for downstream areas in the dry season. The snow mountain stands as the border between the mortal and immortal worlds and between Earth and heaven. In Nepal, mountains are regarded as holy objects.

We spent a pleasant, relaxing night in Machhapuchhre Base Camp, as if listening to a symphony composed of all the mountain sounds. It felt much better than at Everest Base Camp. Without other mountaineering groups, helicopters, rescue teams, telephones, swimming pools, pets or families, we enjoyed a blissful freedom. In the absence of anyone but our small group of trekkers, the mountains seemed to be extraordinarily pure and true.

"I've fallen in love with the mountain. It has become the only edible meal I can enjoy during the day," I said to Bikram.

"Good, the next dish is called 'four thousand, one hundred and thirty metres'. Pearl, can that be your special lunch today?"

We put the large bags on our backs and headed off at dawn for our final destination.

Shepherds' territory

My face had become sunburned and my lungs were sore through coughing, but the experience made it all worthwhile. The path to Annapurna Base Camp was no longer rugged, with sea-buckthorn grass all around and a glistening stream murmuring close by. We walked through waist-high golden grassland wet with morning dew and moved upwards on the rustling clover grass. The smell was delicious. All my sense organs were attuned to each new environment. On a 4,000-metre-high hillock, we spotted violet, strawflowers, primrose, felwort and numerous other fragrant flowers and wild grasses. I was delighted to see white edelweiss and ice blue forget-me-not along with the lemon-yellow shelters pitched by shepherds on the highland and exposed to wind and rain.

Edelweiss is sometimes known as snow grass or snowflakes in the Himalayas. *The Sound of Music* features a song about edelweiss in the Alps. Its umbrella-shaped woolly flowerhead looks like an angel-faced girl, while the forget-me-not that pokes out between rocks on dry, high-altitude mountain slopes symbolises love. Bleating Himalayan blue goats and tahrs were eating flowers and plants on hillocks, buffeted by an icy wind.

Himalayan goats can be found in Kashmir, Nepal and Sikkim. They live at the same altitude as wild gorals and chamois. Their curly horns are extraordinarily beautiful. Strong and vigorous, they can leap and dart around on cliffsides. Unlike other kinds of goat, they are able to climb trees and can sometimes be seen chewing on leaves up a two-metre-high tree, looking like celestial beings. Fights between rams are common in the mating season. The fierce clash of their horns can be heard from far away, something that attracts snow leopards, 'the Lone Rangers' of the Himalayas. Snow leopards can be stealthy, waiting silently among the rocks until the goats are exhausted from their duel.

To protect them from the severe cold, the Himalayan goats' long hair can reach down to their knees. For many years, cashmere wool has been sold in the markets of Pokhara, Kathmandu and Kashmir, and its fine, smooth filaments are prized in the manufacture of Pashmina shawls. Hence, it is reputed as the best cashmere wool. The craftspeople of the Kashmir Highlands make hand-knitted Pashmina shawls with skills that have been handed down over generations. Pashmina shawls are highly sought-after in the West, being warm and as light as clouds, and featuring gorgeous designs. In the 1990s, the supermodel Kate Moss appeared in *Vogue* magazine wearing a Pashmina shawl from the Himalayas, which initiated a worldwide taste for the garment.

Despite living at such a high altitude, Himalayan goats have to guard against predators such as golden eagles and vultures. While relaxing on the grass, I saw a female goat give birth to a kid that managed to wobble to its feet in no more than five seconds. Three black shepherd dogs were guarding the goats. They barked furiously to the sky and bravely drove away one unwelcome visitor after another.

From spring, when the ice and snow melt, to winter, when heavy snow seals the mountain passes, shepherds take their families up into high mountains. Their holy, pastoral world is isolated from politics and the daily concerns of urban life. A shepherd wearing a woollen cloak and holding a staff was sitting beside a stone house boiling milk tea while watching over his flock as if God were looking down on his people sound asleep. When I took off my shoes to give my feet a rest, I rummaged through my bag and found my last two sweets and gave them to the child nearby, a round, suntanned little shepherdess. She asked me: "Madam, which valley do you live in?"

The shepherds live in a pastoral world isolated from the daily concerns of urban life

It was similar to asking the Little Dragon Maiden in Jin Yong's *The Return of the Condor Heroes*: "Are you a member of the Ancient Tomb Sect? How come you've spent sixteen years at the bottom of the Passionless Valley?"

Her innocent question made me reconsider the mystery and beauty of the valley and the poetic quality and essence of the world. I thought the designs of the Pashmina shawls and their colours that reflect the sky, lakes, forests, flowers and leaves could only be expressed by the weavers living in the heavenly Himalayas. The Annapurna Base Camp that I had imagined so many times is not merely surrounded by ice peaks that are bone-chilling, mysterious and life-threatening, but they are at the same time serene, peaceful and harmonious. It was as if the scene came from the pages of *The Little Prince* in which the eponymous hero asks the pilot: "So you, too, come from the sky! Which is your planet?"

A little shepherdess asked me: "Madam, which valley do you live in?"

If I were an artist and was invited to paint the boys, girls, flowers, grass and animals in the Garden of Eden, I would come to Annapurna Base Camp to paint from nature because the world originated from the chaotic and carefree lives of Adam and Eve.

Party for borderless trekkers

There is no blue more beautiful than the blue of the forget-me-not.

After walking for four-and-a-half hours, I was finally standing under the flagpole of Annapurna Base Camp, on which a colourful prayer flag whistled in the blustery wind. Having taken some 160,000 steps, I lay prone at the foot of the Annapurna Peaks. Standing on the top of the world was a true, permanent and specific experience. It made me re-evaluate my trivial life and revealed the splendour of the earth under my feet. I'd been imagining this moment and the passions it would arouse for the past seven days. However, as I stood there leaning against the flag, I did not have the strength to express my emotions.

It was getting dark and the rising fog was reducing visibility further when I put my bags in Room 3 and prepared to take some photos. Just ten minutes previously, the snow mountains were glittering against the blue sky. The weather is highly changeable in the Annapurna Peaks. It is often clear in the morning, windy and snowy at noon and starlit at night. When you are at home watching TV or just lounging around, you never experience the constantly changing natural conditions made by the Creator.

During the rainy season from June to September, rainstorms brought by the strong southeast monsoon frequently cause icefalls, and trekking conditions in Annapurna can become difficult due to heavy cloud and mist or falling ice and snow. From November to February, a violent northwest wind plunges the temperature to below minus 40 Celsius. Heavy snow covers the whole path to Annapurna Base Camp and the huts alongside. Winds can blow at speeds of up to ninety metres a second, strong enough to blow people off their feet.

Only the periods between late April and late May and from September to October offer respite from the wind and rain. During these weeks, however, spells of good weather that last for between two and five days occur only on three of four occasions. Even so, this is the golden time for mountaineering in the Himalayas, with spring being the best season of all. However, due to its remote location and perilous, complicated routes, Annapurna is only approachable in September and October. Avalanches and the ever-changing weather are the main reasons for the its reputation as the 'Killer Mountain'.

Amateur mountaineers are particularly keen to climb Annapurna Base Camp's three 'mountains for hiking': Hiunchuli (6,441 metres), Tent Peak (5,663 metres) and Fluted Peak (6,501 metres). For years, they had been known for their inaccessibility and attracted leading mountaineers from across the world. Hiking on the mountains requires more than just the ability to walk. To climb these mountains, you will need a Sherpa or Gurung guide to accompany you to the base camp. You also need to be have some experience of mountaineering and an ability to use ski poles, ropes, pickaxes and pitons. More important, once you have reached the peak, your body needs to adapt to the high altitude and the changing weather before you are able to return to base camp safe and sound.

Heavy fog and an icy wind blocked our progress at Annapurna Base Camp. Mountaineers, trekkers, guides and porters were all crowded in the sitting room of a tea house, playing Chinese chess or poker, chatting, cooking food, or brewing tea or coffee. It was extraordinary that we were able to get along so harmoniously at such an altitude, isolated in a 4,130-metre giant 'bowl valley' below the snow mountain. I saw Nepalese clansmen and trekkers from different countries getting along famously.

In the tea house at Annapurna Base Camp

Nepal is a meeting place for Indo-Aryans and Himalayan Mongols. Here, the Tamangs of Tibetan descent are horse dealers and warriors on horseback in times of war; the Thakalis in the Kali Gandaki Valley are good at trading, running hotels and selling salt; the Newars are skilful craftsmen, being proficient in handicrafts, architecture and art; the Yakhas are carnivorous; the Rais and Limbus like to live in houses painted gorgeous colours; the Sunuwars live in the valley; the Gurungs and Magars of Tibetan and Burmese stock are the best mountaineers and soldiers, believe in

Shamanism and enjoy a gregarious tribal lifestyle; the most famous Sherpas in Nepal, the Tibetan herdsmen, moved to Solu Khumbu in Nepal five hundred years ago. Those Sherpas who are Tibetan Buddhists have built many magnificent lamaseries and giant prayer wheels. In Tibetan, 'Sherpa' means 'people living in the east'.

It was extraordinary that everyone got along so harmoniously at such a high altitude

As I crawled along like the slowest snail, I wrote 'Fragrance of Nepal, Trekking on the Himalayas, Pearl, 1 October' on a piece of white cloth for trekkers to leave a message. I told them that *Fragrance of Nepal* was my first book on Nepal and that it was China's National Day, the day when families like to get together. The moon that night is rounder and brighter than the full moon in other months because the Earth is at its closest to the Moon. The team of young men from four countries that we had met in Sinuva, along with several porters, suggested we have a match to celebrate.

The Himalayas are home to all kinds of rare animals as well as exotic customs. Each ethnic group has its own form of religious ceremony. However, at Annapurna Base Camp, the sacred land of the Goddess of Fertility, there's a simple celebration that people of different religious beliefs can participate in. I would never have guessed that it came in the form of a volleyball court as vast as a heliport!

Leading mountaineers from across the world are drawn to Annapurna Base Camp

A hundred metres from the hut, a group were happily playing volleyball. Some trekkers had even taken off their shoes, and were running and jumping on the rugged ground barefoot. A heavy fog swirled around and the volleyball was being buffeted around in the wind. I heard cheers ring out.

It would only take a short walk for me to run out of breath, but these players were dashing around without any apparent discomfort. How did they manage it? What made them so powerful?

The existence of what must be the world's highest volleyball court is a testimony to the tenacity and fortitude of trekkers. They are endowed with strength, teamwork, freedom and harmony. I could do nothing but stand in awe and cheer them on.

Wilderness of time

At altitude, people acquire a certain innocence and are purified from evil thoughts. For instance, I have no selfish desires when standing in front of a sheer precipice. Steep precipices stand majestically because they do not have any worldly desires. The path under our feet not only gives us strength and new ideas but also stimulates the imagination and new dreams. It is neither early nor late in the boundless time. I arrived at Annapurna Base Camp on the night of the full moon in the most classical Chinese sense.

There was a mottled wooden chair next to a stone house. A giant Annapurna Base Camp signboard was hung on the granite cliff as large as a house. Light flickered in a number of tents like little boats berthed in a harbour. Wrapped up in their sleeping bags, dozens of trekkers stood in the icy wind waiting for the moon to appear. On one high hilltop, prayer flags danced in the moonlight, with each stone on the cliff glowing brilliant rays of life and the essence of nature accumulating there. As a traveller in a foreign land, I sat on this moonlit night in the snow, lost in fanciful thoughts.

The most eminent American landscape photographer Ansel Adams spent a long time in the wilderness. His photographic collection *Yosemite and the Range of Light* sold 200,000 copies. His work *Moonrise, Half Dome, Yosemite Valley* was auctioned for 17,500 dollars, a record for a photographic work in the 1980s. Like him, I dreamed to explore the night sky.

Many views in Annapurna are unlike anywhere else. Saturn, Mars and Mercury twinkle in the west at midnight and Venus is like a jade plate in the east at dawn. The vast heavens are far from quiet and the constellations drone softly and lightly.

Most trekkers return to Pokhara after witnessing the setting of the Moon and sunrise at the base camp, while the mountaineers pack away their tents and set off for the mountain top. For me, with the air at its thinnest in the dead of night, my cough was getting worse. By contrast, during the day I seldom coughed. I lay down on a plank bed no more than sixty centimetres wide and only one-and-a-half metres long, covered in damp bedding. I felt that, after seven days of coughing, my ribs were about to crack.

When I started to cough phlegm with pink blood streaks, my guide became nervous and asked whether we should go downhill. It would take no more than an hour to return to Machhapuchhre Base Camp and the bright moon in the sky would light up our return trip with no need for headlamps. But I hoped to witness the next day's sunrise, just like the brave mountaineers.

According to Bikram's experience, I had the symptoms of mountain sickness and I would breathe more comfortably at Machhapuchhre Base Camp, some five hundred metres lower. Although he was able to support me and even carry me on his back, I felt extraordinarily peaceful and composed because I could hear my innermost voice. I think the essence of *Prajna Paramita Heart Sutra* is that 'everything tangible or intangible is empty'. If the mind is pure, then external things and internal thinking are all 'empty'. The six 'roots' of sensations (the root of the eye and of the ear, nose, tongue, feeling and mind) are 'pure and clean' (meaning 'free from human desires and passions'), the six 'dusts' (colour, sound, smell, flavour, feeling and mind) and the six senses (seeing, hearing, smelling, tasting, feeling and thinking) will be empty. There's no limit to what the eyes can see or the heart can experience, there's nothing that's not understood and there's no end to ageing and death. So there's nothing to fear.

Just like a young man setting out with an empty bottle, I travelled thousands of miles simply to absorb all kinds of nutrients to nourish my life. The moment I started trekking in the Himalayas, I aimed to climb to a place where I didn't feel exhausted or out of breath. The physical pain seemed to be a cultivation of my soul and the achievements of *bodhi*, or enlightenment, would only be reached in the empty mountain. I would rather sit still until daybreak.

Under the moonlight, my guide opened the louver of the hut, followed by a long wait. A Chinese traveller nicknamed 'Zhu Zhu' (meaning 'Piglet') had left a message on the wall: 'If you hate someone, let him climb mountains alone, drink milk tea every day and stay where he can't take a bath or make a phone call, has to answer the call of nature in the wild, walk on cold, wet mountain paths and loses his willpower. If you love someone, you can climb mountains together, share a pot of milk tea every day and go without taking a bath or wanting to make a phone call. It can be very romantic, even though you have to answer the call of nature in the wild. Long periods of trekking on the mountain path will help you lose weight. Your shared experience of the cold, high altitude and damp will cement your love.' But I thought that, even if the sun or the moon set and my face became pale, I would not hesitate or become suspicious should I gain sudden enlightenment or retreat from the immortal world in a teardrop.

The Thakalis and the Newars are Hindus and they think that, just like men, plants, animals, mountains, rivers, stars and the moon have an interlinked spirituality and that each living creature exerts a subtle influence on the other. The Sherpas and the Gurungs believe that all creatures have animistic spirituality and those that can walk 108 circles around the snow mountain can reach a state of enlightenment. Trekkers of all complexions, races and beliefs long to sit quietly in meditation in the embrace of the Goddess of Fertility.

When the full moon rose from the highest mountain top, it lit up the dim glaciers and snowbanks under my feet, presenting a chilling, dreamy beauty. Annapurna was peaceful but not in total silence. It was warm, full of life and like a deity travelling by moonlight, as if I could touch its clothes when I raised my hand and feel the strong spiritual power of the full moon when I closed my eyes.

There is an old Chinese ballad often sung by wanderers: 'Nothing is more round than the moon, / nothing is more square than a bucket, / and nothing is sweeter than the tenderness of a young girl.' The silvery moon rising above the snow mountain was not the moon in my eyes but the face of perfection, and I was equipped with silvery wings.

DAY EIGHT

LOTUS FLOWERS AND SNOW MOUNTAINS

Mountaineering is a dream for many people as they grow up.

The Annapurna region contains many snow mountains. Seven of them are above 7,000 metres, five of which are called Annapurna. At base camp, when the first rays of light shine on Annapurna I, you can stand on a glacier in great anticipation and see the gradual awakening of one snow mountain after another: Annapurna II (7,937 metres), Annapurna III (7,555 metres), Annapurna IV (7,525 metres), Gangapurna (7,455 metres) and Annapurna South (7,219 metres). Fish Tail Mountain in the centre is famous for its magnificent pyramidal peak and is known as the Holy Virgin Peak because of the ban on climbing it imposed by the Nepalese government.

Annapurna is well known for its range of altitudes and ecological variations, from a subtropical climate at the bottom of the Pokhara Valley to the snow-capped mountains. It is this diversity that makes the Annapurna Peaks one of the most popular places in Nepal for explorers.

It is difficult to imagine the magnificence and splendour of sunrise at Annapurna. The base camp, like a village in the film *2012*, sits at the bottom of a perfectly round natural bowl, surrounded by precipitous cliffs. The amphitheatre is open to the south so the campsite is bathed in sunshine. The cliffs above the campsite are covered with glaciers. The mountains gleam overhead and the dazzling peaks look down on the whole valley, like prowling deities. The slow-flowing glacial drifts are masterpieces of nature. The area's great beauty is gradually revealed over time, and the power of time like a glistening touchstone made me shiver and become lost in thought.

With my body and face bathed in golden light, I forgot my breathing difficulties along with the cold and pain. One female trekker removed her coat and top down to her bra so that the sun could shine directly onto her naked skin.

Walking 400 metres eastwards from the campsite, I saw a silvery glacier covered with moraines like a sinuous sand strip cutting a deep ravine through the surrounding sills. The glacier glimmered dim blue in the shadow of the dawn and the moisture hovered above the glacier like freezing smog. The night before, as I lay in my hut, I heard a light crunch and ringing sound of a furious, gushing windstorm. It reminded me of a serenade, lying on a glacier advancing at a speed of several microns an hour, several millimetres a day, several centimetres a month and a few metres a year.

I squinted at the 8,091-metre mountain top for almost half an hour, trying to imagine what it would be like standing at the summit during an ice storm. However vivid my imagination, its strangeness and holiness were beyond description. A stone monument stood about a hundred metres above the campsite, draped with colourful prayer flags. It celebrated the mountaineer Anatoli Boukreev.

Born in a poor mining town in the Ural Mountains in the former Soviet Union, Boukreev learned to climb mountains at the age of nine. He was a survivor of a tragedy that occurred on Mount Everest on 10 May 1996 in which twelve world-class mountaineers lost their lives. About eighteen months later, Boukreev, who had climbed eleven of the fourteen mountains above 8,000 metres, set out to conquer Annapurna. He tried climbing Annapurna I along a perilous route on the vast southern wall of the peak. To add to the difficulty, he decided to begin climbing in winter rather than in spring. After setting up base camp at 5,180 metres, he headed towards the summit at sunrise on Christmas Day 1997. At a height of 6,000 metres, the harsh rumble of an avalanche engulfed him. The 39-year-old Anatoli Boukreev, who loved mountaineering and exploring great mountains, passed away in the ice and snow.

Everything in this world, including all the wealth, arrogance and glory, can be destroyed in Annapurna, but people remain captivated by the challenge in what was once a forbidden area and look to explore its secret. As a matter of fact, the planning and preparation are more important than the climbing itself. Mountaineering is fraught with danger, and a large part of its glamour depends on its unpredictability. Danger can occur at any time. But without danger, mountaineering cannot be distinguished from hundreds of other sports and activities. It is the danger that makes mountaineering such a great adventure sport.

All mountaineering teams that set out from base camp pass the monument. Some of them pray to God and throw amulets with printed scriptures and religious doctrines into the air for good luck. Each fluttering prayer flag is a blessing to the deities. According to Nepalese belief, the horse is a sacred animal that can speedily take the scriptures to heaven.

Some trekkers leave wild flowers and candles on the foundation stone that contains an inlaid photo of Anatoli Boukreev.

The stone monument celebrating Anatoli Boukreev

Mountaineering is a dream for many young people

When I placed a small stone and raised my head, I saw the sapphire eyes of Anatoli Boukreev were squinting at the snow mountain. His deep eyes were full of mysterious glamour, revealing a determination to eschew home comforts and a heroic refusal to give in to weakness, cowardice, feebleness and the mundanity of a conventional life. His picture made me smile. I was profoundly touched by him and shed hot tears. I felt like I was travelling with him to the great peak. He was a symbol of a free, unrestrained mountaineer with a lofty ambition.

Arrow leaving the bow

On the high, snow-capped mountains, the peaks lit up by the morning sun were reflected in a dark green-and-black icy pond. Snow lotus herbs bloomed all around. It seemed that paradise at the top of the mountains was just a few steps away.

At eight o'clock, after I had taken photos of the sunrise against the biting ice storm, Bikram came into my room, skilfully helped me pack my luggage and told me that he had already prepared hot milk coffee and, once I had drunk it, we could make our return journey. He said that our steps home would be as fast as arrows.

A black Tibetan mastiff had been left at the campsite by a former mountaineering team. It closely followed and sent off each trekker when they departed the campsite. When we passed the shepherds' tents after twenty minutes trekking downhill, three shepherd dogs rushed out to fight the Tibetan mastiff. I ran up and shouted: "Stop that! Go back!" The wounded Tibetan mastiff returned to the campsite.

On looking back, I saw it sit forlornly on a rock surveying the path we were descending covered with golden sea-buckthorn. Before the Buddha was reincarnated and achieved enlightenment, he had experienced reincarnation for a hundred generations. During this time he was, among other things, a beggar, a demon, a crow and a prince. Maybe the intelligent Tibetan mastiff was the incarnation of a certain mountaineer. It watched each departing trekker fondly and sent them on their way.

It took us only an hour to reach Machhapuchhre Base Camp, where I enjoyed a cup of hot black lemon tea on a sun-bathed stone terrace. A handsome Taiwanese man on his way up to Annapurna Base Camp asked me whether the scenery there was beautiful. His face was tanned since he hadn't applied any sunscreen. He said he wanted to tan naturally. I nodded and said smilingly: "Here you can enjoy a celestial body bath."

As we went downhill, I relaxed and broke out into song. I had almost forgotten the wise proverb 'It is far easier to go uphill than downhill'. When we reached a steeply falling section of the path in Deurali, the inflammation in my right knee flared up again. It hurt so much that I had to put extra pressure on my left foot, with my right foot dragging behind. At that time I could understand the words of Sir Edmund Hillary, the first person to ascend Mount Everest: "The key to climbing Everest is not only to reach its summit, but more important, to get down safe and sound."

Numerous mountaineers have had accidents or lost their lives on the descent. Going uphill is tiring but relatively safe, while going downhill is the opposite. With gravity pulling them down, trekkers are in danger of stumbling forward, and this places a great strain on the legs. It is particularly difficult to keep balance on loose stones. My calves ached and my toes were becoming hot and swollen due to the weight of my body.

Bikram said that our steps home would be as fast as arrows

It was raining as we hobbled into the Himalaya Hotel. The weather was almost the same every day: sunny and clear in the morning, followed by the approach of dense clouds from the east at noon and then rainfall. The clouds on the snow-capped mountains also bring violent falls of hail and snow, and snow slides are possible at any time. A plunge in temperature would sometimes be followed by a fierce storm, buffeting me from front and rear. It felt like being in a cold storage facility, and many times my guide had to stand in a freezing stream, instructing me to walk on the stepping stones and pulling me across the swollen watercourse so that I wouldn't wobble from side to side or be blown away by the rainstorm like a kite.

I noticed his rubber shoes soaked in the torrential ice water and the heavy bag on his back. This was a time for friends to pull together. At that moment, I vowed to give him my Gore-Tex windcheater and buy him a pair of waterproof climbing boots on returning to Pokhara so that he could keep warm and dry and be better equipped to help other trekkers.

As I was walked on in the rain, I saw many wild flowers in the rock crevices, such as saffron crocus and light yellow Chinese enkianthus with its clean, tiny flowerheads that somehow manage to bloom in the rain. They lightened my mood and filled me with incomparable pleasure and warmth. It was inspiring to see them bloom so splendidly on the snow mountains.

It's far easier to go uphill than downhill

My guide picked three leaves of a spear-shaped plantain herb and placed them on my chest. It looked like a beautiful logo. I was unaware at the time that ordinary plantain herbs are actually good friends of trekkers. Pilgrims wear them as amulets, while their tender leaves taste like mushrooms and are used to dress salads and vegetables. My guide picked a large handful of them and put them in his pocket. He said they were good for healing bruises, blisters and cuts, and he would help me rub my swollen legs and feet with them in the evening. The word 'plantain' in English means helping to reduce swelling in the feet.

I felt constantly cold, tired and in pain. When we arrived in Doban in the valley at half-past-three in the afternoon, it rained so heavily that it seemed capable of washing away the houses. I had trudged for ten hours to cover just fourteen kilometres. I had developed a fever and my guide rushed to my room and covered me with two quilts. I felt like a refugee shivering in bed. I imagined myself as a broken arrow that had lost its tail feather, totally exhausted. Every day, I seemed to be suffering from one thing or another.

I arrived in Doban, having trudged for ten hours

The significance of serenity

At dusk, a six-member Chinese team arrived at the lodge. They were soaked through, and one of them was pulling a giant suitcase. Did he imagine he was going on a shopping spree in Europe or Hong Kong! It should have been obvious that a porter could easily lose balance when carrying such a large case on a mountain path.

Thanks to the film *2012*, Chinese travellers have become increasingly interested in trekking in the Himalayas. Many choose to visit during Golden Week in October, when the National Day and Mid-Autumn Festival holidays merge. We met several Chinese tour groups on our journey. One group, comprising members from sixteen provinces that had met up online, convened in Kathmandu. They set a great example, taking only simple equipment, behaving sensitively and travelling quietly through villages, displaying the qualities of real 'travellers'.

By contrast, the six members we now encountered shattered the quietness of Doban. They quickly took over the kitchen, noisily began to make tea, assembled the food carried by the porter, including Chinese cabbage, potatoes, pork sausages, rice and tinned meat, lit a large hot pot that smoked out the kitchen, and then took up drinking, singing and playing games. In no time, they turned a serene valley into a tea shop as boisterous as those in Lijiang, ignoring the existence of other trekkers in the sitting room, and seemingly impervious to the silent, saintly snowy peaks towering around.

The other people there might include a Hindu in worship, a Muslim prohibited from eating pork, a teetotal Buddhist, a vegetarian Christian or a pilgrim kowtowing around the holy mountains with a lifelong devotion. The forest, snow mountains and holy land are all quiet places. Quietness was God's will and therefore no one dared to break it.

Most owners of Nepalese travel agencies, shops, lodges and restaurants have a mixed view of Chinese travellers. They like their spending power, especially tour groups, but are frustrated by their table manners and lack of religious awareness. The head of one mountaineering team could stand it no longer and came to ask them: "Could you keep it down a little?"

I thought this was about as direct as a Sherpa could be. But it only succeeded in calming down things for a few minutes before they forgot themselves and yelled: "Take more photos and post them online!"

The Sherpa could do nothing but shake his head and say to his customers: "They don't understand anything about the mountains."

The tranquillity of the Himalayas can easily be destroyed.

I remember my first night in Kathmandu on this trip. I lodged in Tashi Delek Family Inn where I'd stayed three years before. In *Fragrance of Nepal*, I vividly recounted my short stay in Kathmandu. Many Chinese travellers to Nepal have read that book.

I saw Itten, the owner of the inn, which was now packed with Chinese tourists. I didn't expect the inn would be so lively and devoid of Western travellers. Previously, the courtyard where pink bougainvillaea bloomed was a cosy home for travellers from all corners of the world. When there was a power cut, candles would be lit in the corridors and the dining hall, and the guests would chat softly in the yard. But now, Itten said ruefully: "Sorry, Pearl, there's no room for you."

I felt ashamed at the scene in this sitting room in Doban. In the eyes of some Chinese tourists, trekking in Nepal is no different to travelling in Lijiang, Hainan, Thailand or Hong Kong. However, each trekker should ask themselves why they chose to come here, to make merry or to seek a new experience?

Sir Edmund Hillary, who climbed to the top of the world at the age of thirty-three and stayed there only fifteen minutes, devoted much of his energy in the subsequent fifty-five years to helping the Himalayan people, focusing on educational opportunities and environmental protection. Seeing shortcomings in the provision of healthcare and education, and a lack of clean drinking water, he set up the Himalayan Trust that raised 250,000 dollars a year to help the Nepalese construct schools, hospitals, bridges and airstrips.

As the number of tourists increased, rubbish started to pile up in the base camps of Everest and Annapurna, where discarded oxygen bottles, drinks cans and food wrappers quickly accumulated. To address the problem, Hillary visited Nepal no less than 120 times to call on mountaineers and trekkers to clear away thousands of tons of waste. He never forgot the fact that it was the Himalayas that brought him fame.

The most meaningful form of travel is 'responsible travel'. We should practise social responsibility when we travel, for instance by helping the poor, respecting and protecting local culture, conserving wildlife, improving community health and maintaining the local ecological environment. The beauty of the Himalayas lies in its purity, intangibility, naturalness, remoteness and inaccessibility. As trekking has become more popular, we should strictly abide by the spirit of the mountain path and the virtue of trekking. The film star Chen Kun wrote about trekking in Tibet in his book *The Power of Walking*: "In a greater sense, self-discipline should be in the subconsciousness."

One should listen and be open-minded rather than defiant, ignorant and ruthless. A butterfly flapping its wings in Yucatan might affect the ferns in Flinders Ranges in Australia. Trekking in the Himalayas is a journey of mental endurance, continuous learning and spiritual purification. It will make you become reverent and modest.

There have been times when I became unaware of the fact that my soul was hardening and losing its sensitivity. When I sat with a Sirdar, looking up at the starlit sky, he told me that Sherpas believe that two wolves inhabit the body of every person. One is noisy, needy, selfish, extravagant and self-important, while the other is the hidden spiritual life characterised by warmth, goodness, gratitude, humour and tenderness, and is the quiet wisdom heard or noticed only occasionally.

I said in despair: "I ache and feel painful all over. Does it mean that the first wolf is stronger?"

Smiling, he clasped my hands with his thick palms and said: "No, the one you feed is stronger."

I felt that Hillary had somehow managed to nourish the lotus flowers and snow mountains and each of our teardrops and steps could warm the Buddha. How far is it from a wild flower in the foothills to the summit at an altitude of 8,000 metres? It is the distance of a breath. How far is it from the deity in heaven to the beast in our heart? The distance of awakening and a beat of the heart.

As the moon rose solemnly and slowly in the cloudless night sky, my heart calmed down and I felt a lotus-like joy at the mountains giving out unobstructed rays of light in the silence.

DAY NINE

THE ZEN OF WALKING AND THE BEAUTY OF THE BODY

You can appreciate the beauty of the serene mountains that attracted the Chinese artist Xu Beihong.

In the spring of 1940, Xu Beihong, together with some friends, rode horses on a narrow clifftop path and arrived in Darjeeling in the Himalayan foothills. He sketched from nature and tried to capture the landscape of the Himalayas from different perspectives, in different environments and at different times of day. He described climbing the Himalayas as "one of the greatest pleasure in life", where you can feel serenity in the grotesque mountains and the imposing forests.

Nature is an endless source of inspiration. However, some people rarely listen to their innermost voice because an outdoor life requires more spiritual freedom.

I like to refer to car drivers as 'rubber nomads' and hitchhikers as 'leather nomads'. Driven by an innate desire to travel, the latter move step by step and try to establish a real connection with other hikers, guides and porters. They are fascinated by the vastness and power of land, are moved by the laws of Mother Nature and left awestruck by the lofty mountains. On their travels, they embrace each unpredictable day and night, making life as simple and fragrant as the wild flowers, and leave behind their everyday grumbles, pressures, obligations and rules. They manage to re-establish peace of mind by detaching themselves from the constraints and complex emotions involved in friendships, WeChat groups and coteries. They yearn to escape the degenerate, carefree and materialistic world in order to realise the ultimate physical and spiritual freedom.

When you become a 'leather nomad' on the narrow path of the Himalayas, you will find that life becomes more flexible and immortal, shining like the bright stars in the sky. All of nature seems to rejoice in the freedom and simplicity of life. Lying down next to your tent, your heart roams in the boundless universe and you feel awakened under the blue sky; sitting at the foot of a snow-capped mountain, you can delight in the dewdrops forming on the plants and flowers; by standing next to a creek, you will find your heart imperceptibly converging with the burbling water; standing below an icefall, you can purify your heart with its delightful melody; and by meditating in the moonlight, you can breathe in tranquillity and cleanse in its calm beauty.

Everything in the Himalayas can help us cultivate and practise the Zen model. When you are open-minded, the sky appears blue, the grass is merciful, life is simple and time is meaningless in the absence of any commitments, obligations or special ambitions, desires and duties. All that remains are the smallest and simplest needs. You start out trekking when it is light and stop when it is dark. You live in a quiet environment, far removed from everyday troubles and disputes; all you need to do is trek. Your daily experience is to follow the Zen model. Today I'm going to walk ten kilometres, just as naturally as I will take five thousand breaths. The purpose of the trek is to discover beauty on the road and stay sober at all times.

The body in full bloom

Before starting out that day, Guide Bikram asked me how I felt. Actually, I could barely move my right foot due to my swollen knee and one of my toenails being covered in dried blood. Human toes can be divided into Greek, Roman and Egyptian types according to their lengths. A foot with the second toe longer than other four is Greek. People with such feet usually have thin limbs and most beautiful women are blessed with such feet, Greece being synonymous with beautiful human sculptures. The Ancient Romans conquered much of Europe thanks possibly to their distinctive feet, in which the first three toes are almost the same length, showing the benefits of the power of unity. An Egyptian foot is one in which the toe length diminishes from the first to the fifth, with the big toe hurting the most, so Egyptians live close to the banks of the Nile and are unwilling to travel the world. I have Egyptian feet, unsuited to walking, despite the fact that I am on a long journey.

My right leg was covered in rheumatism plasters, but they were not working, so it was up to my left leg to take every forward step. To my amazement, I found that the body is quite incredible, so tenacious, that when my right foot was hurt, the left would help out, without complaint; it would reach out. When the right hand is tired after holding a walking stick for a long time, the left takes over. Just like a long-married couple have a sense of 'the left hand feeling the right', sharing breaths as intimate as two leaves on a tree, sticking together and working closely like the left and right hands of the same person.

The sixth Dalai Lama, Tsangyang Gyatso, wrote the love poem *Never Let You and the Buddha Down* in the Potala Palace, where he used the Zen model. I thought I was walking with all my strength just to see you – my Annapurna goddess.

It was two hundred metres from the Doban Valley to the Bamboo Forest. The slope was steep and slippery, and my right knee couldn't bend at all so I had to walk backwards like a tiger entering a cave. Mountain farmers said to me with a smile: "Walking backwards! Wonderful!"

Despite the fact that they were carrying heavy packs, porters would always stop and let me pass out of kindness and say with a smile "*Namaste didi* [Hello, sister]".

Though my swollen leg was useless as if it was cursed, I smiled and replied "*Namaste*". This familiar greeting on the trail warmed my heart. In the eyes of the Nepalese, God exists in everything, hidden in the trees, rivers, mountains and lakes, as well as in our daily lives and our behaviour. When they greet you, they are actually saluting the gods in and around you.

The Bamboo Forest is 2,310 metres above sea level, while Sinuva stands at 2,340 metres, Chhomrong Khola 1,750 metres and Chhomrong 2,210 metres. Looking at the elevation, you will see that the trail is shaped like the tooth of a saw. The tick sign is used by locals to describe the succession of valleys, referring to descending to the bottom of the valley and then climbing to the hill summit. Covering such a long distance, the journey tortured my lame leg and tested my flagging will.

As we went downhill, it started to warm up and the air turned hot and dry. Climbing another hillside, the air temperature fell by one degree Celsius for every hundred metres and the humidity level also fell. Bikram went ahead, carrying a camouflage backpack on which I draped my sweat-stained T-shirt to dry. Once dry, I replaced it with another wet T-shirt. Ever attentive, he placed a dry towel over my shoulders in case I got cold.

To encourage me to complete the journey, Bikram always urged me to climb each mountain using the poetic Nepalese language. When the going was easy, he would say the trail was 'beautiful'. Otherwise, he would say it was 'so ugly'. When one trekker took the wrong route and ended up on a donkey trail that was full of wild plants, he said the trail was 'sick'. If I asked how far was left, he would say the time to have one or two meals – namely half a day or one full day, which means we had to walk more than ten hours, equivalent to more than ten kilometres. This use of the word 'meal' seemed to be our daily mental nourishment. The Nepalese humour typical of the mountainous area made me feel like the feet were suffering in hell, but the heart was enjoying heaven. Only by trekking in the mountains can you understand this kind of beauty.

Only by trekking in the mountains can you understand this kind of beauty

Indian Buddhism pursues austere and long-lasting cultivation of the body. Under this influence, China has its distinctive branch of Buddhism, Zen, which involves the pursuit of bodily harmony through meditation and sudden enlightenment. On the trail, one kilometre is a long way, two kilometres is really far and leaves you panting, while covering ten kilometres in a whole day is an incredible feat, and fifty kilometres in a single day is an extreme concept and one that only professional mountaineers or guides can attain, but not me. Here, you appreciate the immensity of the external world and realise that a human body can be part of a deep, natural purification.

Only you and your small group of trekking partners know that the size and magnificence of Earth is a little secret under your feet. Every movement, breath and release of pressure can help you recover. Your limbs become thin and symmetric, your muscles are powerful and your body is in harmony with the ground, the sky, the trail and the ancient temple. This is a kind of pure, harmonious, solemn and quiet beauty that arises from the integration of body and nature.

The spirit of trails

At four o'clock in the afternoon I finally returned to the largest village on the Annapurna Base Camp route, Chhomrong. My face was as coarse as sandpaper. It was covered in sunburn blotches the size of quail's eggs. For several days now I tortured my belly, and I had already lost three kilograms in weight. I was now as slender as a princess. On arriving in Chhomrong, I soaked in hot water, took a steam shower, washed my long hair and was given a naked mustard oil massage by a Nepalese masseur. I asked Bikram to go the German bakery and buy a cinnamon roll for a hundred rupees.

Among the goods for sale, I had heard that, aside from some delicious cheese, they also had marijuana paste. Marijuana users from all over the world gather here to share in their enjoyment of the drug. I wanted to try a few puffs myself, thinking that it might perhaps get rid of some of my phlegm and relieve my cough. However, Bikram's concerned stare made me think otherwise. I dared not be indulgent and so, with a sigh, ordered two bowls of fried chicken curry. I ate the meat and chili pepper rice with my hands, my movements dexterous, elegant and pious. I felt it must have looked like I had never eaten before: my eyes were brimming with tears of gratitude. Finally, we brought two bottles of Nepal's best beer, Everest, onto a veranda that overlooked the entire village. Like a well-fed lion, I lay soaking up the sun with all sorts of strange, fantastical thoughts in me.

A man next to me said he was able to distinguish between Chinese, Koreans and Japanese from the shape of their noses. He said that Korean women have flat noses like the actress Lee Young-ae and love travelling alone. He thought I was a strong-willed Korean woman because I trekked alone and had a flat nose.

He made a big mistake this time, though I thought I should write a card reading 'Be unique, be myself" and stick it on my backpack before setting off the next day, and then distribute it to the various hikers I meet on the way.

The roads, paths and hotels in Annapurna have not been repaired for more than fifty years, while meat and alcohol are prohibited in the mountains. This is to preserve the independence, integrity and holiness of the mountains, and to allow people to continue passing through in piety and peace. The paths clean your spirit as well as your body.

The first to come up with the idea of building hiking trails in a remote mountainous area was an American called Benton Mackaye, a minor office clerk in the US Forest Service. He was a gentle and kind-hearted dreamer. At first, all he wanted to do was build a forest trail leading to his architect friend so that he could visit him. Later on, in 1921, he planned a much more ambitious scheme to build a long-distance hiking trail in the United States, complete with hostels, huts and forest villages, which would be "an escape from the mercenary world". The construction of the entire 3,000-kilometre trail, along with bypaths, pedestrian bridges, signs and campsites, would be carried out by volunteers.

In just seven years, these American volunteers, in a spirit of selfless participation, managed to build a 3,499km hiking trail going through the high mountains and wilderness, and taking in the most beautiful scenery and highest ridges. The Appalachian Trail is the world's longest trail run by volunteers. It is the world's first and greatest trail, stretching across fourteen states and five national parks. It can take about six months to complete the entire distance. Similar trails have since sprung up elsewhere, including the Annapurna Trail in Nepal, the Santa Cruz Trail in Peru and the Pacific Crest Trail along the west coast of the US.

Some hikers try to complete a trail in one go, while others do so in sections. One trekker took forty-six years to complete the Appalachian Trail. Ward Leonard walked the entire route, unassisted, in sixty-nine days, covering about fifty kilometres a day. Led by his guide dog, Bill Irwin spent eighteen months completing the journey and he wrote the best-seller *Blind Courage* based on his experiences. One traveller who started his journey weighing 350 pounds had lost fifty-three pounds by the time he finished.

With regard to the imposing Himalayas, the paths walked by teams of laden horses, traders and porters have been in existence for a long time. However, since the start of the craze for hiking and mountain climbing in the 1960s, Nepal's establishment as a national park and the renovation of tea houses along mountain paths, the Himalayan trails have become some of the most beautiful mountain routes in the world.

Maurice Herzog, the first person to climb Annapurna's highest peak, wrote the mountaineering classic *Annapurna*. One British couple made a bet with some friends and carried an ironing board all the way to Annapurna Base Camp One, 5,440 metres above sea level. When they got there, they even ironed a few clothes, an amusing way to combine their domestic life with their love of extreme sports. This reflects the spiritual extravagance and beauty found in the emotional lives of ordinary people.

On the hiking routes of Annapurna, there are very few pharmaceutical or medical facilities. Because of this, a French hiker, a nurse by profession, together with his wife, devoted two years to a special trekking project that covered the entire Himalayan mountain area. Carrying five-kilogram boxes of medicine, they stopped at every village or camp that they passed along the way to bring medical items to treat the local inhabitants with everyday conditions such as conjunctivitis, infected wounds, cuts and blisters. The places where they stayed quickly became emergency first-aid stations. On hearing the news, villagers would queue up patiently to be treated, and the conditions they suffered from were much like the commonplace maladies experienced during the Middle Ages. The French couple displayed a miraculous kind of warmth that is even more important than science and medicine and is able to touch the hearts of their patients.

The medical professionals and nurses who volunteer in far-flung places are there to both admire the scenery and treat illnesses. In this way, they discover the most meaningful kind of hiking journey, and create a true 'spirit of trails'. That is, love and friendship, mutual aid, determination, harmony, purity and tranquillity.

When trekking in Annapurna, the thing that most surprised me was the cleanliness of the paths. You will hardly ever see discarded rubbish; all you are likely to encounter is a clod of excrement left by an ox, sheep or horse.

Outside the villages, there are no bins. All hikers carry their rubbish on their backs until they reach the next village, and only then discard it.

The cleanliness of the paths in Annapurna was striking

Whenever I reached for a sweet, Bikram would stretch out his hand, take the wrapper from me and put it in his pocket, as though concerned that I might not be able to bear the load of a single slip of paper. Every household toilet that we passed on the path, although comprising only a place to squat, would have a bucket of clean spring water for people to wash in. These sorts of toilets are exposed to the elements and are surrounded by colourful plants such as cinquefoil and Mexican marigold. It felt as though the surrounding rocks and stone steps were as clean and pure as those flowers, and there was no foul odour.

I wondered what sorts of customs led to these tribal houses being so beautiful, from the kitchens right down to the toilets. They were free of dust and dirt, and always conferred a feeling of joy in cleanliness and tranquillity. I spent time looking at the women and children, squatting down near streams and mountain springs to scrub their copperware, cutlery and mugs, and I came to realise that, for these devout tribal people, although they might lack material possessions or be short of food, it was imperative for them to have clean tools. It is like when they make offerings to the spirits every morning. All they require is a bowl of clean water, and in the water they would put a leaf, a petal or a wild flower.

When the Buddha was preaching in Jetavana, he saw that the floor was dirty, so he grabbed a broom and began to sweep. He said to his disciples: "Cleaning can make your own heart clean, it can cleanse the hearts of others, and it will also please the gods." These tribal people don't need a vast, gleaming temple to make their offerings to a golden statue of the Buddha; nor do they need to burn a massive stick of incense to pray for inner consolation. All they need is to retain their original simplicity and purity in a shared space with the spirits amid the mountains and rivers. Even without paying respects to the Buddha in a temple, people can still live plainly in the clean, graceful world around them.

At sunset I was sitting in the living room of the Chhomrong Inn. The warm stove emitted a monotonous buzzing sound like the soundtrack of an old film. The household utensils arranged neatly above the stove gave off a soft metallic sheen. Bikram noticed that my feet had begun to blister, and that the nail on the bleeding big toe of my right foot was in a bad state from all the walking. He patiently mashed up some plantain leaves that he had collected and wrapped them, cool and dark, around my foot.

I imagined that my blood was now mixed in with that of the pack horses, oxen and sheep on the mountain path: my own pious, sacrificial offering to the mountain.

Through the translucent glass windows I could see a mountain before me. In the still blueness of the vault of heaven, only the mountain peak stood tall and erect in the centre, connecting with the universe. Who would have thought that part of this beautiful and tranquil scene would exist on such a bitter, treacherous path?

Realising that I had walked this entire path on my own two feet, I experienced a feeling of relief and joy. Ascetic monks in the Himalayas use penance and a suppression of desire to increase their moral integrity. I feel that ascending a mountain via a difficult route is to enter a kind of dialogue with the mountain. In talking with the mountain, you are simultaneously searching for your own strength and temperament. It is like those eminent monks in ancient times: as they played their lute, their souls would also find union with the surrounding snow.

From in among the oaks and maples of the forest, you can hear the endless warbling of the Himalayan cuckoo. The Gurung folk in the inn's kitchen said that, when you hear the sweet cooing of the cuckoo for the first time that year, whatever state you are in at that given moment, you shall remain in that same state for the rest of the year. At that time, I saw the paths of Annapurna were suffused with even more lustre, were more limpid and more softly radiant. It's like the limitless, self-reflecting net of the great god Indra that the Buddha spoke of. As my silhouette pierced through the mountains and streams like a placid packhorse, the bare sound of my feet on the path gave off a kind of limitless, merciful warmth.

DAY TEN

LARGER SPACE, MORE FREEDOM

THE HIMALAYAS WERE SHROUDED by morning sunshine, giving out colourful, fantastic light. Enveloped in rosy halos, the valley and the forest seemed be wearing a gorgeous long robe. Buffaloes bathing in the first rays of morning appeared like a black glaze and sheep were grazing under a thick grove, bleating dreamlike on the path.

More than a billion years ago, a giant continent called Pangea was surrounded by the quiet Panthalassa Ocean. Later, some turmoil in the earth's mantle made the land split, drift and crash into each other. About 470 million years ago, a gigantic force pushed up the mountains like a magic corrugated carpet. Like a magician's playing cards that had been shuffled, the crystalline metamorphic rocks baked and squeezed for thousands of years glistened in strips in the sky.

Only geologists deal in time spans as great as 470 million years or appreciate the scale of such a concept. If you could fly across time at a rate of one year per second, it would take sixteen years to complete the journey.

Ordinary people are unable to perceive the occurrence of any significant geological event. For instance, a 1954 Survey of India revealed the height of Mount Everest to be 8,848 metres, while an official Chinese document released in 2005 stated that the height was 8,844.43 metres. The former calculation related to the height climbed by mountaineers while the latter referred to the geological height. If you can imagine the enormous Indian landmass crashing into an Asian snow drift like an out-of-control bullet train and increasing the height of the Himalayas by three millimetres each year, you will appreciate the eternalness and greatness of Mount Everest.

Only when you start out trekking and then stop can you see clearly.

The British artist David Hockney fingerpaints flowers and grass on his iPhone, capturing the moment when the sun rises behind a mountain peak or river bend. He sends his paintings to a number of friends so that they can receive six of his original works at breakfast. Their minds will be filled with light and space as well as genial, comfortable feelings. Now in his eighties, the artist has found a new way of viewing and presenting the world. His hundreds of distinctive landscape paintings were drawn in the countryside of east Yorkshire, the place of his birth. The ever-changing nature always provides us with unruly colours and new ways to perceive life, filled with infinite inspiration and providing greater space and freedom.

The poetry of packhorses

I fell in love with the sunshine, colours, space, animals, plants and people in Annapurna Base Camp as soon as I started my journey. I felt each living creature there had a God-like face. The secret of Hockney's success was realising that 'teachers can pass on skills rather than poetry'.

Indeed, poetry cannot be taught but only felt in nature and in life. When I walked down from the steps in Chhomrong to the tea house in Taglung, the path appeared to take a fork in the fields. My right foot, bandaged like an Egyptian mummy, seemed to awaken, its energy restored and able once more to help the left foot move. I suddenly felt relaxed.

The stone sign on the way to Ghandruk showed that this was no ordinary path but the one leading to Annapurna Base Camp. A glorious world unfolded as we climbed over high mountains and passed icy rivers, great lakes, deep valleys, paddy fields and villages. Walking among the mountains and their alluring names – Fish Tail Mountain, Tent Peak, Fluted Peak and Poon Hill – made us reluctant to return home. In his *Notes on Literature and Art*, the scholar and writer Qian Zhongshu said: "Some place names can have miraculous, aesthetic effects."

Who can fail to be attracted to 'Fish Tail Mountain' or 'Fluted Peak'? As John Muir, father of America's National Parks, once said: "Who has not felt the urge to throw a loaf of bread and a pound of tea in an old sack, and jump over the back fence?"

Packhorses on the path from Chhomrong to Kimche

From the 1,810-metre-high Taglung to the 1,600-metre-high Kimrong Khola, we encountered packhorses crossing a river on a simple bridge made of straw and sticks. They tinkled as they walked and climbed 620 metres to arrive at the 2,220-metre-high Kumrong Danda. We closely followed them on the narrow, muddy path. From Chhomrong to Ghandruk and then to Kimche, packhorses have been deployed on this path for thousands of years. All items going into and out of Annapurna Base Camp have been carried on this path by mules. We continually stepped on the dung of donkeys and horses that smelled of fresh grass and contained undigested beans and corn kernels.

Ghandruk has the largest Gurung population in the Annapurna Peaks

A liquid gas storage tank costs 1,500 rupees in Pokhara, 1,700 rupees when carried to Naya Pul, 2,000 rupees in Chhomrong having been brought uphill by mule in the absence of any roads, and 3,000 rupees in Annapurna Base Camp where it has been carried by porters since the path is too narrow for mules. A mule driver can make a hundred rupees for delivering a liquid gas storage tank. 'Danda' means height or cliff in Nepali. The village of Danda offers splendid views but the prices there are eye-watering. A small bottle of Coke cost me 160 rupees. Two teams of donkeys meeting there can cause a traffic jam. A Korean trekker dropped a camera lens cap and when he stooped down to pick it up, his guide shouted: "Look out for the donkey." When the path was clear again, the lens cap was in fragments.

Donkeys hold a special position among animals that carry goods and materials. Often derided, they are actually clever and easy to handle. A donkey can transport a load of forty kilograms, equal to the carrying-capacity of four trekkers. All the packhorses and donkeys are well presented, wearing a colourful mask fringed with knitted wool, leaving only their eyes and nose exposed. A small, round mirror positioned at the centre of their foreheads glitters in the sun. The colour of their woollen saddlery changes over time due to the effect of weathering and abrasion. They do the most miserable and tiring work but they are wonderfully attired and have the most amazing strength.

The donkeys, mules and packhorses are lined up in strict sequence. The one in the lead is called the 'head'. It is given the most attention and is dressed with the most care since it has the greatest power and mental strength of the team. The head donkey wears a golden pheasant feather symbolising a bright future or a flag representing success. The mule driver blows a whistle and hums a tune. The special 'language' of the animals rose and fell happily, reflecting a deep mood, and mingled with the sounds of copper bells, silver bells and stringed bells that they were wearing, all combined to create a fantastic music on the mountain path and lightened our mood and increased our tempo.

We followed one of the lads driving the animals. A recording of him singing one of his favourite songs had been set to be his mobile phone ringtone. He moved forward quickly and listened to the popular Nepalese folk song *Resham Firiri*. The toil facing these donkeys must have been alleviated by listening to these songs.

> *The kapok tree bloomed. When did it happen?*
> *The flowers fell like flying white birds;*
> *You must be tired. Do you want to rest,*
> *Or fly to the remote places in your dream?*

On this refreshing morning, with the sound of the hoofs on the serene mountain path, I finally appreciated why we called ourselves 'donkey friends' –a group of trekkers and backpackers that can carry a heavy load and endure bitterness and hardship. Although we looked like refugees from a distance and beggars closer up, we were idlers with nothing better to do than climb mountains. How can ordinary tourists enjoy the hell of carrying like a packhorse while flying like a bird in heaven!

We endured wind and frost on the way but our hearts were as free as a bird. Although the bird is small, it can fly across the whole sky.

A love for dancing

In Danda, we encountered a group of young, upper-class Nepalese who were studying at university in Britain. I thought only foreigners like me would struggle with breathing. But they turned out to be similarly afflicted. We walked on the blue stone path, passed fields of golden corn, zigzagged for four kilometres along the valley floor and came to our destination, Ghandruk, at an altitude of 1,990 metres. Ghandruk has the second largest Gurung population in Nepal and the largest in Annapurna Peaks, housing 270 families from this tribe. 'Ghandruk' means vast, wild forest in Nepali.

The mountains, grassland and fields that surround this densely forested area with its comfortable climate are protected by numerous Buddhist deities. The temples facing the snow mountains were built in the architectural style of the Ghandruk's Tibetan ancestors. This serene and rich land is an ideal tourist destination. The village elders sit around on a terrace. The fluttering, heart-shaped banyan leaves greet each passerby. Pink galsang flowers, golden marigolds and colourful pincushions thrive on both sides of the path. They were so fabulous and the villagers were so quiet that you had to slow your pace to truly appreciate the scene.

My guide took me to directly to the Hotel Milan in the highlands. The blue courtyard, wooden building and balcony, and roof paved with smooth tiles brought me great warmth, like an exhausted bird returning home.

Hotel Milan has a history of more than twenty years. It is a typical Gurung family inn. Its hostess Shanker served us two cups of strong Masala tea. She was sitting among the flowers on the balcony, basking in the sun and quietly watching us enjoy the herbal tea. Her son was making *chhaang*, a kind of beer made in a round barrel in the yard. It is the most popular home brew in the Himalayas. Made with barley, millet or rice and spring water, it has a relatively low alcoholic content and can be drunk hot or cold. The aroma drifting from the barrel made me tipsy before I even tasted it.

The Gurungs arrived here from western Tibet. Believing in Shamanism and Tibetan Buddhism, they are ethnically related to Tibetans and Burmese. With high cheekbones and perfectly round faces, they look like Mongols and are good at mountaineering and hunting. Many of its young men join Britain's Gurkha regiment. They send back home their army earnings made overseas, which accounts for this area being more developed and more prosperous than other parts of Nepal.

Sorathi is danced primarily by girls and unmarried young women

Shanker's son making 'chhaang' in a round barrel

The sound of the frame drum rises in waves, going beyond the limits of my memory

We saw a volleyball court in the village where many children were playing. To my astonishment, their movement and knowledge of the rules seemed quite advanced. It was the same with other students in the mountains. Nepalese students from the mountains or the cities wear British-style school uniforms. Their shirts, ties, shorts, leather shoes and socks are all neat and tidy. This shows the value placed on education in a poor place like Nepal.

The Rodi is a distinctive aspect of raising children in Gurung society. It is something like a youth club. A male takes charge of teenage boys while a female counterpart looks after the girls. They live together in a Rodi during the winter and summer holidays, working and playing together.

There are usually several Rodis in a large village. A Rodi generally comprises between a dozen and fifteen teenagers, and members of the same Rodi work together in the fields or collect wood in the mountains. Sometimes, the members of a Rodi will ask those in another village for help with work, and a Rodi composed of young men will walk to a remote village to visit another one composed of girls. When they stay there for a couple of days, the girls will kill a chicken or a sheep and cook delicious food. They sing and dance together and establish innocent friendships and sometimes love. They leave the Rodi at the age of eighteen.

Bikram spared from the physical burden of carrying a backpack

Close to completing my trek to Annapurna Base Camp on schedule

Ghandruk has a Tibetan Buddhist temple that faces two snow mountains

The team we encountered on our journey were members of a Rodi. The parents of this affluent group from the top of Gurung society owned villas in Kathmandu and sent their children to study in Britain. The youngsters returned home during the holidays, carried heavy backpacks and trudged across the Himalayas to boost their stamina and experience the splendour of the mountains and rivers that nourish them. They are known as the 'rich second generation' of overseas returnees. But they too are bestowed with a kind, unswerving and philanthropic outlook and spirit typical of the great Himalayas.

Most Gurung women wear glistening nose rings and red coral necklaces. Unlike women from other mountainous nationalities, those I met were vivacious and cheerful and often talked or played jokes on travellers. That evening, on the day of the new moon, my guide took me to dance in the moonlit courtyard of the Gurung Traditional Museum.

The Gurungs love dancing, especially the classic folk dance known as the Sorathi. Their season for dancing stretches from the Spring-Welcoming Festival of the Goddess of Wisdom in January to the autumn full moon in October. Dancing takes place after the farm work is completed or when the hail stops, on full moon and new moon days, and at weddings and funerals. Sorathi is danced primarily by unmarried girls. They first clean the ground with dried cow dung, then close their eyes and mouths, sit solemnly and quietly on the ground so that the deities would possess them and give them permission to dance.

The girls wear all kinds of garlands, nose rings, earrings and bracelets. Their bare feet move to the beat of a drum and they wriggle their limbs lithely and gracefully, showing great charm and sexual allure. The sound of the frame drum rises in waves, reverberating in the dark night of the Annapurna Peaks and going beyond the limits of my hearing, eyesight and memory.

A free heart

I was near to completing my trek to Annapurna Base Camp on schedule. The imposing Annapurna mountains towered behind me. The temple draped with colourful prayer flags was watching over the mountain. The smooth snow mountains standing between 6,000 and 8,000 metres were like the 'seats of deities' and swirling clouds in the film *2012*.

Bikram and I sat facing each other in the courtyard. With the chanting of 'Om Mani Padme Hum' flowing slowly from the old tape machine, I appreciated for the first time that my guide was clean, handsome and brilliant.

His body was now spared from the physical burden of carrying a backpack. I thought he must be looking forward to the prospect of hurrying home to see the arrival of a new life and to bring with him his love and tender care. Over the previous ten days, he had impressed me with his ability to carry that heavy bag on the mountain path. I always encouraged him to move on at his own pace and not to wait for me as I limped on behind. But whenever I reached a mountain pass, there he was waiting for me. The quiet patience and warmth made me realise the sentiment of 'I will never leave you or forsake you'.

He treated me with great sincerity. His amber eyes, long curly hair and strong backbone helped protect me and overcome difficulty in this mountainous region. Sir Edmund Hillary said no one could climb Mount Everest without the help of a Sherpa. For my part, I thought that was also true for anyone trekking in the great Himalayas.

. . .

As we walked that path every day, it was our entire world. We took big strides, raised our legs to climb and flared our nostrils to inhale the refreshing air. With each footstep we took in the fragrance and essence of the plants. In a place dominated by forests and mountains, the trees filled my senses and the pure white snow mountains enriched my imagination. With no crowded highways, car exhaust fumes or noisy factories, trekking is a luxury and an opportunity to stand aloof from worldly matters.

All trekkers feel their blood surge while on the path, and their excitement can be seen in the radiance of their faces. Like burning torches, their faces are lit up by the golden, purple-red and cerise leaves in the mountain forest. Even though danger lurks in the forest and unexpected disaster might occur on the path, you can fly against the wind, turn as light as a sword, sit at the foot of a snow mountain to watch the turning world and enjoy the dream-like sunshine.

The trekking route to Annapurna Base Camp covers a distance of 220 kilometres. We had good reason to feel proud of our achievement. We had defecated in the forest, passed by muntjac deer, flown with vultures and slept with leeches. Although I had coughed up blood, lost consciousness in a rainstorm and damaged my big toe nail, we derived profound harmony, pleasure and confidence in ourselves. There are so many paths in this world that I cannot walk all of them, but I thought I would always be a person trekking in the mountains.

I was a 'leather vagrant', a trekker without borders and without wheels. Nevertheless, before long, I felt flustered and my feet itched. As Jean-Jacques Rousseau stated in *Émile, or on Education*: "As far as I know, trekking is the only form of travel more pleasant than horse riding." As someone who belongs to nature and advocates freedom, I pledged to return there and live a life of travelling in high mountains.

NOTES

THE GREATEST EXPENSE IS SEEING A DOCTOR

On the eleventh morning of my journey, we started off from Ghandruk and arrived at Kimche after two hours of trekking on the mountain path. I saw Indian-made Bolero SUVs and brightly coloured buses with paintings of Lord Shiva on them parked on a small sand bank, and donkeys waiting to transport cargo. I didn't think any trekker would have the energy to walk any further. The bus fare was 120 rupees but it was unlikely to depart soon. The SUV had a capacity of twelve, charged 500 rupees for each passenger and departed once it was full. Many short-haul trekkers come to Kimche and return after a short tour in Ghandruk. It was China's National Day holiday and there were throngs of Chinese tourists. I quickly persuaded a large group of Chinese unwilling to walk in returning to Pokhara by vehicle.

After we returned to the Himalaya Hotel at noon, my guide took my backpack to my room. We gave each other a hug and said goodbye. My eyes were wet and I said I wished he would be my guide on my next journey.

Bikram hurried to the hospital because his baby would soon be born. I told him that I would take a short rest and visit them in a couple of days. The moment he left, I began to wash myself, along with my clothes and shoes. Then I had an extravagant meal of spicy boiled beef in the Sichuan Emei restaurant opposite the hotel. That night, I began to cough violently and was woken up with a start by a loud shriek. I opened the door to ask a waiter what was going on, and it turned out that two Chinese tourists were making love at maximum volume. I was half dead with fright. The serenity of the mountains had disappeared in an instant.

At six the next morning, I packed, checked out of the hotel occupied solely by Chinese tourists, moved to the Peace Eye Guest House diagonally across and asked the waiter to take me to hospital, fearing that I had got pneumonia.

The waiter took me on the back of his moped to a hospital where letters of gratitude from Western travellers were pasted on the corridor walls. I later understood that it was a private hospital run by an Indian. First, a male nurse wearing a Sikh turban took my temperature and blood pressure. Then a bespectacled Indian doctor checked my lungs with a stethoscope, made sure there was no infection or fever and prescribed three different types of medicine made in India and costing 4,000 rupees. Then, the doctor gave me a prescription and medical insurance form and told me that I could apply to the insurance company for reimbursement once I arrived back in China. I hadn't expected that the medicine would be so expensive. However, since I had not been diagnosed with a serious condition, I went back to sleep in the hotel somewhat relieved.

I recuperated for three days in my room, still coughing violently. When I rode a bicycle to take photos, I suddenly got vertigo, blurred vision and tinnitus. I informed Nakhi, the boss of the Peace Eye. His hotel had once appeared in *Lonely Planet* and therefore Western travellers were fond of staying there. He was warm-hearted and told me that one of his friends was a good doctor who had helped his family for several years. I believed him and he took me to a clinic on his motorbike.

This doctor was also Indian. He asked me to stop taking the medicine prescribed by the previous doctor and diagnosed that it was the trekking that had caused my extreme weakness. He asked me to take extra vitamins and fruit and not to go trekking for a week. He then prescribed some different medicine made in India costing 1,800 rupees.

Later on, Basanta told me that it was quite expensive to see Indian doctors and anyone who took me there would invariably get a kickback. It would be better to see a doctor at a hospital owned by the local government. The medicines had cost me 5,800 rupees in total, equivalent to the monthly salary of a waiter. Yet I didn't feel any better even by the fifth day. I got angry and decided to take the initiative. I asked a young Kashmiri man called Adil to take me to a local pharmacy on his motorbike and bought a bottle of cough syrup and local vitamin tablets made in Nepal that set me back 200 rupees. I then decided to set out for a pilgrimage to Jomsom early the next morning.

Much better to walk on a clean path than to continue taking medicine in Pokhara. One of life's essentials is to go through fire and water, live an unworldly life and achieve enlightenment. I decided it was the right path for me to follow.

ITINERARY

Bus route
Pokhana to Phedi (23km, 1hr)

Trekking route
Phedi (altitude: 1,130 metres) to Dhampus (altitude: 1,650 metres, 8km) to Pothana (altitude: 1,890 metres, 4km) to Deurali (altitude: 2,100 metres, 4km) to Bheri Kharka (altitude: 2,150 metres, 6km) to Tolka (altitude: 1,700 metres, 4km) to Landruk (altitude: 1,620 metres, 3km) to New Bridge (altitude: 1,410 metres, 4km) to Jhinu Danda (altitude: 1,750 metres, 3km) to Chhomrong (altitude: 2,210 metres, 3km) to Chhomrong Khola (altitude: 1,750 metres, 3km) to Sinuva (altitude: 2,340 metres, 5km) to Bamboo (altitude: 2,310 metres, 2km) to Doban (altitude: 2,500 metres, 2km) to the Himalayan Hotel (altitude: 2,900 metres, 3km) to Deorali (altitude: 3,200 metres, 3km) to Machhapuchhre Base Camp (altitude: 3,700 metres, 4km) to Annapurna Base Camp (altitude: 4,130 metres, 4km)

Return route
Annapurna Base Camp (altitude: 4,130 metres) to Machhapuchhre Base Camp (altitude: 3,700 metres, 4km) to Deorali (altitude: 3,200 metres, 4km) to Himalayan Hotel (altitude: 2,900 metres, 3km) to Doban (altitude: 2,500 metres, 3km) to Bamboo (altitude: 2,310 metres, 2km) to Sinuva (altitude: 2,340 metres, 2km) to Chhomrong Khola (altitude: 1,750 metres, 5km) to Chhomrong (altitude: 2,210 metres, 3km) to Taglung (altitude: 1,810 metres, 1km) to Kimrong Khola (altitude: 1,600 metres, 3km) to Kumrong Danda (altitude: 2,220 metres, 3km) to Ghandruk (altitude: 1,990 metres, 4km) to Kimche (altitude: 1,640 metres, 4km)

Bus route
Kimche to Pokhana (60km, 3hr)

Mileage/Duration
220km/11days

CHAPTER III

PILGRIMAGE TO JOMSOM

Early Tibetan scriptures and epic Indian tales all mention the amazing Himalayas. This is the place where deities live at high altitude and mortals can find paradise in a secret valley, with the mysterious breath pervading the pinnacles of temples that penetrate the sky, in an antiquated, dull-red monastery, in the chants of mandala scriptures and around the possessed Shaman...

Sometimes, we are excited by incompleteness. That night, I really saw the moonlight in Mustang reflected in Kangaroo's eyes. The moonlight apart from the snow lotus on the icy mountain was extraordinary. Mustang is like an oasis, the Garden of Eden, Babylon and the world we lose in the boisterous mortal life. We have to trudge on, cast a distant eye at it, appreciate the wild flowers in the valley housing deities, wave our hands and leave with melancholy.

DAY ONE

ARRIVING WITH MY FEET ON A LOTUS

Pokhara Municipality would not exist without the Himalayas. Trekkers and backpackers from all over the world come to Pokhara for enlightenment and to steel themselves for the rigours ahead.

Nepal is one of the best trekking destinations in the world. If you have ever camped in your back garden, lit a barbecue, sung karaoke or looked at the starlit sky, you too will fall in love with trekking. It needn't take up much time. Nepal is a small country, sandwiched between two huge ones, China and India. However, it has the world's highest mountains. There is a saying: 'Let the Himalayas change you.'

Sir Edmund Hillary visited Nepal 120 times in his remaining fifty-five years after becoming the first person to climb Mount Everest. The Nepalese call Mount Everest 'Sagarmatha', meaning 'Sky Goddess' and some believe Noah's Ark washed up in the mysterious Himalayas. What is its great charm? Its charm rests in the fact that trekkers can discover things in Nepal that can't be found in other countries.

Early Tibetan scriptures and epic Indian tales all mention the Himalayas. They describe both deities and mortals finding paradise in its secret valleys, in the soaring temples, in the old, dull-red monasteries, in the chants of scriptures and in the healing powers of shamans...

Rolling mountains and stunning terraces put people in a reverie. Taking a break at the top of a mountain, fording a river and receiving 'Namaste' greetings and smiles are some of the true moments of deep, hidden feelings that trekkers experience. High and low, and incomparably vast, the mountain landscape can be all-consuming and energy-sapping. Even simple food such as curry and *dal bhat* eaten hastily by the common people are delicious in a land where fresh meat and vegetables are in short supply. Many trekkers are drawn to the Nepalese people, just as much as the mountains and temples. They have lived on this land for generations, getting up at sunrise and going to sleep at sundown. Despite the arrival of tourists, they continue to live in their villages and maintain their traditional lifestyles, while retaining a friendly and charming disposition. By living a simple and uncomplicated life, the Nepalese show travellers how to be tolerant, treat others well and have self-respect.

The wonderful natural scenery, its distance from the busy world and the lightness of body and mind can make people reappraise their complicated, busy urban lives. Mountaineering and trekking are addictive and hugely rewarding, and there should be more of it.

Rivers of Naga

The pilgrimage to Jomsom is one of the most popular trekking routes in Nepal. Starting from Pokhara and moving upwards along the Kali Gandaki Valley, I passed Poon Hill where I enjoyed a panoramic view of Annapurna and came to Muktinath, the second largest pilgrimage site in Nepal.

Bikram was no longer my guide because of the arrival of his baby, who was called Dawa, meaning 'Moon' in Nepali. Instead, Basanta arranged for his brother Bishnu to be my guide. Bishnu, twenty-nine years old and 1.85 metres tall, had long, thick, curly hair and a moustache that made him resemble the Italian mountaineer and adventurer, Reinhold Messner. He looked more like an Indian of Aryan extraction than an ethnic Tibetan.

Basanta assured me that if I became ill in remote Muktinath, Bishnu, as strong as a leopard, would carry me with ease.

My backpack now weighed fifteen kilograms, containing additional items such as medicine, thermal clothes, sweets and chocolate. We estimated the journey of about five hundred kilometres would take ten days to complete if we used a vehicle for part of the route. Bishnu once served in the Gurkha regiment in Qatar and could speak English fluently. When we met, he said he would be happy to carry my large backpack. He suggested I carry my camera bag and he would meet me at seven the next morning.

From Pokhara we sat in a vehicle for ninety minutes, moving westwards and following the limpid Seti Khola before arriving in Nayapul, the starting point of pilgrimages to Jomsom. The small Gurung village was swarming with trekkers who had been transported there by minibuses, SUVs and Suzuki taxis. Rafters on the Modi Khola also gathered there and were busy making preparations before setting out on the river. Food stalls and tea houses were set up in bamboo huts selling hot Chinese tea eggs, milky tea and doughnuts.

The Gurung people are good at climbing. Dozens of bamboo pack baskets were placed on the roofs of the stone houses. These baskets are used by porters to carry trekkers' luggage weighing thirty to forty kilograms. Setting out along the mountain stone paths, they moved upwards, step by step, along the Bhurungdi Khola.

In Birethanti, we passed through the checkpoints of the Annapurna Conservation Area Project and Trekkers' Information Management System.

The village also had a bakery, a bank, smart hotels and cafes. Seeing the inspector stamp and date my two passports for trekking in the mountains, I smiled to myself in anticipation of the journey ahead.

Rafting is one of the most exciting ways to travel in Nepal

Bishnu suggested I offer two sweets to Naga at the roadside so that this mythical being, half human, half snake, would protect us during our journey over mountains and across rivers. In Chinese mythology, the snake is a symbol of danger and insidiousness. But in Nepal, where Hinduism is the main religion, people worship the Naga because they believe it can control the rain in monsoon seasons, just like the Dragon King, the God of Rain in Chinese mythology. Legend has it that the Naga, worshipped by Gurkhas, sat on a cushion with nine snakes coiled around which protected Nepal from torrential rains and flooding for a period of twelve years. Therefore, on the Naga Panchami festival in July or August each year, Nepalese Hindus will paste colourful images of snakes on their walls and devoutly consecrate sweets, rice and milk to the Naga, in the hope of being granted favourable weather.

Everyone starting out on their journey felt excited, light-footed and full of energy. The clean mountain air was like an oxygen bar that provided relief from industrial pollution.

Most of the more than one hundred rivers in Nepal originate in or pass through the Himalayas, cross the rugged land, flow among forests, wind through the Terai Plains and finally pour into the sacred Ganges and the Indian Ocean. Like blue veins, the rivers connect the high mountains and the plains, turbulently or quietly pouring from the highlands and creating an incomparably wonderful feeling.

The Himalayan rivers are regarded by the Nepalese as sacred. Human ashes are transported by these rivers and finally taken to the Ganges. Many religious bathing ceremonies are held at the intersection of two rivers. Water brings life and reincarnation but it can also be terrifying and dreadful. Therefore, the Nepalese are seldom seen swimming in rivers no matter how hot the weather.

In 1976, an American man named Al Read went rafting on the Seti Khola and started to make a map of the river. From then on, Nepal gained a reputation as one of the best places for rafting and canoeing. The streams plunging down steep mountains, the large areas of primitive wilderness, the fascinating expanses of sand and the roaring waves make rafting or walking alongside the river so exhilarating.

The Nepalese have beautiful names for all the rivers protected by the Naga. For instance, meaning 'white river' in Nepali, the Seti Khola originating in South Annapurna got its name because of its soft, milk-white upstream waters that flow over limestone. The source of the Kali Gandaki Khola is in the snow mountains to the north of Mount Dhaulagiri, where the water has cut through black rocks and argillite to create a number of canyons. Along its course from north to south, the river carries large quantities of pitch-black sediment. Hence, '*kali*' means 'black river' in Nepali.

We were passing through a deep valley formed by the 'blue river', the Bhurungdi Khola. Since the Himalayas were created, the Bhurungdi Khola has been an undulating mass of blue-black water, rushing on in perpetual movement and forming the distinctive valleys in Pokhara Municipality. Passing it from above, it looked like a trench rather than a steep, serene valley. The river itself was not visible, only a gurgling sound could be heard. We continued our trek in the ever-changing valley, panting for breath.

Bishnu carried my large camouflage backpack with his smaller bag for carry-on clothes dangling in front of his chest. I referred to us as the

'Kangaroo Group'. Carrying two packs, one in front and one behind, he looked like a female kangaroo in the Australian outback. The most useful Nepalese word I learned was '*bassnu*', meaning 'let's stop for a breather'.

That morning, I weakly shouted '*bassnu*' about a dozen times and the tall, robust 'kangaroo' would stop reluctantly, looking at me panting heavily, and then reached out his strong hand and pulled me ahead on the path.

Sad songs

At noon, we ate a plate of fried noodles with tomato sauce on the north bank of the Bhurungdi Khola. Having climbed a distance of five kilometres, my knees were stabbing with pain. We stopped at the river bank near a bamboo forest, a small waterfall and a drawbridge made of rattan. I no longer cared whether we would reach the campsite that day. Tired as a pile of cotton, I took an afternoon nap on a bench outside a tea house.

'Bang!' the sound of a fig falling, followed by 'thud', a pile of birds' droppings splatting onto my arm. I was sleeping under a Bodhi tree where the Buddha was first enlightened.

Some 2,500 years ago, the twenty-nine-year-old Prince Gotama Siddhattha of Kapilavastu (now Lumbini) in Nepal eschewed his comfortable imperial life and gave all his jewellery, fine clothes and horses to his carter Ghtem. He also cut off his own beautiful curly hair, the last symbol of his social class and royal family status, and left his wife, children and home in his quest for enlightenment.

He practised asceticism for six years, sat under a Bodhi, looking haggard, and explored an abstruse, serene, non-extreme and fulfilling path. Finally, he decided to give up his ascetic state, bathe in the Nairanjana River near which musical instruments were being played, accepted fresh milk from the shepherdess Sujata, found the 'middle way', established authentic wisdom and changed the religious world for the next two thousand years.

I was fascinated by the thought of the simple figure of the Buddha barefoot on the bank of the Sacred River in the Himalayas. Gotama Siddhattha did not use any high-tech tools in those years. He only pursued negative escapism and exploration in the wilderness and forests. I thought that, if we didn't follow his example, we would never experience the harsh journey or achieve enlightenment.

. . .

It was not just the Buddha who picked flowers smilingly in the Himalayas but God Shiva of Creation and Destruction. With the arrival of the ancient kingdom of Lichchhavi in the fifth century AD, Hinduism was introduced to Nepal. The emperors of the ruling Malla dynasty believed in Hinduism, and they built many Hindu temples and invited Indian Brahmins to make sacrifices. Consequently it was Hinduism and not Buddhism that finally became the state religion.

The Hindu classic *Rigveda* exhibits beliefs in several deities and the propitiation of several divinities associated with the sky and the atmosphere. Citizens were classified according to their castes, the four main ones being Brahmins (priests, gurus), Kshatriyas (warriors, kings), Vaisyas (farmers, traders) and Shudras (labourers). However, in Nepal, the caste system was less rigid than in neighbouring India, and the boundary between castes was not as strict.

Today, Hinduism, Buddhism, Islam, Christianity, Jainism, Shamanism and Bahaism are all popular in Nepal. There are many beliefs and many castes. It is difficult to imagine that sixty-one ethnic groups, five more than those in vast China, are living in a country as small as a 'Chinese yam'. Besides, the diversity of the different nationals is quite perplexing.

However, once you start to become acquainted with Nepal, you can tell a lot about a person just through their name, including their social status, occupation, ethnicity and home town. For instance, 'Jaya Gurung' implies that the person comes from Ghia and is of the Gurung ethnic group; 'Dawa Sherpa' from Dawa of the Sherpa ethnic group; 'Mingmar Tamang' from Mingmar of the Tamang ethnic group.

Family, ethnic group and caste are still the three major elements of Nepalese life. Anyone violating the traditions handed down over thousands of years might be expelled from the family and society in general. Nepal is one of the poorest countries in the world. In addition to the influence of its special geological conditions, the people devoutly believe that human beings cannot control their fate and that everything is determined by God. For this reason, Nepal boasts 'as many temples as houses and as many deities as people'. Religions exert a profound impact on people's thoughts, behaviour and lifestyles. All kinds of belief mix together in a giant religious melting pot. Fatalism helps the Nepalese deal with poverty and lead a virtuous life, but it stifles entrepreneurship and taking the initiative.

My guide Bishnu came from a Brahman family in a mountainous area. His overseas military experience and handsome appearance would be lucrative assets in the city, but he loves the mountains where he grew up and he is content working as a mountain guide. I summed up his features with three words ending with '-ing': climbing, flying and sleeping. I could often work out the nationalities and religious beliefs of the villagers I encountered on the way simply by looking at their faces and clothes.

An acolyte painting auspicious 'tika' on the foreheads of women

The first day was the toughest for all the trekkers. Kangaroo saw that I only walked twelve kilometres in an eight-hour period, compared with an average for a trekker of seventeen or eighteen kilometres. The distance I walked each day got gradually shorter, and I was relieved to stop to lodge in a hotel in Tikhedhunga around half way.

Tikhedhunga, at an altitude of 1,540 metres, sits on a hillside and is home to about sixty villagers, most of whom are Brahman. Nepalese usually live together in a big family. Sometimes, an entire small village is composed of one big family. In Nepalese Hindu society, the custom of arranged marriage is still maintained. Although Western values and lifestyles have a big influence in the cities, a great majority of villagers still keep to traditional customs and habits. Both sides of the marriage should belong to the same caste or ethnic group.

Nepal is a patriarchal society and many ethnic groups still regard girls as an economic burden. They must remain virgins before marriage and they must pay a substantial dowry. Twice as many boys as girls receive an education. Women live a tough life and their mortality rate is higher than that of men. They usually work harder and longer than men, but receive less pay. In rural areas, girls are the last to have meals and menstruating women are often locked up in a cowshed for a period of four days, although the practice was outlawed in 2005. In Nepal, if a woman fails to produce a child in ten years, her husband has the right to marry a second wife; after the husband dies, the widow is not allowed to marry anyone but the brother of her late husband, with the properties inherited by her son. The old tradition of *sati*, in which a woman had to jump into the funeral pyre of her late husband, was another bad social custom. It was abolished in the 1920s.

Now, millions of Nepalese men have to leave their home town or village and make a living elsewhere, sometimes in foreign countries such as India or Malaysia. Trekking for days in the Annapurna Peaks, I found that women laboured both at home and in the fields. They are genuine 'leftovers'. I stayed in Mamata Lodge, *'mamata'* meaning 'lovely' in Nepali. It was a family inn run by three sisters. It was cold in the mountains in the evening, so I stayed huddled in the kitchen to warm myself and watched them cook rice and mutton using firewood. One of them, a twenty-year-old named Sunita, cooked and affectionately watched Kangaroo.

Usually, a guide would take his clients to stay in the same inn in each different place they stayed. I knew that this rural girl had been waiting for Kangaroo to pass by their lodge and cast an affectionate eye over him. I jokingly asked Kangaroo why he had chosen this lodge and whether it was because of the three 'azaleas' (girls as beautiful as azaleas).

Kangaroo smiled and just said the girls were good cooks.

At that moment, the radio was playing a sad song sung by a Nepalese man and woman. I asked Kangaroo what they were singing about.

He said that the husband was the god and source of everything in the life of a Brahmin woman and that, if he were to die, his wife would not marry again, wear colourful clothes or a red 'tika', a mark on the forehead that represents 'good luck'. The husband sang: "I'm dying. How can I have the heart to leave you? I hope you can still wear colourful sari and a tika every day after my death."

In the rural kitchen, I shed tears for the deep love of this Nepalese husband. He was like my own husband, always encouraging me before I went on a long journey. He sent me off at the airport and told me: "Take care."

I would save every penny on my journey while he repeatedly told me by email not to worry about money and he would top up my bank account. Couples who have loved each other for a long time don't need to speak sugared words but instead talk about the most important issues in life. I thought sympathy, kindness, true love and fair treatment are important to all people, irrespective of faith or social strata.

I hope that, when I next travel to the Himalayas, I will arrive with my feet on a lotus, love a soul-stirring love like ordinary Nepalese men and women, and return enlightened by Bodhi and spiritual purity.

DAY TWO

GOD IS THE LIGHTHOUSE IN THE ECLIPSE

THE NEXT MORNING MY LEGS AND FEET, which are accustomed to a sedentary urban lifestyle, began to get swollen, painful and out of control. Kangaroo was puzzled why a fragile person like me was so crazy about trekking.

Actually, this is a question that all trekkers must answer: why do we trek? Why do we put ourselves through this? Why do we do practise asceticism like the Buddha?

When you unfold a map, you see grey shadows representing mountains, blue lines for rivers, green patches for plains, thin twigs for forests, patches of small dots for deserts, black dots for cities and fine grains for villages, as if the whole world is nothing but a palm-sized piece of paper.

Many people are bored with their lives, encircled in a dot or a small patch, breathing in polluted air, drinking recycled water, suffering from headaches, struggling for survival, busying themselves with their houses, cars, jobs, money and children, repeating their routines, day after day. However, when you step on a mountain path, ford a river, cross a valley, pass through a forest, climb a mountain, stay in a village or rest in a log cabin, you'll find that the sounds of the wind, rain, thunder and birds and your groans, breaths and whispers are closely linked with your life and throb with your pulse.

The rivers, mountains, forests and valleys are no longer insignificant signs on a map. They are quiet, silent and soundless; they are splendid, wonderful and amazing; the villages, cattle, sheep, paddy fields, porters and girls are no longer pale, fragile and sorrowful. Instead, they are vivid, lively, fragrant and gorgeous.

Each living creature has its own mission. We should experience the integration of our body and soul in nature and let our souls link freely with the only divinity of the cosmos.

Sometimes, a trek can activate spiritual resuscitation. It requires only a pair of walking shoes, a backpack and a sleeping bag. It empowers us with the land and makes us inseparable from it. We feel that we've never lived such a real life before.

Sense of happiness in trekking

Kangaroo told me that we would climb over the high mountains in Ulleri and walk eighteen kilometres to the village of Ghorepani, towering into the clouds.

Setting out from Tikhedhunga, we nervously crossed a narrow

suspension bridge over the Bhurungdi Khola at an altitude of 1,520 metres. We climbed about 3,300 exhausting stone steps and took a short rest in a large village called Ulleri, home to a number of Marga people.

Whenever I became exhausted, I would distract myself by giving a funny name to each tour group I encountered. That day I renamed our Kangaroo Group as Pink Group since I was wearing a pink straw hat, pink T-shirt and Factor 50 sun cream. Then we met a young man from Hong Kong and a cool, long-haired Nepalese guide. I generously called them the Lady Hunter Group.

Along the way, they stared amorously at the female trekkers they met and referred to them as old or young, ugly or beautiful. We met a great variety of trekkers, a loose, harmonious group of strange, impulsive people of different ages, professions and complexions, speaking different languages yet experiencing the same weather, discomfort, hardships, mood and scenery on our journey to Poon Hill. The charming scenes and the hilarious flirtations made the mountain path soft and agreeable to the feet.

On the way, I learned new Nepali words from Kangaroo, such as *kiete* (girl), *kita* (boy), *dualya* (wife), *dullya* (husband), *didi* (sister), *bhai* (brother), *kam* (dew), *path* (leaf), *nilo* (blue), *chorote* (smoke from chimney), *aggo* (firewood), *banda* (cabbage), *kacharo* (cucumber) and *allu* (potato). They were all lovely details in the daily life of each trekker.

Kangaroo proved himself to be an experienced guide, always encouraging me to walk more. I kept on asking: "How long left?" He told me that we would arrive in Banthanti in half an hour or reach the 2,460-metre-high Nangathanti Village in an hour. But in reality it would take us two or three hours.

'*Thanti*' means 'rest house' in Nepali, the place where animals and plants live and multiply. In the forest, the old oak trees were astonishingly beautiful. The bodhi trees growing from the crevices in rocks intertwined, their brown branches extending in all directions and their golden leaves reaching for the sky. All these magical things reminded me of scenes from *The Lord of the Rings*.

In the afternoon, in Nangathanti, we met an old couple from Colorado. They had been climbing bravely with the support of trekking poles. Our team was always at the rear. Noticing a stream clear enough to see our reflections in it, I renamed our party the Submarine Group.

It is a human instinct to get close to mountains and rivers. The ancient Chinese advocated 'reading thousands of books and travelling thousands of miles' and that 'wise men love travelling in mountains and moral men prefer travelling on water'. I longed to be a submarine lurking in the blue water and forgetting any thoughts of returning home.

The American couple would stop every few minutes for their son and their Nepalese daughter-in-law. But I didn't see either of these younger people throughout the afternoon. Most of the time, the couple turned back and walked downhill to wait for the children. Kangaroo provided them with moral support, saying that they were young grown-ups and would surely catch up soon. The old couple finally broke down in tears.

Their son had married the Nepalese girl the year before. They invited the girl's entire family to travel to the west coast of the United States. This time they had made a special trip to Poon Hill to see the sunrise in the company of their son and daughter-in-law. But the girl who was born in a mountainous area in Nepal was not helping them at all and instead constantly asked them to buy new walking shoes and outdoor jackets. In defiance, she stayed in the tea house and refused to walk any more, and their son left his old parents to stay with his inconsiderate wife.

The old couple sighed: "We've taken good care of our son since he was a little boy, but he no longer cares for us." Kangaroo unloaded our backpack and turned round to find the young couple.

A person's life can be like climbing a mountain. In childhood, our parents support us to overcome difficulties and reach the next peak. But can we accompany our parents when they get old and need our support to help them complete their journey?

The mountains are silent and the sense of happiness from trekking and the pleasure of life have nothing to do with material goods. Any happiness derived from material goods is ephemeral. Only peace of mind, good nature, generosity and harmony between two lovers can lead to spiritual and mental wellbeing. We hope to pass through the polar regions and traverse mountains in the hope that each step of our life will be wonderful, meaningful and affectionate.

Night sky in indulgence

At 6pm, we arrived at the campsite in Ghorepani having climbed more than three thousand stone steps to get there. It was the ultimate test for my poor knees. It was also the day I covered the most ground. Fortunately, my trekking poles helped bear some of the strain.

Ghorepani appeared to be a small, prosperous village where people from all walks of life congregated and internet cafes, tea houses, lodges, tents, packhorses and horse manure could all be found. I washed the dirty clothes I had been sweating in over the previous two days, but as I hung them up to dry, the clothes rack at the Snowland Hotel collapsed and fell onto my sore right foot.

I cried out and scolded the lodge keeper and Kangaroo who were playing pool, slammed the door with my injured foot and stormed out of the hotel in search of a restaurant. I didn't know why I had lost my temper, but I had calmed down by the time I warmed myself by a fire in the kitchen of Dhaulagiri Lodge.

I put it down to ignorance and the arrogant, wilful personality of an urban woman. In addition, my extreme physical fatigue made me mentally ill-equipped to cope with the tough environment. I wasn't strong or generous enough to face unexpected accidents and hardships. I had become a selfish, city 'animal' that indulged in creature comforts and had lost the ability to survive in the natural environment of human beings. When I turned round and looked out of the window reflected by the snow mountain and saw the figure of Kangaroo emerging into the cold night, I burst into tears.

Kangaroo said that he had been searching for me in the log cabins: "I'm your guide. How could I allow my client to get lost? I will always follow you."

Our friendship developed over the long journey. Many trekkers treat their guides or porters as servants or as laden donkeys, without any respect or care. I felt ashamed that I, too, had inadvertently become arrogant and imperious.

Dhaulagiri Lodge was set up by a Tibetan couple in 1995. Their five children were busy in the kitchen helping them cut up vegetables and cook. One of them, a nineteen-year-old girl, was the liveliest. She served the tables and added firewood while dancing and singing folk songs like an innocent, beautiful nightingale or perhaps like a Franz Schubert serenade. I referred to their kitchen as the Dancing Kitchen. I decided to pull up my sleeves and cook a dish of fried chicken with green pepper for Kangaroo.

Seeing me busy cooking, everyone burst out laughing. I realised that trekking could really make one acquire a new identity.

That night, Kangaroo and I returned to the 2,870-metre-high Snowland Hotel. There was no hot water or indoor bathroom. A cold wind blew through our fingers and hair. But when I pulled back the curtains, I saw the starry night, and the profiles and shadows of mountains, woods and villages. It was not a Chinese wash painting with subtle shades of colours but more like Vincent van Gogh's violent *Starry Night*. The giant, swirling nebula was like a dragon flying across the night sky, a mass of exaggerated starlight, and the incredible, divine bright orange moon of a lunar eclipse seemed to echo the words of the romantic French writer Victor Hugo: "God is the beacon of the lunar eclipse."

God says there should be light, and so there is light. But each planet is a single entity, just like human beings in this world. So the stars can sparkle, face each other from afar, light up each other's soul, show the colours of their life with a smile, love and watch over each other, seek light and warmth but they cannot meet each other. When two drifting planets collide, I firmly believe they must do it out of a crazy, destructive love.

It had been years since I had seen such resplendent starlight. Bright blue and yellow, large and small, the stars and planets rotated and burst forth in the universe. Where else but the Himalayas could one see the night sky emit such divine rays of light?

The mountains were in an uproar, the moon and the nebula were rotating, and it seemed as if I could reach out of the window and catch a handful of stars. I longed to fall sound asleep like a fish, a bird or the drunken Chinese poet Li Bai in the embrace of stars.

DAY THREE

BIDDING FAREWELL MEANS ETERNITY

I WOKE UP EACH MORNING to the music of Xu Wei. The rock star's ethereal, lofty melody, 'My heart once drifted in the wind and flowed freely in my dream', always lifted my mood and stirred my body from the perfect lotus position.

His hoarse, low but warm voice moved me for no apparent reason. Throughout his career, he has always sung about 'flying', 'travelling', 'freedom' and 'happiness'. From a rebellious rock'n'roll youth, to a gloomy young prodigal, an innocent, humane singer and a warm, self-enlightened poet, he became calmer, kinder and warmer over the years. But his soft, free heart always soared in the flickering starlight. Whenever I heard his songs, tears would flow down my cheeks and I would yearn to travel to a sunny place.

Xu Wei's songs are in tune with the mental state of trekkers. Carrying a backpack and walking alongside rivers, mountains, lakes, forests, valleys, paddy fields and villages to the snow mountains, your mind is at its most free, most naked and most powerful state. It is a thorough physical test in terms of stamina, endurance, perseverance and emotions. When you embrace nature intimately and directly, you can enrich your mind at the rhythm of nature and let your soul in its entirety be soaked in the blue sky and white clouds.

Kiss of Poon Hill

Ghorepani is one of the finest sights in the Himalayas. '*Ghore*' means 'horse' in Nepali and '*pani*' refers to 'water'. For centuries, Ghorepani has been a courier station in Annapurna Peaks, where travelling merchants, packhorses and porters pass through. Trekkers seek out Ghorepani to see the sunrise at Poon Hill. Kangaroo knocked on my door to wake me up at 4.30am when the dawn was still hidden in the starlit night.

We reached the peak after walking on the steep, winding path for more than an hour. It was almost completely dark, with only weak starlight around. Groups of trekkers were gathered to see the sunrise, looking like devout pilgrims on their way to Mecca.

The peak of Poon Hill at an altitude of 3,193 metres offers a commanding view of the sunrise in this region of eight Himalayan peaks, two of which are above 8,000 metres. From west to east, they are in sequence Mount

Dhaulagiri (8,167 metres), Tukuche (6,920 metres), Mount Nilgiri (6,940 metres), Annapurna South (7,219 metres), Annapurna I (8,091 metres), Hiunchuli Peak (6,441 metres), Glacier Dome (7,193 metres) and Fish Tail Mountain (6,997 metres). Sunrise cannot be seen on overcast or foggy mornings; only the fortunate can appreciate such a soul-stirring moment.

Pilgrims and trekkers visit Poon Hill numerous times in the hope of finding a clear sky. All those watching the sunrise face the same direction, like the images of the Buddha.

Pilgrims and trekkers gather at Poon Hill in the hope of watching the sun rise

When the first glow lit up Fish Tail at 6.10am, some started praying, mumbling to themselves and gabbling on and on; some lovers from distant countries stood in the golden grass, tearfully hugged each other and kissed. How many times in life can one have a commanding view of eight world-class snow mountains covered in brilliant light!

The sky looked like a glorious temple of God, the mountains appeared to be wearing noble, rosemary lotus crowns, the blue, rolling mountain ranges wore colourful garlands, the leaves were dyed crimson, golden, cerise and purple-bronze, and the meadows, flowers, rocks and human bodies glittered like pearl earrings. It was like seeing the world of Monet's *Impression, Sunrise*.

Kangaroo suggested to me: "Pearl, you're a writer. You should give a warm, touching name to each of the eight mountains rather than refer to them according to their shape or height." He didn't know that everyone had an indescribably beautiful image of the Goddess of Snow in their mind and that we would all remember the majestic scenery for the rest of our lives.

Being called 'Mummy'

Leaving Poon Hill, the peak of pilgrimage, we walked downhill for the rest of the day. With Chitre standing at 2,420 metres, Phalate 2,390 metres, Shikha 1,980 metres, Ghara 1,780 metres and Tatopani Village 1,190 metres, the journey covered a distance of up to twenty kilometres and a fall in altitude of nearly two thousand metres.

In the forests and valleys at different altitudes, eight types of azalea flourished. Various kinds of cold-resistant and drought-resistant azalea grow on the hillsides, forest edges, precipices and alpine meadows at high altitudes of the Himalayas in Nepal, Bhutan, Sikkim, Burma and north India. The azalea, like Xi Shi (one of the renowned four beauties in ancient China), is the most beautiful of all flowers. With red, purple, white, pink and blue varieties, the Chinese affectionately refer to it as the 'Indian azalea' while the Nepalese call it the 'sympetalous flower' because its five soft petals are fused with the stem.

The people of Yunnan Province, China, like to cook the petals of the great white rhododendron and the common rhododendron with pigs' feet. It is said to make women beautiful and helps to soothe the nerves, harmonise the blood and remove freckles. The Nepalese believe that women who like sympetalous flowers are mostly sincere and Cupid comes when azaleas bloom all over the mountains.

When Kangaroo picked a pink sympetalous flower and inserted it in my hat, I immediately forgot the ache in my legs, and my body was filled with endless power and love. I began to learn to cherish and care about others. I asked Kangaroo to put down his small bag dangling in front of him and carried it on my back instead so that he would have a better view when walking downhill. When I walked downhill with two small bags on my back, other porters I met on the way laughed because I looked like a mummy kangaroo.

. . .

Covered with sweat, we finally crossed the dark green Ghar Khola which, like a maiden, was passionately embraced by the black Kali Gandaki Khola in Tatopani. I once dreamed of taking a hot spring bath in Tatopani after finishing trekking on the mountain paths. Tatopani, a village built along the river, means 'hot water' and 'hot spring' in Nepali. But when we arrived there in the evening, there was no room in any of the lodges. I didn't know whether it was because I looked like an indigenous Nepalese woman due to my olivaceous skin after three days of exposure to the blazing sun or because I carried two bags on my back like a porter, but a sun-tanned girl gave me the only vacant room in the Himalayan Hotel. It was actually just a storage room in the corridor, without a window and containing only two beds.

"Is there a bathroom or hot water in the hotel?" I asked.

"No."

"A toilet?"

"No."

Kangaroo and I burst into laughter.

The Eagles wrote a classic song called *Hotel California*, which describes a musician driving on a dark desert highway, with the cool wind in his hair and the warm smell of colitas rising up through the air. He finally saw a shimmering light. His head grew heavy and he had to stop for the night. A girl standing in the doorway greeted him and he thought it could be heaven or perhaps hell. Then the girl lit a candle to show him the way. He heard voices in the corridor and he thought he heard them say: "Welcome to Hotel California."

I thought myself less fortunate than the character in the song because the girl lighting the candle seemed to lead me to a hell I'd never encountered before. Kangaroo joked: "This is a 'five-star hotel' for us porters. She mistook me as a guide and you a female porter."

Some trekking companies offer the services of women porters to female clients. I didn't care a scrap if I had been mistaken for a porter. I put aside the bags and ran to the balcony outside the hotel to take photos of the sunset at Mount Dhaulagiri.

While squatting on the ground and watching the golden rays of light sink slowly over the ice-cold snow mountaintop, I heard a crisp voice: "Mummy, coffee's ready." It was a little boy, only nine years old. At first I thought he was the son of the boss. But when I saw him serving tea, cleaning tables and washing dishes with an apron around his waist, I realised that he was a servant hired by the hotel. Kangaroo told me that one in four Nepalese workers were children who had left their parents in the mountains and lived in hotels, tea houses or restaurants to alleviate the family burden.

I didn't know who the little boy was and continued to take photos. Then he gently pulled my sleeve and repeated: "Mummy, coffee is cold."

My face blushed because I had never given birth and no one had ever called me 'mummy', especially in front of my handsome guide and so many trekkers taking photos. I left with him in embarrassment.

The boss's little daughter had just begun learning Indian dances, and she was practising in the dining hall. Then the little boy excitedly ran to my dining table and said: "Mummy, go dancing." I didn't know why he kept on calling me 'mummy'. Maybe because I looked like his mother, I wore long *kurtas* favoured by Nepalese women or perhaps he simply missed his mummy. But by then, I had become accustomed to it, and a stream of maternal love swept over me.

I treated every child to a drink after I had been called 'Mummy'

The coffee revived me. Putting away my luggage, I went to find a hot spring. The ideal hot spring I had been longing for was actually a large pool of hot natural water surging constantly from the Kali Gandaki Khola. Trekkers, porters and local children all played in the river. The water was warm and comfortable, in which my aching joints and muscles could relax. It was understandable why the hotels were all packed. It seemed that trekkers regarded Tatopani as a place to relax after days of hard walking.

There was a tap outside the pool for people to wash their clothes and hair. I wore my bikini, half kneeling on the ground, and used shampoo to wash my body and hair. Everyone looked at each other as if we had returned to the era of the Garden of Eden, when Adam and Eve covered up their embarrassment with fig leaves. The inverted image of the snowy Himalayas was a picture of perfection and serenity. I could not help plunging down to the warm depths.

The green water was velvet smooth and wonderfully buoyant. Eyes closed, I floated on my back and all the negative oxygen ions in the limpid water made me slightly numb.

I then heard a terrified shout: "Mummy!" Turning around, I saw a boy's head bob up and down in the water. Instinctively I paddled over to him but I made slow progress. Exhausted, I made my way to the little boy, pulled him to the bank and patted his back.

Since the river was holy, many locals did not swim in it out of respect, while others couldn't swim at all. So they were shocked to see a near-drowning boy and did not know what to do.

It was fortunate that I was able to hear the panic in his voice at that crucial moment. I never wanted to have my own child because I suffer from hypotension and often feel dizzy and faint, and my roving lifestyle made me reject the idea. Even so, after that experience in Nepal, I would never again feel it odd for a child to call me 'Mummy' like that.

Hair in flames

Returning to our 'five-star hotel', we could not help laughing. Without hot water, electricity, a window or toilet, I said in the new Nepali I'd just learned that Tatopani should be renamed Tisupani, meaning 'land of cold water and grimness'.

Meat is usually unavailable in mountain lodges, and only eggs, tomatoes, potatoes, rice and Nepalese lentil soup are served. Hindus do not eat beef and Muslims do not eat pork. But we had lost too much energy and, as a Christian, I could do nothing but shout that I wanted to eat chicken.

Bear Grylls is well known for his inventive recipes in *Remote Survival*, a documentary broadcast on the National Geographic channel. His ingredients for survival recipes include raw snake eggs, ants and raw fish. Some dishes were so disgusting that even he found them difficult to swallow: fresh killer scorpions, mussels and maggot soup, frog legs and snails, whip scorpions and Saharan goat testicles. Dessert is an assortment of special 'cheese' dishes: weevil larva and mucus mixed with honey.

Copying Bear's pet phrases, I said to Kangaroo: "Look, there's a creature. We can catch it from behind and eat it after cutting its head and tail. It will taste better if it is grilled. The delicious chicken will be crisp." The programme showing brave Bear swallowing anything and everything is popular around the world and up to two billion people have shared his passion for the wild.

"Just a minute," Kangaroo responded, as he turned around and headed for the village to find a chicken.

The mountainous regions of Nepal suffer frequent power shortages and they often strike in the log cabins in the evening. As I rummaged to find a candle in my pack and lowered my head to light it, my long hair hanging down loosely in front of me caught light. Seized with terror, I flapped with my hands. The fire spread onto my robe and the right side of my hair was scorched.

This time, I kept calm and did not howl or make too much noise. When Kangaroo returned to my room and smelt the burning, he grabbed me, looking more terrified than me. He then got a small bowl of vegetable oil from the hotel owner and rubbed the burned hair with his hands.

The hotel owner asked me: "Didn't you see the notice on the wall: 'No candles in the room'?"

Once, a trekker left his room with a candle burning. In the wind, the candle was blown down and the whole building caught fire. The villagers spent an entire night putting out the fire. But taking sympathy for my plight, the hotel owner said he would waive the cost of the room that night.

We can never predict what might happen during a trek. A detailed plan for the outdoor life sometimes goes awry. Occasionally, getting lost or making mistakes can result in a struggle for survival, or cause my beautiful hair to go up in smoke. Even experienced trekkers can drown or get lost, slip or lose their sense of direction. But as long as we keep calm, the most difficult predicament can be solved.

There is a popular phrase in Western countries: 'Every cloud has a silver lining.' There is a similar Chinese saying: 'Just as the weary traveller despairs of finding a road, a village appears and the shade of willows and riotous flowers beckon.' A trek is a journey brimming with life and death, imagination, disaster, wonder, fun and craziness. Sometimes, you accidentally encounter a stranger or become detached from a companion. But as long as you are flexible, you can experience a life of extraordinary significance and incredible beauty.

DAY FOUR

A BROKEN JAR CAN ALSO REFLECT LIGHT

Can you picture the look of a boy when you part from him?

As we carried our backpacks, bathed in the light of the rising sun at Mount Dhaulagiri, and walked on the stone path in Tatopani, the little boy of the Himalayan Hotel was leaning against the door frame with his body half hidden in the shadows, watching us with his gloomy eyes. He was not the little boy I saved when I was swimming the day before, but the one who called me 'Mummy' for the first time in my life and filled my blood with warm, maternal love.

I didn't know he would be standing there so early in the day.

Numerous trekkers and travellers walk on this path where packhorses have passed for a thousand years. He cast his transparent, amber eyes on me, just like the black light at the bottom of a well holding sweet water. As my tears welled up, Kangaroo said: "Pearl, he's saying goodbye to you."

After climbing the mountains, some mountaineering groups discard their belongings and guard dogs at the campsite, some trekkers abandon a guiding dog or sick porter halfway and some guides might have affairs with lodge landladies and abandon them when they find they are pregnant. At that time, I thought of myself as a brutally mean mother about to abandon her child. I wanted to fly to him and give him a big hug. I didn't want him to continue working in the lodge; he should join me on my travels. But my feet were firmly attached to the stone path, and I could not move a step. I didn't even dare hug him goodbye for fear that I should do something silly!

Kangaroo went forward, patted him on his shoulder and tenderly put a small coil of rupees in his palm. But he reacted like a child pricked by a rose during play and instinctively took back the hand waving goodbye.

I knew that I wouldn't return there in future, step into the same stream or meet again, just like the lyrics of *Hotel California*: "I had to find the passage to the place I was before... You can check out anytime you like / but you can never leave." I only hoped that he would become a trekking guide when he grew up and would soar forever above high mountains and in the blue sky like an eagle.

It's difficult to estimate the number of high mountains and the time it will take to complete a journey and the number of strangers encountered on the way. But I'll always remember the banana trees on the slope and the innocent face of the little boy in the shadows of the dense lemon leaves.

The deepest valley in the world

Some scenery can be experienced only by walking, and some sentiments are generated only on the journey.

Being in my company for three days, Kangaroo found that I was accident prone, ill equipped for outdoor survival and likely to fall into baffling, unexpected troubles every day. So he watched my actions on the mountain road carefully.

At a launch event for a new travel book, readers often ask me: "Is it safe for a woman to travel alone in a foreign country?"

Since childhood, we've lived in an environment equipped with burglar alarms and security doors, but our levels of fear still increase. Several indoorsy girls ask me: "Aren't you afraid of being robbed or raped when you trek alone?"

Each time, I would reply: "As long as you cherish love and understanding, and have a smile on your face, you'll find the world is much more beautiful than your imagination."

I have met all sorts of trekkers on my travels. Mostly, they are in groups of three or four and hire two porters. A trekking group of four South Korean girls once exclaimed: "How come your guide is so handsome and patient with you?"

Usually, porters do not accompany their clients but only carry the luggage and walk separately; but the guides will follow their clients, help them with their basic needs, provide them with information and ensure their safety. However, they will not carry any bags for them. From my very first step on the mountain road on that first day of trekking, I knew how lucky I was. Kangaroo not only carried my backpack, but he also waited for me no matter how slowly I walked.

I asked him whether he was aware that many female trekkers fall in love with their guide in Nepal. He nodded, but then added: "They should like each other. We have our own constraints."

Your guide is your eyes, your hands and feet, your security and safety in a dense forest. They are usually well built, have a good complexion, a robust smile and bright disposition. All these things make them different from most urban men. They are like raw jade, an untamed beast, a refreshing spring or a strong breeze. It is difficult not to be touched.

But there is big difference between love, friendship and appreciation. Love can span differences in culture, race, age and social status. For thousands of years, love has existed at different levels and in different realms: universal love, maternal love, sex, kindheartedness, friendship and tender affection... As a reporter, I once interviewed a victim of a rape in a mountain area. After trekking from Poon Hill and returning to Pokhara, a Japanese woman reported to the police that her guide raped her on the way. The guide was imprisoned for a month and his guide licence was revoked. He was set free after paying bail, but no one would hire him afterwards.

Did any lodges report theft? Was any trekker robbed? Any murders reported in the press? Almost none! So far, I've not heard any stories of trekkers' money or possessions being stolen. Generosity, patience, kindness and tenderness are some of the best attributes among devout Buddhists. Their belief is the reason why they have planted two important seeds: the first is for kindness and love and the other is for reverence. In the Himalayas, moral and religious forces are much stronger and more effective than any legislative constraints or sanctions.

I set out intending to treat my guide as a brother and everyone I met on the way as equals. So I travelled with a magnanimous mind, enjoyed good luck and made many friends.

Tatopani is near the floor of the Kali Gandaki Valley. Trekking more than a hundred kilometres along the valley with the altitude rising about 1,570 metres, you come to Jomsom, the largest courier station in the northern wilderness. Kali Gandaki Khola is famed as a 'black river'. I have never seen a river given to such capricious moods. Like a black goddess, it roared down from the snowy Mount Dhaulagiri in the north. The river channel weaved and leaped at the bottom of the valley, flowed through different terrains and changed direction. The black water had carved out a deep ravine between Annapurna I and Mount Dhaulagiri. It was the Kali Gandaki Valley, known as 'the deepest valley in the world'. Until you walk on the mountain path above the valley, you cannot imagine that the two giant mountains both at an altitude of more than 8,000 metres are only twenty kilometres from each other and the altitude of the Kali Gandaki in between is no more than 2,200 metres.

We walked on the mountain path lined with lemon trees, orange trees and grapefruit trees, each giving off a subtle, refreshing scent. We saw many packhorses carrying heavy loads. When the tinkle of bells came from the dense forest, packhorses would soon emerge, panting heavily under their loads of gas tanks, salt, tea leaves, potatoes, apples and grain.

Porters moving slowly across the Kali Gandaki Valley

There were no highways or modern vehicles in Poon Hill, and the locals made a living doing what they have done for centuries, delivering goods as porters or with donkeys. The donkey drivers would follow their animals closely behind while blowing the Nepalese flute. The more callous owners would often whip their donkeys, throw stones at them or shout at them. Some donkeys' skins were blood-stained due to the heaviness of the loads they were carrying. But carrying loads is their destiny until the day they drop dead on the mountain path. Many porters face the same fate. Some carry a large metal frame containing chicks bought from Pokhara a hundred kilometres away, and the entire contraption could weigh as much as fifty kilograms. They make an arduous journey to sell them in lodges on the mountain top so that hungry trekkers can have meat to replenish their lost energy.

The menus on offer on the route to Jomsom are Westernised. Delicious local apples are made into all sorts of pies and you can even enjoy a cold beer. So if you are minded to complain about the high price, spare a thought for the porters who carry the food to the high mountains and who then take back the empty bottles and cans. When I saw the porters plod by me endlessly, I felt sorry for them. We are all human beings, but they live the miserable life of a working animal.

Kagbeni, one of the most popular Nepalese films, tells the story of two young porters who betray each other and then take out revenge in order to win the love of a girl. Usually, a trekker will provide financial support for up to seven Nepalese. Porters are the pillars of the country's trekking industry, but they are often put into a vulnerable position. Some trekking groups operate on a tight budget and only care about their own personal comfort and enjoyment, ignoring the interests of the porters who help them. In the high-altitude areas leading to the base camps of Mount Everest and Annapurna, some porters do not have thermal gear and wear only thin cotton-padded clothes and sandals.

Each spring, the bodies of some porters are discovered as the snow melts and the flowers come into bloom. They might die of overwork, disease, acute mountain sickness or exposure to the cold. So when your porter gets ill, please don't feel it is enough to pay him for his services and then leave him alone. Porters are also human beings. We should love them dearly in the way we love the flowers, trees and birds during our trekking.

Road revolution

Each time we encountered packhorses or donkeys, Kangaroo would direct me to the inside part of the mountain path which was comparatively higher or ask me to stop to let them pass; when the donkeys and buffaloes were going downhill, he would grip my hand for fear that they might knock me off the path 'as narrow as chicken intestines'. We originally planned to start off in Tatopani, cross the world's deepest valley, pass Jomsom and then on to Muktinath, offering a good view of the West Kali Gandaki Valley and the holy temple, visit the traditional villages of the Thakali and Tibetan ethnic groups up to Upper Mustang District and then return to Pokhara to complete the pilgrimage.

But from Tatopani at an altitude of 1,190 metres, the trekking paths and mountain roads for packhorses and packdonkeys that have existed for centuries have been gradually replaced by the now completed Baglung Highway. Humans always favour the easy option. By building roads to enable tourists to reach their destination quicker, they have destroyed forests, mountains and rivers. After the Qinghai-Tibet Railway opened, many rural paths, lodges, restaurants, animal migration routes and lively bazaars vanished in an instant. The same was true on my walk from Tatopani, along the uneven rural road with dust swirling around.

There were no trees reaching to the sky or quiet mountain paths for trekkers to take shelter from the sun, and there were no blue or pink lodges or tea houses for trekkers to visit. The world-famous trekking route, the mountain path recommended in so many editions of *Lonely Planet*, had changed into a monotonous road devoid of porters and trekkers, to be replaced by small vehicles and motorcycles roaring past.

The decision to build the Baglung Highway was controversial. Trekkers from all over the world voiced their disapproval because it traversed Annapurna and Mount Mahabharat, some of the best and most popular trekking routes in the country. To those wanting to leave behind their urban lives and enjoy Nepal's primitive natural scenery, the sound of car engines was doubtless exceedingly irritating to the ear.

I once summarised my times in Nepal as being the influence of three 'religions': Hinduism, Buddhism and tourism. Tourism is the country's most important source of income and trekking tourism in particular. However, with the highway now open, the number of international travellers visiting Jomsom began to decline. International travellers have switched to other tourist destinations due to the worsening environment and the large number of pilgrims visiting in the summer.

Despite the valid arguments put forward by trekkers about preserving an ancient civilisation, it must be admitted that the highway has opened an area that had been closed for thousands of years, lowered the prices of goods and made it possible for locals to access cheap electric appliances from abroad, along with everyday items such as blankets, thermos flasks and batteries. It has also meant that children could go to school and see the outside world more easily, and for women to sell produce including apples, pomegranates and figs at the roadside.

The highway also made it possible for the remotest villagers to pilgrimage in Muktinath, bathe and wash their sins in the water gushing from the 108 springs located at the foot of the snow mountain and complete their lifelong ambition. Modern roads mean that the residents of Pokhara can now make the pilgrimage in only two days rather than the ten to fifteen days previously.

Hitherto, few were able to make the journey on foot.

A most uncomfortable journey

The Chinese government helped Nepal build the Baglung Highway leading from Pokhara to Jomsom. Due to the annual flooding of the Kali Gandaki Khola in the monsoon season and the extraordinarily precipitous and complicated geological structure in Mount Dhaulagiri, the entire highway is quite different to most other highways. It is actually more like a broken rural road or a farm track. Landslides and falling debris are common in many areas. Road maintenance requires investment in expensive heavy-duty equipment. But the area remains backward and travellers are often required to change buses to get from one part to another, or to walk round sections impassable for vehicles.

With dust covering our faces and in our mouths, we walked about two hours and could not find a lodge to have a rest or a meal. Roaring vehicles carried international travellers past places where previously they might have rested and spent money. So the lodges that formerly had courtyards, flowers and grass disappeared in no time. Kangaroo and I were forced to sit by the road, rummaging in the bag for Oreo biscuits and Dove chocolate. We ended up having a dusty picnic on the grass by the road with three buffaloes for company.

When we came to Dana at an altitude of 1,450 metres, I decided not to go any further. I asked Kangaroo to hitch a lift from a bus. It was difficult to travel on the road from Dana to Maurice Herzog's base camp. In 1950, the mountaineer Herzog led a French team to Annapurna I, the first time that a mountain at an altitude of 8,000 metres had been scaled in human history.

I originally thought that things would improve after catching the bus. But the stone steps rising up the precipitous mountainside were so alarmingly dangerous that I felt dizzy and nervous. The steps were narrow, broken and slippery, sometimes so narrow that they left no possibility for offering a route of retreat. We had to continue in order to catch the next bus.

The bus that we boarded was crowded with pilgrims and other travellers. Porters sat in the aisle piled up with backpacks. Wandering Sadhus wore scarlet headbands, held holy canes stained with 'fresh blood' and crowded in the bus with trekkers. They painted the canes red like the one used by Bodhidharma, which was said to kill monsters and turn calamities into blessings. The problem was that, when the vehicle bounced and bumped, the 'holy' canes would bash into other passengers, leading to raised voices of complaint.

Pilgrims and trekkers getting a ride on the Baglung Highway

At the famous Rupse Chhahara waterfall, a whole mountainside had been washed away by the river. The highway was blocked and had been beyond repair for two years. This meant everyone had to get out of the vehicle and walk. They went over mountains and hills along a deserted trekking path. The porters were clutching large backpacks while the donkeys bore a load twice their own bodyweight. Locals were carrying motorcycles so that they didn't have to walk on the other side of the mountain. By contrast, once I was set on the trekking path again, I started to feel more comfortable, relaxed and safe.

When we trekked to Ghasa, the first village inhabited by the Thakalis, the gradient was too steep for a minibus so we transferred to a Bolero.

Bolero was an orchestral piece composed by the French composer Maurice Ravel. Its romantic, unrestrained rhythm of castanets puts listeners in high spirits and makes them feel relaxed. I wasn't expecting that a Bolero SUV would only depart once twelve passengers were on board. The fare was 400 rupees per person. The SUV was refitted as a van with seats facing each other, like a truck designed to carry pigs. The porters were at the rear of the vehicle while the tall Westerners were forced to tuck their legs under their seats like rabbits. Occasionally, we would bump our heads on the roof; it was not a happy journey.

After a while, some trekkers who couldn't stand it any longer jumped off and decided to walk. The rise in altitude and the swirling dust raised by the jolting vehicle made it difficult to breathe.

At 1.30pm, we arrived in Jomsom at an altitude of 2,760 metres. We hastily ate tea-flavoured eggs and Tibetan-style bread in a tea house, transferred to another SUV and headed for Muktinath.

The Dasain Festival

Jomsom is the last Thakali village and the administrative centre of Mustang District. Here, trekkers have their licences checked before they can enter the mountains. There were many lodges, hotels, shops, hospitals, a garrison, an eco-museum and a small airport. The airport is one of the most dangerous in the world. An aircraft carrying Indian pilgrims crashed there in May 2012. Fifteen people on the plane died while six somehow managed to survive. The airport runway is only 600 metres long and twenty metres wide, which poses a severe test of the aviator's skills.

Two races in Nepal are especially impressive. One is the indigenous Tibetan Sherpas who are particularly skilled in mountaineering and the other is the Thakali people, with Mongolian features and an aptitude for doing business. The Thakali live in the Thak Khola Valley floor between Annapurna and Mount Dhaulagiri. It is both the logical route for Nepal-Tibet trade and the dividing line between Hindu culture in the mountains in central Nepal and Buddhist culture in the northern border region. South of Jomsom is an expanse of dark and luxuriantly green subtropical forest; north, there is a harsh, arid plateau. Because the area is a melting pot of different religions, the Thakali believe in Buddhism, Shamanism or Hinduism. Young women are still trafficked as brides. Standing at the crossroads of different customs and territories, the people of Jomsom are quick-witted.

The Thakali build their houses of stone and set up many roadside lodges on all the major roads. The roof terraces on the lodges are used to dry grain and store goods. Many passersby take advantage of these lodges to stay the night or to have tea or meals.

When the rainy season arrives in summer and autumn, floods block traffic routes in the south. But at that time, the melting ice and snow in the cold highlands in the north makes the roads there passable. The Thakali take this opportunity to buy Tibetan-made lake salt, square brick tea, butter, goats, yaks, wool, blankets, turquoise and musk transported across the Sino-Nepal border. The items are stored and then sold in India after the rainy season; similarly, southern merchants will take their cereals, sugar, kerosene, spice, cigarettes, paper, cotton and cloth there after the autumn harvest. However, the roads in the north are sealed by ice and snow at this time of year, and merchants have to sell the goods to the Thakali or barter salt, butter and wool with them. The intelligent and capable Thakali make use of their special location and climatic conditions to monopolise trade in the whole valley region.

Most of the hotels, restaurants and tea houses are run by affluent Thakali in Pokhara Municipality. They also lend money and organise shipments by packhorses. The villagers around have been gradually reduced to the role of contracted workers, grooms or household servants. Porters, domestic animals and packhorses still bustle along Jomsom's narrow passages, as they have for centuries. The Ancient Tea Horse Road and the Grain and Salt Road present a scene of melodious hoof beats and jingling bells.

The most important national festival in Nepal is the Dashain Festival. It is similar to Christmas in the West and China's Spring Festival. With the advent of the pleasant post-monsoon season, the sky is clear, the air is fresh, the rice has ripened, the flocks and herds are fat and strong, and the people far away from their home town hurry back to get together with their families. The Dashain Festival lasts ten days and begins on the night of the full moon in late September or early October. To celebrate it, people should prepare for the Durga Puja prayer ritual, night bathe in the Sacred River or the river nearby, and water barley seeds with sacred water. The elderly will make an auspicious red tika mark on the foreheads of children to celebrate the goddess Durga on a lion conquering the ox-headed King Mahishasura.

Many animals are sacrificed during the Dashain Festival

Durga is worshiped by most Nepalis. Her shrine can be seen on mountaintops, in fortresses and in palatial buildings. Since Durga is a bloodthirsty character, a large-scale bloodletting ceremony is held during this festival. Affluent households kill buffaloes or sheep as sacrificial offerings to the deities while the poor might kill a chicken or a duck. I asked Bishnu, a Hindu, why five kinds of animal should be killed for the Dashain Festival. He told me that Hindus regard the killing of these animals as symbolic: the buffalo, goat, sheep, chicken and duck represent anger, greed, stupidity, cowardice and indifference, respectively. Sacrifice shows that people should overcome these human weaknesses and defects, and elevate their spiritual purity.

More than two thousand birds and cattle are killed in the imperial palace during the Dashain Festival. The extravasated blood on the floor can be several inches thick; the royal army of Nepal will brandish swords to military music and hold a sacrificial ceremony in the Cortes Courtyard on Kathmandu Durbar Square. Foreign visitors should arrive early to secure a position to see the bloody sacrificial scene. Fresh blood is sometimes sprayed on the wheels of cars or other motor vehicles. All sorts of offerings are placed in front of cars to ensure safe driving and prevent accidents in the following year. Each aircraft belonging to Nepal Airlines will have a goat as an offering. Ordinary Nepalese do not eat too much mutton at ordinary times but plenty is cooked during that festival.

Each year Tibetan herdsmen in China send large numbers of domestic animals across the border to 'support' the Nepalese in celebrating the festival. Flocks of sheep and goats are dyed in different colours so that they don't get mixed up. The shepherds carry solid food, blow loud whistles and walk from the land of snow and wilderness in Upper Mustang at the Sino-Nepal border, in the direction in which the Kali Gandaki Khola flows and then south to Pokhara and Kathmandu. The migration often lasts more than a month.

A sheep weighing about twenty kilograms can be sold for more than ten thousand rupees. We frequently gave way to the sweeping flocks and waited for the dust to settle. Looking at the sheep and goats with hoofs broken through walking and like prisoners in exile, I felt my heart filled with wordless sympathy and compassion. They had no other choice but to make this final journey of more than a thousand kilometres. Enjoying their last days in the sun, their fatigued bodies gave off a mysterious and tragic appearance.

The French film director Jacques Perrin once made a trilogy of 'heaven, Earth and man' films: *Travelling Birds*, a documentary about a bird's dream of flying, *Microcosmos*, a film showing the happy life of worms and *Himalaya*, a feature film exploring the close relations that exist between human beings, animals and nature. As we approached Muktinath, the destination of pilgrimage, I thought that the Himalayas known as the 'roof of the world', in addition to the abundant religions and amazing sights, was also a land of mystery and profundity. The story of *Himalaya* takes place in a village called Dolpo in northwest Nepal. The most important event in the calendar for the people in this isolated mountain village is when the tribal chief leads the driving of flocks and herds carrying lake salt produced in their village over the mountains and to exchange for cereals traded by another tribe.

The Himalayas does not only include the story of a tribal chief in childhood, the soul-stirring legend of the tribal people, alienation in foreign lands and the remote, mysterious sounds of heaven but also the amazing endurance, courage, obstinacy and resolve of the people as well as numerous sad, beautiful and pathetic lives.

Moved to enlightenment

At sunset, the Bolero sped onto the dry, desolate highlands and reached Muktinath at an altitude of 3,800 metres.

Jumping out of the SUV, I felt top-heavy and struggled to catch my breath due to the strong wind and biting cold. Muktinath, seated in a corner of the Himalayas and protected from the elements, is a paradise for followers of both Buddhism and Hinduism. Businessmen, ascetic monks and tribal people from Nepal and India can be seen everywhere. Numerous Buddhist and Hindu temples have been erected in a dense wood. One hundred and eight springs gush from ox-head taps in front of the ancient Bishnu Mandir. The same number is also sacred in Tibetan Buddhism: 108 deities in the worlds of the past, present and future can eliminate 108 kinds of worry and tranquillise the body and mind. It was amazing to see a jet of burning blue flame fed by underground natural gas. This was the famed eternal fire of the Holy Land.

It is miraculous that the monasteries and temples of the two major religions in Nepal are united and Hindus worshiping Shiva, the God of Sex, and Buddhists with a pure heart and few desires can walk together under the sun over the Himalayas. Such things are rare in other countries and territories.

You might flush with shame at the sight of the reliefs and scenes of sexual intercourse between male and female deities embracing each other closely on a wooden figure of Yab-Yum (meaning father-mother) carved on the temple pillars. As a matter of fact, both Hinduism and Buddhism were hugely influenced by Esoteric Buddhism (Tantric doctrines) in the Middle Ages. 'Tantrism' is a Sanskrit word referring to the basic warp in spinning. Esoteric Buddhism advocates the philosophy that all things on Earth are intertwined with people's behaviour. Being secretly handed down, it has an air of mystery and was therefore called '*mi jiao*' (meaning 'secret religion') in Chinese.

Esoteric Buddhism holds the view that the human body is the epitome of the universe, universal life is the product of the integration of masculine vitality (symbolised by Shiva) and feminine 'shakti', the sacred integration of male and female deities can create and maintain all things in the universe and therefore sexual intercourse between males and females is a way of cultivating the mind and enables practitioners to realise 'the integration of yin and yang' and 'unity of heaven and man' to obtain liberation and bliss of soul through it. The contribution of Esoteric Buddhism to the growth of Nepalese religions rests in the fact that it blends the characteristics of Hinduism and Buddhism and helps with their integration. The general worship of Śāktaṃ, a sect of Hinduism, brought forth the building of numerous goddesses in the pantheons of Hinduism and Buddhism. For instance, since the Goddess of Snow Mountains Parvati (wife of Shiva) and Goddess of Auspice Lakshmi (wife of Bishnu) sit on the left or on the left leg of their husband, Shaktism is also known as 'the left-hand sect'.

As a consequence, Shiva is able to wield considerable power. He is both a disciplinarian and a symbol of lust. He had sex with Parvati for a hundred years and his seminal fluid poured into the River Ganges. That is why the Ganges comes from heaven; Shiva's smiles are white and the glaciers and snow mountains were accumulated by Shiva's smiles. I'm afraid that Shiva would be little more than a zombie without shakti.

Swayambhunath, where two religions blend, is a collection of shrines and temples located on a hill to the west of Kathmandu, while Muktinath is a highly venerated temple in the Kali Gandaki Valley. I think the combination of earth, water, fire, yin and yang endow them with the most important religious significance. These places are still lively and deeply moving thanks to the constant blessing of the deities, Buddha and Bodhisattva and the worship of millions of pilgrims in an endless stream. We can smell the gracefully burning incense smoke in the burners ignited by Buddhists and see the young monks with innocent faces move up and down in prayer. We can also sit beside a tranquil stream, watch the proceedings of a Hindu cremation ceremony, smell the burned corpses and indulge ourselves in the slow Vedic chants of senior priests...

Muktinath is a venerated temple, sacred to both Hindus and Buddhists

The snow-capped Himalayas penetrate the azure canopy of the heavens. Their unadorned beauty has been a constant for thousands of years. It made me think that Buddha Sakyamuni chose to be born on Earth, the blue planet, among all the planets in the cosmos and in Nepal among more than 200 countries and regions, in the land of the Himalayas. His birth, leaving home, ascetic practice, Nirvana and final enlightenment, like the appalling mutation and continual existence of the universe at the very beginning, informed me of the starting point, the experience and the end of life.

Nepal still keeps its traditional culture and religious tolerance; that is the great virtue of the Nepalese people.

Kangaroo filled his small bottle with pure water from the sacred spring to take home. I saw a few disciples cast coins into the spring water and some Sadhus wash there to purify their bodies and remove their sins. As a Christian, I also plunged my arms into the sacred spring.

What biting, icy water! But at least it was much cleaner than the warm, turbid Ganges. When I wrote *Yoga Code in the Holy Land of India*, I bathed in the Ganges in the city of Varanasi along with tens of thousands of other people, with the river filled with bacteria, saliva and garbage. When that thought sprang into my mind, my dust- and grime-covered body was recharged with extraordinary bravery.

. . .

Muktinath leaned against the towering mountain ridges and it was a grand site from a distance. Thorung La, at an altitude of 5,416 metres, is one of the highest mountain passes in Nepal and one of the greatest strategic passes in the world.

Since the mountain road from Muktinath to Thorung La is steep, the Circuit Trek in Annapurna proceeds anti-clockwise. After arriving in Muktinath, we continued in the opposite direction along the pilgrimage route to Jomsom. Setting out from Besi Sahar at an altitude of 820 metres, we walked along the edge of Annapurna for about ten days to the foot of the 4,420-metre-high Mount Thorung Phedi. Trekkers spend the night in one of two lodges and prepare for a sprint the following day. About 200 trekkers gather there every day during the peak season, so the beds are hard to secure and some trekkers are afflicted with acute mountain sickness.

It took nearly eight hours to climb from the foot of Mount Thorung Phedi to the mountain pass. The mountain road is exceedingly precipitous and the high altitude and heavy snow are additional challenges for trekkers. When the mountain pass is covered in heavy snow, it is almost impossible to find the mountain path to Thorung La. The mountain path from Thorung La down to Muktinath is rugged and involves a fall of up to 1,600 metres, so many trekkers set off as early as 3am from the foot of Thorung La. Due to the cold weather and prolonged exposure to the snow, it is certainly the most challenging section on the Annapurna Circuit. It can only be tackled by tough and experienced trekkers.

But the majestic, imposing primitive scenery of the Himalayas does not disappoint. When you stand on top of the clouds at Thorung La and watch the dancing prayer flags at Muktinath, the golden light on the pinnacle of the temples, and the luxuriantly green white poplars, pine trees, bubbling springs, curling incense smoke, flocks and herds and their faint bell tones, you could be forgiven for believing it to be the legendary Shangri-La, the pure and lonesome land in the west where the soul rises.

This pure land is the most solemn Buddhist place where the sun sets. The purity of Buddha and of Buddhist nature comes from innermost comfort and pleasure, cheerful acceptance, sexual capacity and composure after a myriad of hardships and difficulties. The Himalayan religions may tell you how to act when in great difficulty, and the snow mountains help to endow climbers with endurance and willpower.

Greatness often comes from overcoming challenges, and trekking provides us with the time, space and adversity to really know ourselves.

Having arrived at Muktinath, trekkers stay in the nearby town of Ranipauwa because the temples themselves do not provide accommodation. The word 'Ranipauwa' means 'nest of the queen and the queenlike residence'. There's a checkpoint in this small Tibetan village for the registration of trekkers, most of whom come from the US and Europe, especially Germany and France. I noticed that I was the third Chinese person to arrive there that year. Pride surged within me.

The scenery in Ranipauwa is similar to that in Tibet, Ngari and ancient Zhada seven hundred years ago. Trekkers were lying down on the red-white-black Tibetan roofs, drinking clean and mellow *chhaang*, eating home-made apple pie and basking in the sun. Their bones seemed to be softened by the chants of the mandala having trekked for so many miles. It is said that the most auspicious time to pilgrimage in Muktinath is on the night of the full moon in late August because this is the time of the Yartung Carnival when Tibetans hold horse races, drink wine, sing, fall in love, gamble and dance to their heart's content.

I had been asking myself a question during my time in Nepal: why do people go on a pilgrimage? Why do I drift from place to place, homeless and miserable?

If I hadn't been away on a pilgrimage, I would not have gone on this inner journey or experienced any enlightenment. If I hadn't been travelling, I wouldn't have experienced this sweet and bitter life along the way or found the place where my body and soul belong. In Sanskrit, 'Buddha' means 'enlightenment' and 'realised beings'.

Sometimes, a journey in search of spirituality is long and requires great endurance. A small sign can indicate a great trend and a single water drop can reflect the sun's brilliance. For trekkers, the time for happiness and sorrow in the journey awakens the torrents of soul and belief. The dust, stones and broken cans can reflect the brilliant rays of sunlight. After repeated attempts, we can achieve sexual and spiritual recognition, gratitude and satisfaction.

As long as we have a dream and a firm faith in our heart, we can be moved by the sound of our footsteps during our travels.

Kobo Daishi (744-835), a major figure in the history of Japanese Buddhism, once wrote a verse: "Triloka [Three Realms] is like a guest house and only the heart is the home to return to." The world is just a place for us to rest during our journey. However far we go, the innermost being is our ultimate paradise.

DAY FIVE

LIFE IS A DEEP-ROOTED ROVING

BLUE IS A WARM COLOUR when the champagne rays of light spill over the icy peaks and snow-capped mountains.

At half past five in the morning, I set out for the mountaintop where a temple is situated. The oxygen levels were low and the temperature was bitingly cold at an altitude above 3,800 metres. However, in my innermost being, I was eager to be with each sunrise and yearned for the solitude and serenity brought by the high mountains, in the same way that I love the everyday spinning of prayer wheels and the chants of scriptures by the monks and disciples.

The temples in Muktinath are scattered above the Kali Gandaki Valley and face two world-class snow mountains, Annapurna and Mount Dhaulagiri. The 'Goddess of Fertility' Annapurna was the first 8,000-metre mountain that mankind has ever climbed. The word 'Dhaulagiri' literally means 'genial' and 'white mountain' in Nepali. The Buddha was sat on the ground, serene and solemn, with the wind and clouds swirling around him; the gods in heaven, including God Brahma of Creation in Hinduism in charge of the universe, God Bishnu of Protection, God Shiva of Destruction and the deities in charge of the sun, the moon, the stars, wind, rain and life, all walked in the fabulous shadows cast by the high mountains.

The brown faces and saffron robes of the Buddhist nuns sitting in the Marme Lhakhang scripture halls with their legs crossed were rocking back and forth in the shadow of butter lamps. They sang an anthem in both Nepali and Tibetan: "Ah, the silent flowers in the Orient, you should leave the crowds and advance along the secret, saintly way and arrive at the golden throne of the Buddha. In the face of the silence and the mercy of the gods, you are our last force to rely on."

The otherworldly chants were serene and transmitted far away in the light of the sunrise. Pigeons flew swiftly above and danced like shadows amid the tinkle of bells made by the disciples.

The acts of transcribing, holding and chanting scriptures are called the 'merits and virtues of scriptures', for which the Buddha will bring us a splendid life in return. The Buddhist nuns in Muktinath pray for the peace and purity of the people as they sleep and have maintained the holy, mysterious tradition for hundreds of years. When people wake at dawn with sympathy, purity, mercy, kindness and braveness in their mind, they will begin the new day briskly and happily. When you stand on the snow mountain and pray facing the east, your Buddhist nature will be awakened by the rising sun and will bloom naturally like flowers under the sun. At that time, you seem to live in every moment. Without the limitations of time and space, you will find the whole universe shining with its beauty, existence and energy.

Each year we should go to some special place to see the sunrise. When the sun rises slowly over the horizon and the light gradually spreads over the mountains, it seems that the centre of the world is overflowing with warmth, tranquillity and gracefulness and generates the feeling that life is a real gift. This simple pleasure can bring us enduring enlightenment and pacification. I had been curious about the origin of the word 'Nepal' and hadn't known until I came to Muktinath that it means 'land of wool' in Tibetan and 'land of caverns' in Sikkimese.

In ancient times, Nepal was indeed abundant in wool and caves, where many saints and ascetics practised and lived. The Himalayas was even the place where the God Shiva of Destruction and Revival lived. The word 'Shiva' means 'mercy'. As a yogi, he sat on a piece of tiger skin in meditation with his legs crossed day and night to pray for blessings for the world. When we travel to Nepal, to the beacon of Buddha Sakyamuni, the source of life as inspired by spiritual longing, we should not merely take photos of the relics and the Buddha there, drink mouthfuls of holy water and take a cold bath, but also make good use of the time in the Holy Land and sit under the bodhi for a few seconds, minutes or hours in meditation.

However long we sit in meditation, the Buddhist nature, like the glory when the sun sheds light on the golden mountains, will help us pursue spiritual eternity, tranquillity, freedom and liberation and establish a habit of purifying our mood and accumulating wisdom and blessings in the mind. The eminent monk Dzongsar Jamyang Khyentse Rinpoche of Bhutan wrote in his book *Pilgrimage*: "Pilgrimage provides a way to practise Buddhism."

Pilgrimage offers us an outlet to show mercy, devoutness and reverence during trekking. These states of mind can be seen everywhere like the wind, rain, sunrise and sunset; pilgrimage makes us grateful that there is indeed a tranquil, pleasant way to relieve us of our mental and physical pollution.

Enjoy the beauty of a roving life

Brilliant rays enveloped the entire town of Ranipauwa at half-past eight in the morning. I was wearing a hat with a braid at the back as I left the peak-top temple and went downhill.

Some Tibetan residents had opened their red-and-black wooden doors and hung up mysterious ammonite fossils known as Saligram. Kangaroo said that, if we were lucky, we would turn over some black stones on our journey and find our own Saligram.

I remembered an anecdote in a book: when a person consulted the French Enlightenment thinker Voltaire about this kind of fossil, he said that its discovery in the Alps proved that a grand oyster banquet had been held when the crusade marched towards the Middle East. However, to Himalayan locals, such a fossil is the incarnation of the God Brahma of Creation and is proof that the Himalayas was originally a handsome blue ocean, known as Neotethys.

As a matter of fact, time is infinite in the universe, but it can also be the shortest of times since we may become dust or ashes at any moment. We can see a world in a grain of sand and appreciate paradise in a wild flower. Sometimes, life is just an instantaneous phantom and the purpose of our life is to pursue happiness, imagination and transcendence.

Like me, a group of ascetic monks known as Sadhus had also woken up early that morning. They stood on the path in the biting wind and begged like the Buddha who was living in Jetavana monastery just outside the ancient Indian city of Sravasti. When it was time for the Bhagawan to eat, he would put on his cassock, hold his bowl like other monks and walk from Jetavana to Sravasti to beg for food. After eating, he would tidy his cassock and bowl, return to his residence, wash his feet, sit on an auspicious mat with his legs crossed and begin to sermon.

The idea behind begging for food in Buddhism is that those who can give alms to begging monks are brought together by fate, and the monks make many friends in the process. Similarly, in Hinduism, the Sadhus wander everywhere equipped only with sticks, blankets and aluminium pots, have no regard for life, death, bitterness and joy and pursue the ultimate end of life – liberation. These dignified people appear ragged and unkempt, have no fixed abode and very little in the way of money. When I rummaged through my purse and gave all my Chinese money to the Sadhus, they were so happy that they took me as their sibling and fellow sufferer, wanting to take a photo with me with the renminbi in their hands.

The donor forgot the act of giving and the recipient forgot the acceptance. We even forgot the alms and only enjoyed the happiness of sharing. At that time, the Buddha in the temple behind me no longer seemed to be a bronze statue carefully carved by Nivar artisans. He did not blink or breathe. He accepted the water and rice we put out as if for a pet every morning and accepted the lamp or flower from us in the evening. He permeated the air we breathed and the incense smoke around us. I felt as if I had existed as a Himalayan person for centuries.

Happiness not shared is not true happiness. Happiness exists only when it is shared. Our most important moment is when lives similar to ours mix closely with us. I told Kangaroo we would walk to Kagbeni Village rather than take the 'pig cage' truck. Once again, I switched from being a 'rubber vagrant' to a 'leather vagrant' like a Sadhu walking on foot.

The dawn meant rebirth, seemed to be the third eye on the God Shiva of Destruction and Salvation and ushered in the true life. I had a scene of the wilderness in my mind and thought the land was always something we could rely on. I wanted to listen to the inner call and go out on a path in my dream to enjoy the beauty of vagrancy, just as Lin Yutang once said: "A true traveller must be a vagrant who has experienced the happiness, temptation and long journeys of vagrants." I prefer the riding saddle to the saddle of an SUV, the starlit sky to the warm roof, the rugged paths leading to the unknown world to the broad bituminous roads and the profound silence in the wilderness to the noisy cities. I like to experience the weight of my body and the world through walking.

Sometimes, life is an unforgettable vagrancy.

The mountain bikers are coming

Actually the mountain bikers who were approaching from far away were much braver and crazier than me.

In addition to vagrancy and pilgrimage, riding mountain bikes is one of the most popular activities in the Himalayas. From the high mountain paths to the low Terai Plains, riding on mountain bikes is a practical and challenging mode of transport on rural Nepal's muddy roads and paths.

Mountain biking developed in the 1970s in California as a way to cope with the state's rugged, rocky paths and steep mountain roads. In the mid-1980s, mountain biking was introduced by Westerners into Nepal. With typical gradients of fourteen per cent, the Himalayas is an ideal place for riding.

The wilderness, the ever-changing terrain and the rolling mountains of the Himalayas provide great possibilities for adventure. Thanks to variable-speed gears and tyre tread patterns that grip the surface, riders can experience the wonders of daily rural life on mud paths without having to go on roads. Riding is also a great way to visit temples and the various ethnic settlements that have existed since medieval times. It is an excellent way to tour Nepal by combining cycling with taking spring baths, rock climbing, paragliding, rafting, temple tourism and bush walking.

Wandering happily together with a group of ascetic monks known as Sadhus

Muktinath, at an altitude of 3,800 metres, is a blessed place for pilgrims to meditate, enhance their insight and cultivate themselves gracefully. It is also a great place for cycling.

I stayed in Hotel Mount Kailash, along with a 39-year-old French cyclist called Andre and his Nepalese guide Raj. We bathed in the first rays of the morning sun, enjoying coffee and apple pie, with the snow-covered Mount Nilgiri lighting up before us and colourful prayer flags dancing in the wind.

Cyclists and guides start their adventure in Ranipauwa

Andre had come via Ranipauwa, Jomsom and Tatopani. An exploration company had transported his mountain bike and guide to Ranipauwa in an SUV and the cycling adventure to Tatopani started from there. Before departure, Raj helped the excited Andre check his tyres and brakes.

During morning tea, Andre, said: "Nepal has two hundred and forty mountains at an altitude above six thousand metres. So when you ride on high-altitude mountain paths with white clouds passing by, Pearl, it feels like you are cycling on clouds."

I reckoned this must be his best cycling experience. I high-fived Andre goodbye and jokingly warned him not to crash into the two-metre high boulders in the valley and thereby win the Best Collision Award for 'survival in the wild'. Afterwards, Kangaroo and I carried our full backpacks loaded with bottles, Tibetan bread, gloves, hats and walking pole, and walked directly to Jharkot along a small goat path.

Some riders sped by and gave out elated screams. Trekkers, cyclists, SUVs, flocks, herds and shepherds shared the same gravel path. There were numerous Alpine-style sharp bends. Guide Raj, a 22-year-old muscular young man, had been cycling for five years. He proudly waved to me: "Pearl, you should leave the wilderness by bike or on foot. The alternative is to be carried out in a 'pig cage' truck, and that is the worst choice of all!"

Excited children in remote villages ran out and shouted: "Here come the speedy cyclists!" Seeing the cyclists in their colourful outfits, gripping their handlebars and standing out of the saddle, I thought it was like the moment when the spirit leaves one's body.

Cyclists sped by and give out elated screams

Che Guevara, the Marxist revolutionary, might have remained an obscure physician rather than an international guerrilla fighter having cycled thousands of miles in five South American countries over a period of nine months. I thought that one day I would return to Nepal and 'fly' like them in the clouds.

Life should be an adventure so why shouldn't I lead an adventurous life!

Mustang, Nepal's forbidden place, opens up

Two hours later, Kangaroo and I walked along a gravel path and into Jharkot. It looked like the Gyantse Fortress on Mount Zong in Tibet.

With precipices on three sides, Jharkot looks towards the vast, dried-up Jhong Khola and to the rocky peak of Yakgawa Kang, 6,482 metres high.

'Wakang' is revered by the mountain people and gives them great power. Drinking butter tea to warm myself in front of a window reflecting the snow mountains, the wilderness and the village, I found that many trekkers were unwilling to stay in Hotel Ranipauwa because it was crowded with pilgrims. Instead, they would stay overnight in quiet, simple Jharkot and pay religious homage in Muktinath the following morning.

The houses there were painted white and the windows looked like the eyes of pandas. The villagers had the broad faces and single-fold eyelids characteristic of Tibetans. There were also white-and-yellow pagodas, dark red Mani stones, well-trodden circumambulation paths and dancing prayer flags. The locals grow barley, and drive mules and horses. Once the barley is harvested, it is put outside in small baskets so that the husks are blown away in the wind. They sang and worked continuously. Although this is Nepal, strong Tibetan traditions and customs prevail. In ancient times, Jharkot was a bridge between India and Tibet, and it boasted the shortest route from the Indian Plains to the Himalayas. Therefore, it was strategically and economically important, especially in the trade of salt. People bartered salt from the salt lakes of northern Tibet for cereals from the Indian plains and valleys. Even today, the hoofbeats and bells of packhorses can still be heard on the desolated path of Jharkot.

Wise Tibetans do not just use yaks and donkeys to carry bags of salt, tea, grain and apples; they also have sheep carry them. Each sheep can carry a ten kilogram bag containing salt or wool, for instance, which was heavier than my own backpack. Some sheep are sold along with the commodities they carry, as a job lot.

When I stood on a deserted wall in Jharkot and cast my eye over the Jhong Khola, I could see as far as Upper Mustang, the forbidden area in Nepal under a strong, pure and glowing red-orange sky.

Few people can clearly describe the remoteness and mystery of Upper Mustang. The English writer James Hilton wrote *Lost Horizon* in 1933. It tells the story of four Westerners travelling on a plane that crashes in the valley of Shika Snow Mountain in Tibet. There is a pyramid-like snow mountain and a lamasery named Shangri-La. The people and nature there adhere to the virtue of 'moderation' and live a peaceful, serene and happy existence.

Since the book's publication, Shangri-La became another term for Utopia, Garden of Eden, Babylon, 'a fictitious land of idyllic beauty'.

Numerous people have tried to find the real place. Hilton once said there was no such place as Shangri-La in reality because it only existed in the imagination. Nevertheless, this did not stop some countries from trying to find their own Shangri-La. India said it existed in Baltistan in Kashmir, while Nepal thought it was Mustang in the north of the country. In the Chinese province of Yunnan, Zhongdian County was renamed 'Shangri-La County' in 2001 because Zhongdian means 'the sun and the moon at heart' in Tibetan.

Mustang was once forbidden to foreigners for more than half a century. In 1991 it permitted an American photographer to enter this secret area in north Nepal, and his images brought Mustang to the whole world.

Mustang is a sparsely populated, primitive area at an average altitude of more than 2,500 metres. It is so remote that even the Nepalese travelling there are often mistaken for foreigners. In history, Mustang used to be an independent kingdom, but it was not the original name for the area. The locals call their territory 'Lo', a Tibetan word meaning 'southern land' and 'fertile plains', and the people that have lived there for generations are known as 'Lopas'. Different branches of the Tibetan ethnic group are often named after the places where they live with the suffix 'pa' added, meaning 'people'. For example, 'Sherpas' in Tibetan means 'people living in the East' and 'Khampas' means 'people living in the Kham region'.

Lo, founded by the warrior Ame Pal in 1380, has been governed by twenty-five kings and was part of the ancient Ngari Prefecture. During the fifteenth to seventeenth centuries, thanks to its advantageous location in the Himalayan Corridor, it was a prosperous Buddhist cultural and artistic centre and a place through which salt mined in Tibet was transported to cities in the Indian subcontinent. In those years salt was one of the most precious commodities in the world. Packhorses and caravans laden with salt and wool were carried on rugged mountain paths. Managing a salt trade route at that time was like controlling an oil pipeline today. Lo made a fortune by controlling the trade caravans passing through its territory.

However, in the late eighteenth century, Lo's economy gradually declined with the production of cheaper salt in India. The small kingdom worshiping Tibetan Buddhism was conquered by the Shah dynasty believing in Hinduism. Prithvi Narayan Shah was the founder of modern

Nepal and made Lo part of Nepal's territory. However, Lo remained the only autonomous kingdom in Nepal and had its own king and national banner.

In 1951, Lo officially joined the Kingdom of Nepal and was renamed Mustang Autonomous Region. Mustang was divided into the upper and lower parts. Upper Mustang was the territory north of Kagbeni to the northern border in Tibet, China, while Lower Mustang was the area south from Kagbeni through Jomsom to south Ghasa. Upper Mustang is the former Kingdom of Lo, with its centre in the capital Lo Manthang.

Geopolitically, Upper Mustang District was the most sensitive strategic zone, involving China, Nepal, India and the United States. This was the border across which the Dalai Lama and other Tibetans fled to Nepal and India in 1959 and the last hideout of the Dalai's rebels. In 1960, overseas powers set up the so-called 'Chushi Gangdrug' forces in Upper Mustang and launched a ten-year military harassment campaign on the border with Tibet, China. The chaotic situation in Upper Mustang was not resolved until 1972, when King Birendra of Nepal succeeded to the throne. The Chushi Gangdrug was annihilated by the Nepalese government army in 1974. In 2008, the Kingdom of Nepal changed its regime and became a federal republic. The former king of Lo was deposed in Lo Manthang Rural Municipality, the kingship of Lo of more than six hundred years was officially terminated and Jigme Palbar Bista, the last king born in 1930, became an ordinary Nepalese citizen. He died in 2016.

For environmental and political reasons, Nepal did not allow foreigners to visit Upper Mustang District. As a result, it had a very low international profile. The imposing statues of mandala in the temples of Upper Mustang gradually collapsed while the exquisite murals peeled off. This country with a brilliant culture was forgotten by history. In the Himalayas, the only things that moved were the passing clouds in the rainy season and the yaks when the snows were forty centimetres thick in winter.

In 1991, the American photographer Taylor Weidman was given a special permit by the Nepalese government to travel in the Upper Mustang. He recorded the precarious lifestyles of many different world races in his 'Vanishing Cultures' project. In his book *Mustang: Lives and Landscapes of the Lost Tibetan Kingdom*, he wrote: "Mustang District, hidden in the rain shadow of the Himalayas, is one of the remotest places in Nepal. The southern part of the former Lo is surrounded by the world's highest mountains and closed Tibet lies in the north. Since the fifteenth century, this small Tibetan kingdom has remained unchanged. Now, Mustang

District might be the best example in the world of a place that has retained the traditional Tibetan lifestyle."

Mustang is a sparsely populated, primitive area, known by the locals as 'Lo'

In 1992, Upper Mustang allowed restricted opening to the public. Foreign travellers can enter after paying 500 dollars for a permit. It receives 3,000 foreigners a year. The capital Lo Manthang of the former Lo was selected by UNESCO as a world cultural heritage site. As one of the best-preserved ancient cities in the world, secret Upper Mustang District famed as a 'Himalayan gem' became the best example of primitive Tibetan life.

Now, this closed, restricted place is ready for change. Restaurants, tea houses, coffee shops, stores and hotels are appearing in remote, high-altitude villages. Backpacking foreigners travel back and forth on the rugged mountain paths and the outside world is exerting a greater influence on Upper Mustang.

Crossing the worry-free land

On Google Earth, you can see the whole Mustang District stretching more than eighty kilometres from north to south and forty-five kilometres at the narrowest from east to west. Shaped like the long, elliptical leaf of the ashoka tree, it surrounds the Kali Gandaki Khola on the northern snowy Himalayas. Like a deep blue main vein, the river occupies the passageway between Annapurna and Mount Dhaulagiri, traverses numerous valleys from north to south, turns east and finally pours into the Ganges.

Innumerable tributaries including the Dhimi Khola, Yak Khola, Qumona Khola and Lunpa Khola look like countless fishbone-shaped lateral veins that flow down from the snow mountains on both sides. The ancestors of primitive tribes always lived beside rivers. The tributaries that flow in the valley provide abundant water, an even terrain and relatively fertile land for human settlements to grow and prosper.

Ashoka trees, also known as worry-free trees and Buddha trees, have a holy, symbolic meaning in South Asia. They bloom in spring, when a torch-like golden inflorescence covers the whole canopy. They look like golden pagodas from a distance, but on closer inspection, the long, thin leaves droop like soft feathers cloaked in a purple cassock dampened by rain. They got their name 'worry-free' trees for their bright colours, freshness and fragrance. Two thousand five hundred years ago, Prince Siddhartha of Sakya was born under a worry-free tree in Lumbini in south Nepal, got enlightened and finally became a Buddha under a heart-shaped bodhi in Bodh Gaya, India.

The wonderful birth and enlightenment of the Buddha correspond with the belief and state of mind of the Lopas in worshiping Buddhism. There are places in the real world that correspond with the spiritual paradise of Buddhists, such as Lhasa in the minds of Tibetans and the Holy Mount Kailas. Could any other place be a more appropriate homeland of the Lopas than this land in the shape of the worry-free leaf?

Jomsom is situated at the place where the stalk meets the stem. It powerfully supports Lower Mustang District. Kagbeni is the starting point of the main vein. It is the entrance to Upper Mustang District. Lo Manthang Rural Municipality, situated at the top of the main vein at an altitude of 3,840 metres, is in an area of innumerable mountains and valleys. The walls that surround Lo Manthang are enveloped by the light and shade of the Middle Ages. The pagodas with sand-coloured spires look like the florid canopies of worry-free trees, presenting a view of 'Shangri-La' covered by a carpet of flowers hidden in the valleys.

I have left only fragmentary notes about Upper Mustang in my writings.

During my pilgrimage, Kangaroo asked me: "Pearl, suppose you could travel through time and space, which would be your next favourite destination?"

I naturally cast my eye like that of a wild horse at Upper Mustang District on the horizon and looked at the sky as violet as burned ceramics. There, time conquered everything and the trip to Upper Mustang made me hold my breath and sigh.

After leaving Jharkot, we took the remote path to Kagbeni. It was rather desolate, with few trees and not much in the way of grass. It reminded me of the road to the desert in ancient Zhada in Ngari Prefecture. At that time, my husband and I tried unsuccessfully to extract our car from mud in Zidaban at an altitude of 5,400 metres. We eventually managed to get it out thanks to an armed policeman.

Most of the path sections here were made of gravel and perched along the sides of valleys, so slipping was a danger. Any fall might cause the earth and stones to give way and I would end up dirty and dishevelled. But don't think the riverbeds were not worth seeing. The area was soul-stirring, which gave me valuable time to enjoy 'stillness' and reunited me with time, history and nature.

For thousands of years, the land seemed to have been cleaved with a sword by the Kali Gandaki Khola. The fences on both sides of the valley were marked with the ripples and waves of the river over the years. Ammonite and shellfish fossils could be found occasionally among the stones, the steep mountains were like giants, and the cliff walls in the far distance were fused by the scorching sun with their colours changing in the shifting light and shadow. The magnificence of the mountains and wilderness areas compare favourably with the Grand Canyon in the US.

Unique to this area, thousands of man-made caverns on the untrodden route hang on steep palisades. Some solitary ones looked like the open mouth of a lion, some like the Secret Garden chorus, and others like the dim windows of an apartment eight storeys high. Wild in appearance, they are among the greatest archaeological mysteries of the modern world.

What kind of nation could create these caverns in such a remote location? How on earth could human beings climb these cliffs in distant times? By rope? By scaffold? Or by excavating stone steps?

Archaeologist have made a conservative estimate that there are about ten thousand caverns in Mustang District. What secret history will the mysterious caverns dating back thousands of years reveal?

But for the efforts of generations of explorers, few might have been interested in these caverns in this most out-of-the-way corner of Nepal. In 1981, the mountaineer Pete Athans came across these caverns by chance and was deeply interested. Many caverns stood against the skyline and seemed accessible only to birds. Athans, who had reached the summit of Mount Everest seven times, didn't get a permit from the Nepalese government to enter Mustang until 2007. Known as 'Mr Everest', Athans regarded Nepal as his second home. He said that Mustang had become the greatest challenge in his adventurous life. An expedition headed by him and the American writer Broughton Coburn made repeated climbs of the tumbledown cliffs to explore these man-made caverns, and they made amazing achievements.

They discovered an eight-metre-long mural describing the life of Sakyamuni Buddha and depicting the exquisite portraits of forty-two great practitioners in the history of Buddhism. Eight thousand ancient handwritten manuscripts were collected in another cavern, with the contents ranging from Tibetan Buddhist doctrines to legal literature and involving religious and worldly themes. Most of the objects date back more than six hundred years, which proved that Lo had been an important place for trade and Buddhism during the thirteenth and fourteenth centuries.

Like other archaeologists, Pete Athans' team were desperate to discover any caverns containing pre-historic relics so as to shed light on questions such as who were the earliest settlers there, where did they come from and what were their beliefs.

The culmination of their epic journey came in 2010 when they discovered the most valuable historic site so far in the form of clusters of tombs and caverns in a place near Samdzong Village, close to the Sino-Nepal border.

In these tombs, they found coffins with exteriors painted in orange-and-white patterns, including portraits of horse owners carved on coffins made of padauk wood. They also found the skulls of child slaves and horses buried with the dead, along with twenty-seven skeletons that had been cut with a knife. These remains could date back as far as the third to eighth centuries.

It seemed that posthumous executions, involving the ceremonial mutilation of an already dead body as an unofficial punishment for wrongdoing, might have been practised here by Buddhists. Sky burials are still performed by citizens in Upper Mustang. It involves the remains of the departed, including their bones, being cut into small pieces, wrapped with *zanba* (roasted highland barley flour) and fed to vultures. Tibetans hold the view that celestial burials that involve lighting incense sticks will facilitate the arrival of the *dakini*, a type of sacred female spirit, to the celestial burial platform. The corpse should be offered respectfully to the deities so that they can remove the sins of the departed before his soul is taken to heaven.

Supposedly, in previous centuries, the flesh of human corpses was removed from the bones, with the whole skeleton taken to the caverns and placed in a coffin. The sacrificial objects buried with them were quite exquisite, most of them sourced from other places, including bamboo cups with delicate round handles, large copper crucibles to brew highland barley wine, colourful burial masks and beads dyed in at least six colours and produced in places as far away as modern-day Pakistan, India and Iran. The coffins themselves were skilfully made from superior black hardwood from the tropics, with each plank cut perfectly to size for quick assembly in the tombs. Everything ready, the corpse-carrier would slowly climb out of the cavern mouth.

How did the people in those years accumulate such dazzling wealth in a place devoid of trees? How did they display their wealth and social status with these exceptional handicrafts? The answer is salt. The salt trade channel in the Himalayan Corridor at that time was just as important as the oil reserves in the Persian Gulf are today.

Athans told the journalist Michael Finkel that he was more excited about discovering these caverns than reaching the summit of Mount Everest. He returned most of the collections discovered there to the present owner of the caverns, namely, the villagers of Samdzong. The Mustang people should take pride in the history of their ancestors. According to archaeologists, these caverns had different uses in three separate time periods. First, they were used as tombs more than three thousand years ago and then as residences a thousand years ago. In about the fifteenth century

AD, most cavern residents moved to settle in traditional villages with these caverns then used as meditation rooms, lookout posts or storerooms. In recent centuries, when civil war broke out in the Kali Gandaki Valley, the caverns were used as hideouts from battle.

The remains kept silently in the caverns have helped to rewrite the prehistory of Mustang. Maybe it is the cradle of Tibetan culture. After all, Nepal means 'land of wool' in Tibetan and 'land of caverns' in Sikkimese.

Sitting and watching the world revolve

The Mesopotamia Plain, situated between the Tigris-Euphrates river system, is the cradle of Western civilisation and was called 'the Garden of Eden' in *The Bible*. Babylon between the two rivers meant 'Damocles', namely, Gate of God, where the incomparably imposing tower of Babel was erected. It is said that it is the temporary home of deities on their way to the mortal world and the lodging place of mortal men and women going to heaven.

Amid the wild wind and fine sand carried in the air, as we passed through Kagbeni, the portal to the trouble-free land in Lo, I wondered if it would be like scenes from the film *Kagbeni* by the Nepalese director Bhusan Dahal. The marvellous Nepalese music and the wild scenery in that film made people long to climb that mountain path. However, what would the magical wizard help me to find?

Kagbeni is an oasis village at the meeting point of the Jhong Khola and the Kali Gandaki Khola. *'La'* means 'mountain pass' or 'gate' in Nepali, while *'beni'* means 'river rapids' or 'junction'. Kagbeni rests at the junction of two ancient trade routes. On our trekking route, we turned left, went through Muktinath, the Holy Land of Hinduism and Buddhism, and came to the hinterland of the Annapurna Base Camp. For four days we trekked northwards to Lo Manthang Rural Municipality and then westwards for two days to Simikot, opposite Xieerwa, the border port in Pulan County, China. Large numbers of Indian and Nepalese pilgrims traverse the Lipulekh Pass at an altitude of 5,300 metres and enter Mount Kailas and Manasarovar Holy Lake in Ngari Prefecture for pilgrimage.

Holy Mount Kailas is regarded by millions of people as the spiritual centre of the universe and is worshiped by sages and praised by poets. It is the sacred homeland of gods falling to the mortal world from heaven. For centuries, Mount Kailas and Lake Manasarovar at its foot reminded people of the classic scenes depicted in Genesis, the Garden of Eden and the place where Noah's Ark berthed and the primitive ocean where the universe was born. Hence, it became the holiest land of Bön, the Tibetan folk religion, Tibetan Buddhism, Hinduism and Jainism (see Pearl Hong Chen's *Across Paradisal Tibet*) and meanwhile Xieerwa border port served as an important place for Chinese and Nepalese businesspeople to trade in wood, wool and other commodities.

Kagbeni is a land of idyllic beauty permeated with the scent of Tibetan incense

The fact that pilgrims have died on their mountain climb shows the gruelling nature of trekking in this area. Advancing in the vast, desolate Valley of Horses and along the exposed riverbed, I felt cold, dry and tired in the sun. Time passed quickly. I thought Kagbeni was still beyond reach. At that time the 'remoteness' I experienced was only a concept of distance but I came to appreciate that it is also connected to the state of one's mind. You initially think a place is remote because it's difficult to access, but once there, you no longer think that way.

A strange wind blew in the Valley of Horses that made both pilgrims and trekkers complain incessantly. Each afternoon, gusts stirred high up in the air above the desolate valley while Himalayan vultures and bearded vultures hovered overhead. Kangaroo reminded me time and again: "The wind is coming." He was an expert in local topography. He asked me to quicken my steps and try to avoid walking on the riverbed in the afternoon. But I didn't take his advice. I stopped to take photos, took a rest, drank water, ate apples and consequently delayed the journey.

During the following two hours' trekking, I was tortured by a strong wind that I could barely withstand despite covering my head with a scarf like a bandit. The force of the wind was similar to that experienced by bungee jumpers, fierce and skin-cutting.

Bungee jumping takes no more than a few seconds but the wind here would blow for hours on end. The bag on Kangaroo's back seemed to anchor him to the ground, stabilising him in the strong gale. With only a light bag on my back, I was being tossed around like a torn kite. I used to associate Ngari in Tibet as a highland area of strong winds. In the nineteenth century, the French explorer Fernand Grenard wrote in his notes of travelling across Tibet: "Tibet is a land of unique geology and strong winds."

The barren land before my eyes made me feel that I would stumble forward in the gale. Looking at the horses galloping alone in the dark wilderness with their manes whistling and the eagles flying freely in the sky, I felt tiny, fragile and lonely by comparison.

On seeing me suffering, Kangaroo put the backpack at the mouth of a cavern, let me shelter from the wind and tried to flag down a lift. The SUVs travelling down to Muktinath were all crowded. Finally, a large tractor stopped close by. The driver had just been unloading fertiliser but still charged us 200 rupees per head. I had no time to complain. Without any seats inside, Kangaroo had to lean tight against the tractor driver and stood on the left tyre foot peg. I climbed onto the wheel rim of the left tyre. A Nepalese man who was also getting a ride was perched over the right tyre, helping me secure the big backpack with one hand and holding my hand with the other.

Perched on top of the tractor, the wind was even stronger than when I was walking. I felt as if my head would pierce the blue sky. In addition, the bumpy road surface and the splashing water as we crossed the river made me feel like I was falling apart and dried by the wind like a pile of broken bones in a cavern. I thought that, of all the different types of vehicle, tractors could change a person most thoroughly.

. . .

Having been jolted for half an hour, we got off the tank-like 'beast' near Kagbeni. The villagers were harvesting millet on the lowlands near the river, casting enchanting pale pink shadows in the wind. Previously, I had suffered a miserable experience in the wilderness but now I found myself in a magical place. Medieval castles stood at the entrance to the village and the ruins of lookout posts could be seen on both sides of the mountain pass, overlooking the corn fields and narrow riverbeds. Tibetan-style dwellings hugged close to one another on the banks of the Kali Gandaki Khola, which no doubt helped protect the inhabitants from the afternoon winds.

To my surprise, many villagers in Kagbeni were able to speak several languages, including Tibetan, Nepali, Hindi and English. The ancient post houses in the 'secret kingdom' seemed to have formed an international transport hub. There were many tea houses, coffee shops, lodges, prayer wheels and prayer flags. Terraced fields stood upon terraced fields at the foot of the snow mountain. Desolate Shiwandashan Mountain stood tall ahead and all kinds of flowers swayed in the light shadows. When I walked along an ancient sand-coloured lane with crumbling stone walls on either side, I discovered that traditional Tibetan culture still influenced people's daily lives. Although living far from Lhasa, they still held Tibetan Buddhist ceremonies for weddings and funerals. They were not just ethnically Tibetan; they lived life at the same slow rhythm as their forebears did hundreds of years ago. It remained a land of idyllic beauty permeated with the sounds of wind and horses and the smell of Tibetan incense.

We stayed in Hotel Shangri-La, close to the central pagoda. After our mountain permits were checked at a log cabin of the Annapurna Conservation Area Project, we rented a bay horse and got ready to start our journey to Lo Manthang the next day. A cool man wearing a traditional hat adeptly took out a sheepskin bag, attached it to the horse and fed it with beans. Its mane was smartly braided, with multi-coloured tassels tied to the plaits. The man and his horse were travelling companions, following and loving each other.

The kitchen in the hotel was referred to as the 'cosy kitchen'. Travellers crowded here to take shelter from the wind, warm themselves and relax. The porters were roasting potatoes mixed with sesame, vegetables and spices, which made the travellers very hungry. There are seven thousand Tibetans in Upper Mustang District. They like chatting with one another in a circle every Wednesday evening and tell stories about the ancient Lopas. Portraits of the twenty-fifth king and queen of Lo were hung on the earthen wall of the kitchen. A woman was picking small stones from a bowl of rice, her hair adorned with traditional ornaments made of coral stones and turquoise; outside, we saw a monk quietly guarding his monastery and a statue of the Buddha. A young man was riding a horse on the valley path, while old women sat in a row spinning prayer wheels and men were packing fertiliser bags on horseback ready to take them to the fields.

A steady stream of horses and people passed through a narrow gate.

We sat there, watching the comings and goings, greedily absorbing the fragrance of coffee and worry-free flowers.

Moonlight of Mustang in his eyes

As I took off my clothes to bathe in the evening, I found that my body was covered in red blotches. When my skin came into contact with hot water, the blotches spread quickly, and became painful and itchy. I looked like a patient afflicted with lupus. I wondered whether it was because I was allergic to the mushroom and yak steak I ate the evening before in Muktinath. Maybe the wild mushrooms were poisonous. Buddha Sakyamuni preached and roamed in India at the age of eighty. Some scriptures record that he ate poisonous mushrooms for dinner served by a blacksmith and passed away due to diarrhoea. Even the Buddha was prone to disease, suffering and ageing.

Kangaroo came in and checked the wheals on my neck, arms and back. He said it might be rubella or an allergic reaction to the wind or the fibre bag of fertiliser on which I'd sat. He insisted that we should get a ride to find a clinic in Pokhara the next morning. That would mean changing vehicles four times and a jolting journey of up to eighteen hours. But we must hurry. He had served as a guide for six years and had never encountered such a case. He immediately fetched saline water from the kitchen and helped me to clean and disinfect the skin, and relieve the itching. I was overwhelmed with fear. I didn't know what virus I had contracted and when I could return to Kagbeni. But I was unwilling to give up on our trek in Upper Mustang.

What a dilemma!

. . .

With the stars shining like little gems in the dark blue night sky, it was spiritually painful and depressing to leave in this manner. As the mountaineer Reinhold Messner said: "Reaching the summits of all the world's mountains above eight thousand metres is not worth my pride. All my successes are not worth my pride. There's only one thing that I'm proud of and that is my survival."

Maybe only fear can lead to fearlessness. But now all I could do was sit helplessly before the dried yak dung bonfire and watch the old women weave yak yarn while humming Lopa melodies. The phrase for weaving woollen yarn is '*suo nan*', a symbol of happiness. The basic wooden weaving contraption squeaked beside me. The simple task of spinning was a source of great happiness to the old women, the inherent happiness at hand which was to live in the moment and was the easiest to be neglected. I thought that anyone arriving in Kagbeni, even a hundred years from now, would probably find the same *suo nan* and the same leisurely happiness.

A large expanse of sugarcane outside the stone wall of the hotel looked like a mysterious garden. The owner had cut down some cane for us travellers to chew and increase our vitamin intake. We sat in a yard covered with fig and apple trees to see the stars and hear the constant flow of the Kali Gandaki Khola in the quiet village. Kangaroo borrowed a flute from the hotel owner and began to play his favourite flute music, *Banko Badh*.

I knew that Kangaroo was born in a small Brahman village called Ghachok in the Annapurna Peaks. The students there had to spend three hours travelling to and from school every day. He had served in Nepal's royal infantry, as a guard in the Qatar flying club and a trekking guide in Pokhara at the age of twenty-three. The Chinese poet Haizi said he had lived a happy life by feeding horses, chopping firewood, facing the great sea and watching the spring blossom. When I exclaimed that I dreamed to live such a serene, simple rural life, Kangaroo put down the flute, watched me with his affectionate brown eyes and told me that he had a similar log cabin with a courtyard in his home village of Ghachok, and I could live there for the rest of my days if I wanted to!

I later found out that the lyrics sung by Kangaroo were "Oh, auspicious birds, wandering airborne travellers, did you see my small village on your way here? Banko Badh, my lovely Banko Badh, you give me the oxygen to breathe. I make the lattice window, the panel door, the log cabin and the sedan to marry my bride..." On that quiet night in the wilderness, my tears started to well up.

In his poem *Thank You*, Hu Shih (1891-1962), a Chinese philosopher, essayist and diplomat, wrote: "Thank you for your coming to relieve my loneliness in the mountains, accompany me to watch the mountains and the moon, and live a life like gods."

I knew that, without Kangaroo, this brave Nepalese man who was accompanying me every day, my stumbling trek would be incomplete. But I'm a wandering Chinese woman, how could I become a tribal girl in the mountains of Nepal? Kangaroo was the epitome of so many friendly, soulful Nepalese men. We were like the sand in the Valley of Horses that gradually became glistening pearls. I knew that my memory of him would deepen with every I step I walked, and that I would miss him more and more.

Although I could not reach Lo Manthang on this occasion, I was determined to go back there on a future trip. Mustang District was like an oasis, the Garden of Eden, Babylon and a world lost in our noisy, mortal world. We could only trudge on, have a distant view of it, appreciate the wild flowers in the valley housing the deities and then wave our hands and leave with a heart imbued with melancholy.

ITINERARY

Bus route
Pokhara to Nayapul (42km, 1.5hr)

Trekking route
Nayapul (altitude: 1,000 metres) to Birethanti (altitude: 1,000 metres, 2km) to Hile (altitude: 1,510 metres, 9km) to Tikhedhunga (altitude: 1,540 metres, 1km) to Ulleri (altitude: 2,080 metres, 3km) to Banthanti (altitude: 2,250 metres, 4km) to Nangathanti (altitude: 2,460 metres, 6km) to Ghorepani (altitude: 2,750 metres, 5km) Poon Hill (altitude: 3,190 metres, 1.5km) to Ghorepani (altitude: 2,750 metres, 1.5km) to Chitre (altitude: 2,420 metres, 4km) to Phalate (altitude: 2,390 metres, 2km) to Shikha (altitude: 1,980 metres, 3 km) to Ghara (altitude: 1,780 metres, 4km) to Tatopani (altitude: 1,190 metres, 5km) to Dana (altitude: 1,450 metres, 3km)

Bus route
Dana to Ghasa to Marpha to Jomsom to Eklai Bhatti to Muktinath (100km, 8hr)

Trekking route
Muktinath (altitude: 3,800 metres) to Jharkot (altitude: 3,500 metres, 3km) to Khingar (altitude: 3,400 metres, 3km) to Kagbeni (altitude: 2,840 metres, 7km)

Return bus route
Kagbeni to Jomsom to Pokhara (200km, 18hr)

Mileage/Duration
500km/6days

CHAPTER IV

EVEREST DRUMMER

Most trekkers passing by Solu region advanced along the road opened up by Expedition Everest in earlier years. Egor once agitated me: "Pearl, be unique, be yourself. It is our lifestyle." Indeed, going to Mount Everest was not to seek a specific mountain but to find numerous possible ways of existence. 'Distance' became a perceptual word to me, offering infinite appeal.

I came back to my ordinary urban life. Even though I didn't climb mountains, when I busied myself in the crowded metro where butterflies flapped their wings or I suddenly felt sad, I would raise my head, seek the green mountains, cast my eye at the sky above concrete buildings and look in the direction of the mountain top…

DAY ONE

DEPARTURE: SMELLS LIKE TEEN SPIRIT

From misty, damp Pokhara to mazy Kathmandu, I could smell humans and beasts in the air. Kathmandu was seriously polluted by vehicle exhaust fumes, soot and dust. Sacred cows, sheep, dogs and chickens ambled on the narrow lanes, their smell mixing with the strong aroma of spice and fresh juice. Then there were the smells of the Himalayan snow, the pheromones of excited travellers and the incense burned in worship to the Hindu deities and the Buddha.

Immersed in the noise and strolling among the two thousand temples and shrines, the five hundred hotels and pubs and the hundred markets selling perfume, spice and fresh flowers, I felt my individuality might vanish in the morning glory of this extraordinary city.

This is the capital city of Nepal, the city of fantasy, Kathmandu.

It was the sixth time I had been here since 2007.

I returned and made plans for my next trip.

A plane from Kathmandu to Lukla crashed on 28 September 2012 and all nineteen people on board died. Subsequent flights from Kathmandu were cancelled for several days and travellers waited restlessly. Even in normal circumstances, flights to Lukla are often postponed or cancelled due to bad weather.

Everest Base Camp is the ultimate destination for many trekkers. It is like Mecca for Muslims, Jerusalem for Christians, and Kailash for Hindus and Buddhists. It is a fairyland in mid-air. Anyone travelling from Kathmandu to Lukla, the starting point of the journey to Everest Base Camp, has two choices. First, they can take a vehicle from Kathmandu to Shivalaya, trek in the valley for a week before arriving in Lukla. The journey may be long and boring, and is therefore shunned by most trekkers, but it is the safest way to travel. The more popular alternative is to fly directly to Lukla, which takes only thirty-five minutes. However, Lukla is the one of the most dangerous airport in the world.

After Era Tours Nepal confirmed with me that I was not able to fly the following day, the soul-stirring words of the old tribal chief Lei Ting in the film *Himalaya* rang in my ears: "When you have two options, choose the more difficult one." So I decided to get a refund for my air ticket and take a vehicle to Shivalaya the next day. I asked Era Tours to book a Sherpa porter there. Thoughts of the air crash persuaded me of the merits of trekking from Shivalaya to Lukla. I reckoned the more difficult path may be preferable so long as we had sufficient courage and faith to overcome the difficulties.

Encountering Egor

Just like in our daily lives, trekking involves many tests, accidents and surprises.

At 10.30am, after a difficult two-hour journey, I finally sat down in the Ever Cafe Bar and was enjoying my first latte of the morning. The air seemed calmer and everything was quiet and comfortable. I had stayed the previous night at the Northland Lodge in the centre of Thamel District and had been kept awake by the unrelenting percussion music in the bar and singing in the dance hall. After the coffee, I quickly packed my bags, checked out before noon and transferred to the cheaper and quieter Kathmandu HI Thamel Hostel.

While I was having coffee, a tall man wearing cobalt blue climbing gear came in and sat at the table diagonally across from me. I stood up and snapped a photo of the morning sky over Kathmandu. That man stood up, smiled and said: "Let me take a photo of you and the sky."

After thanking him for his help, I quickly left because I needed to buy some clothing from an outdoor shop along with some emergency food and medicine. Having met with various accidents on my trek in Annapurna and Jomsom, I realised that I had been naïve and poorly prepared. But this time, I would trek to the base camp of Everest at an altitude of 5,357 metres, 1,227 metres higher than Annapurna Base Camp, where the air would be much thinner than I had previously experienced.

Mount Everest is world-famous. It is the most brilliant image of Nepal and the reason for the wide popularity of Everest Base Camp. However, the trekking route has many other attractions apart from being famous, including the unique rural life of the locals and their religious traditions.

In ancient Tibetan scriptures, alpine valleys in Solu and Khumbu regions were regarded as holy places, a refuge from the chaos caused by war and disaster, and a secret place where saints and eminent monks practised. The area for mountaineering is divided into South Everest and North Everest, with the former being in Nepal and the latter in China. Although both sides of Mount Everest are routes for climbing, the southern trekking route to Everest Base Camp is recognised as the most classic and beautiful, with its history dating back to the eighteenth century. However it was not until 1924 when mountaineering expeditions really took off. A British expedition headed by Edward Norton climbed Everest from the southern slope. They all died in an accident, including the famous mountaineer George Mallory. In 1953, Edmund Hillary and Sherpa Tenzing Norgay became the first two mountaineers to reach the summit of Everest and they took the southern route on the mountain ridge. In 1975, Japan's Junko Tabei became the first woman to reach the summit. Like other famous mountaineers, she also chose the southern route.

My own route began in the village of Shivalaya and it took eighteen days to trek from the lowlands inhabited by Nepali-speaking Hindus to the highlands of Tibetan Buddhists. As I sat in the Peace Garden Bar in Kathmandu HI Thamel Hostel in the afternoon, I listed in my notebook the following four problems I might encounter:

1. On average, one of the nineteen small airplanes flying from Kathmandu to the Himalayas crashes each year. All trekkers drawn to Mount Everest like to meet challenges. The moment you buy an air ticket, you've actually purchased a death permit.
2. During the eighteen-day trek, lodging and catering standards will be poor and hot baths are unavailable in most areas.
3. The average altitude of most path sections is above 4,000 metres, the upper limit for human survival, and any trekker is likely to be afflicted with acute mountain sickness.
4. Dangerous snow slides might happen at any time and accidental burial in ice holes can occur when you cross snow slopes and glaciers at Everest Base Camp.

As my anxiety increased, I met the tall man again. He had a straight-edged nose, light blue eyes, Putin-style short hair and a tattoo in the shape of eagle on his left arm. His black T-shirt had the word 'Zagreb' printed in red, its meaning unclear to me. At first sight, I thought he was a typical Slav because of his rather melancholy features and facial expressions. But when I raised my head and met his eyes, we both felt surprised. He was walking into the Peace Garden Bar in the most brilliant afternoon sunshine, with the fastest internet connections in Kathmandu. We simultaneously asked: "Hey! How'd you get here?"

"Pearl from China!"

"Egor from Croatia!"

This time, we had enough time to introduce ourselves. Egor asked whether he could sit at my table. I smiled and responded: "Sure!"

At first, I imagined Egor was a football player. Standing 1.95 metres tall, strongly built and well-coordinated, he looked like a Croatian footballer kitted out in their famous red-and-white strip. After chatting for a while, I learned that he was thirty-one years old and had travelled to Nepal alone. He was a drummer and his rock band had released two albums in Europe. All too often, rock musicians are drug addicts, philanderers or suicidal. I said: "You came to climb mountains? How dangerous!"

He was instantly amused, his eyes shining with joy.

It was the first time that Egor had come to Asia and it was his first day in Kathmandu. He was staying in the Blue Horizon Hotel, packed with mountaineers, and he planned to take a vehicle to Shivalaya the next day. Unlike me, he hadn't hired a porter and intended to finish the whole journey to Everest Base Camp carrying his bag of twelve kilograms in fifteen days.

Kathmandu has five hundred hotels, five hundred coffee bars and restaurants, a million local residents and five hundred ancient lanes. It also receives no fewer than five thousand foreign travellers every day. How was it possible to meet the same person twice in different coffee bars in different streets in different areas on the same day!

I used to travel alone because I liked to walk quietly, enjoy the solitude, watch the flowers bloom in the morning sun and listen to each drop of water in the ripples of the sunset. At that time, I imagined myself as a rock that had been in existence for thousands of years, a plant, a leaf and a speck of dust flying in the cosmos...

For many years, I refused to have a mobile phone, write blogs or use WeChat... I wrote *On the Road: Stories from American Universities* on a bed in the HI Thamel Hostel, *Fragrance of Nepal* in a stone house in the Himalayas, *Yoga Code in the Holy Land of India* by the Ganges and *Across Paradisal Tibet* and *Across Paradisal Xinjiang* during a cycling tour of Tibet and Xinjiang. It was a lonely journey but a unique world.

But now, I suddenly wanted to travel on Noah's Ark with the dove and olive branch in the company of a sunny man to explore the next unknown world of ice and snow. I couldn't help asking myself: Is he a 'Spiderman' sent by God to save me!

Forever young on the road

With no more words, I secured a brave knight to act as my 'bodyguard'. It would cost twenty dollars a day to hire an efficient guide. Egor jokingly said his ambition was to find the entrance to the Ark at the southern side of Mount Everest. The next day we met up as agreed at the Ratna Park bus stand and took the first bus to Shivalaya at 6am.

The Ratna Park bus stand did not have any English signs and in the hazy dawn it smelt of diesel fumes and animal urine. I'm an experienced traveller in Nepal and had taken local vehicles many times. Failing to understand the signs in Nepali, I asked: "Where's the shuttle bus to Shivalaya?" A Nepalese pointed out the bus we should take.

It was about 200 kilometres from Kathmandu to Shivalaya. Before the highway to Shivalaya opened in 2010, Jiri Municipality was the terminal station of all the shuttle buses. So Jiri was the traditional starting point of trekking to Everest Base Camp. I told Egor that, on my first trip to Nepal, my husband and I drove an SUV from Lhasa across Khasa border port to Jiri. I could not help exaggerating my experience to Egor. Looking into his blue eyes, I sensed he was beginning to fall for me. On that previous occasion, the chassis snapped on the next vehicle we travelled in and we had to return to Kathmandu to have it repaired. But by then my desire to travel to Everest Base Camp had waned.

Our bus would travel seventy-eight kilometres north-westward on the Arniko Highway to the Sino-Nepal border, arrive in Lamosangu, and then turn east and onto the rugged road to Jiri. We bought an 'express' tickets for 550 rupees but the bus frequently stopped to pick up passengers. I bet Egor that the journey would last at least fourteen hours and we would travel at an average speed of no more than ten kilometres an hour. Egor, on his first visit to Nepal, did not believe me. But I was relieved to be leaving the smothering air of Kathmandu and to be able to breathe freely. The buses in Nepal were all painted red or green. Each time I got on one, I would feel as happy as a country girl chasing the sun and going to market.

The mountains in the east of the Himalayas are abundant in wild animals and plants. The local monsoons begin very early and end quite late. So the climate is comfortable and damp, and it is greener and more vibrant than other parts of Nepal. Although it was late October, the paddies on the valley floor were golden yellow and tallowy plantain trees were heavy with fruit, presenting an exuberant view. The autumn wind was full of expectation. However, we were slowed down by numerous checkpoints, mostly looking for contraband. Some vehicles on the way to the Sino-Nepal border illegally carry antelope leather, sandalwood and musk.

I played a dirty trick on Egor by telling him that they were checking if there were criminals or anti-government forces on board, the 'Maoists' in the east who might want to take him hostage because he was tall and distinctive-looking. As expected, when we were about to arrive in Jiri in the evening, a group of Maoists holding up some red flags stopped the buses and charged each one entering the mountain 200 rupees as a 'protection fee' and gave a receipt to each driver. Although most Nepalese were not satisfied with the government headed by the president, Ram Baran Yadav, they placed equally little hope in the Maoists and peasants. They felt they acted like bandits and the Chinese government did not recognise their claim to be Communists. However, the buses were allowed to travel on after giving some money and no one was taken hostage. It was not thrilling at all!

Egor remarked that Kurt Cobain, lead singer of Nirvana, had the greatest influence on him. Kurt was born into a poor family and had an unhappy childhood, but before eventually committing suicide he managed to become one of the most influential rock musicians of recent times. Egor said inequality and suffering were prevalent throughout the world, yet people could overcome their difficulties. I didn't understand why this sunny, handsome Croatian standing beside me would say such things, just like I didn't appreciate the typical worries of people from his country.

I asked Egor why he had come to climb mountains and whether it was because of Mallory's famous saying about Everest: "Because it is there." He said it was because of Marco Polo, the legendary explorer who some Croatians say was born in their country and changed his name in Venice.

Egor's hometown, Korcula, is in an island in the Adriatic Sea off southern Croatia. It is claimed that Marco Polo was born there in a small three-storey stone building in 1254. The seventeen-year-old Marco Polo braved the wind and rain to sail to the sunny Orient. It has been more than seven hundred years since Marco Polo made that famous journey. But *The Travels of Marco Polo* that aroused the curiosity of Europeans about the Orient still inspires ordinary travellers to explore new lands.

I hadn't expected to meet someone like Egor at a time when I was no longer young. It seems that youth is not defined simply by age but instead by our mental state and outlook. The young seem to prefer a life of adventure rather than the humdrum.

As I chatted with Egor in English, the sun had set, the bus was passing Jiri Municipality and was now on a farm track. There were no lights on the mountain road and it was dark all around. Few vehicles passed and it was extremely quiet. Throughout our journey that day, the Nepalese driver was accustomed to turning up the music to maximum volume. At last, even the drummer Egor shouted that he couldn't stand the noise any longer, and he threatened to jump out of the bus and continue on foot.

It reminded me of the time when I first took a shuttle bus to Lumbini, the hometown of the Buddha. It was similar to when I first heard Nirvana's *Smells Like Teen Spirit*. Kurt's rough, broken singing nearly drove me mad. But after a while, I started to hear the song's beautiful rhythm and experience the primitive impulse and candour in his hoarse voice. I have spent a lot of time in developing countries and regions, and my experience of cycling in Tibet and Xinjiang proved useful at that moment. My husband once commented that I was the bravest passenger. I sat on the bonnet, accompanied the Nepalese driver to read the road atlas lest he should be distracted in the dark night, and I asked him to turn down the music.

I bet with the driver that the light in the distance must be from a minivan, and I would treat him to Nepalese dumplings if not. But it turned out to be a motorcycle taxi. Egor joined in the game too. Our 'clumsy' English made the locals in the bus laugh happily.

Maybe the darkness heightened my sense of smell. I was able to make out the refreshing scent of wild animals in the air outside the windows. Everything was serene and harmonious. We talked about Che Guevara, who was a global idol of proletarians and rebellious youth. His portrait with a red star on his beret was pasted on the bus door. We also discussed polygamy among Sherpas, about which I was most curious. Finally, we got onto the subject of fireflies.

I had never seen so many fireflies in one place. They lit up the night sky above the Himalayas like a glistening palace reflecting a fantastic beauty of serenity. In my childhood, I collected fireflies in a glass bottle and carefully held them like stars. But the fireflies in the Himalayas looked like mini angels, flying with small lanterns to warm us in the eternal dark night.

It was almost 9pm when the bus jolted into Shivalaya, the final destination on the highway to Everest Base Camp. From here, we had to walk. I saw the porter waiting for us loyally in the muddy puddles of the bus station. His name was Pasang, eighteen years old, and about the same height as me. The names of Nepalese are quite informative. Sherpa is both an ethnic group and a family name. Their names even reveal their days of birth. For instance, Dawa means Monday, Pasang Friday, Nyima Sunday. I was pleased to find out that the exploration company had dispatched a 'Friday' to me.

After following Pasang across a fifty-metre bridge suspended over the Khimti Khola, we came to the village where lamps flickered. The Sherpa lodge that Pasang had booked for us looked like an ancient castle and charged only a hundred rupees for each room. I suddenly felt Pasang to be a considerate young man. In Chinese classical fiction, lodges are often the scenes of murder or robbery on dark, windy nights. At the time, it was drizzling and chilly outside the lodge. Thinking that God had sent two shepherds to protect me, I wondered what other surprises were in store.

It seems that, during a journey, there are always things we can't smell if we wear perfume, paths we can't walk on if we wear high-heels, scenery we can't see when we lie in an attic and people we won't meet if we stay indoors. That may account for our desire to walk.

DAY TWO - SEVEN
———

LOW ALTITUDE: THE SKY TURNS
BLUE BECAUSE OF YOU

"As long as someone knows where to go, the whole world will give way to him!" Waking up in a damp Shivalaya and packing my luggage, I suddenly thought of the words of Michael Jordan.

This was the route taken by Sir Edmund Hillary when he scaled Mount Everest from Jiri and the traditional trekking route to the base camp. After France's Michel Paccard conquered the highest Alpine peak, Mont Blanc (4,810 metres), in 1786, the Europeans started looking towards the Himalayas, and mountaineering increased in popularity in Europe. Westerners have dreamed of conquering Everest since the 1920s, and the development of mountaineering also reflected the evolution of Alpine expeditions in Europe. But unlike in Europe, Himalayan expeditions involve greater difficulties, more effort and increased costs. Treks at unprecedented altitudes and involving a high degree of difficulty can last months.

In 1953, Edmund Hillary and Sherpa Tenzing Norgay became the first mountaineers to reach the summit of Mount Everest. Their achievement inspired many others. In addition to professional mountaineering teams, ordinary people began to challenge the limits of their endurance and achieve records of their own. In 1978, the Italian Reinhold Messner became the first mountaineer to climb Everest solo and without oxygen cylinders. In 1998, the American Tom Whittaker became the first amputee to successfully reach its summit. His right foot was amputated following a car accident in 1979. Also in 1998, Bear Grylls, despite having injured his back, became the youngest Briton to reach the peak and come down alive at the age of only twenty-three. In 2001, the American Erik Weihenmayer became the first blind person to climb the mountain. In 2010, the thirteen-year-old American Jordan Romero became the youngest mountaineer to reach the summit of Everest. In 2012, seventy-three-year-old Tamae Watanabe of Japan became the oldest female to do so.

The walking capacity of a person decides his world. Hillary said he gained power from the high mountains, and he constantly challenged his own limits, which encouraged many other people to become mountaineers.

When a sixty-three-year-old woman trekked more than 2,000 kilometres from New York to Miami, a journalist asked her whether the idea of trekking had ever scared her and what gave her the courage to go on travelling. "I do not need to be persuaded to trek," she answered. "It is something I do every day."

Travelling to remote places

Yes, sometimes you must take the first step and then have the possibility of continuing step by step. In fact, the trek from Jiri to Namche Bazaar was hard and humid, and it took about a week to complete. The route did not meander along a valley like in Annapurna but cut across valleys. Trekkers went down one side of a valley, crossed a river, then climbed up the other side, before going downhill and then up again. On reaching base camp, you would have climbed almost 9,000 metres in total, higher than the altitude of Mount Everest.

After Lukla Airport was repaired, most people wanted to avoid the Jiri route and instead tried to catch a flight to Lukla and from there trek at high altitude to the base camp. This meant fewer people setting out from Jiri. Some say that the scenery from Jiri to Lukla is not so beautiful, but I disagree. Although there are no majestic snow mountains on this section, the fast-flowing rivers, rolling valleys, plunging waterfalls, delicate streams, exotic flowers and rare plants, birds and animals are all beautiful.

About 150,000 Sherpas live in Nepal, accounting for just over half of one per cent of the total population. Their traditional habitat is in several narrow valleys at the foot of the eastern approaches to Mount Everest, that is, in the present Solu and Khumbu regions. 'Sherpas' means 'people living in the Orient' in Tibetan. They were originally a branch of the Qiang ethnic minority of Tangut five hundred years ago. The leader of the Qiang ethnic minority of Tangut founded the Western Xia dynasty about a thousand years ago. After the Mongols extinguished the Western Xia dynasty, a branch of the Qiang ethnic minority of Tangut moved south to Muya, Xikang. When Kublai Khan, the fifth emperor of the Yuan dynasty, marched south to conquer Dali, a city in Yunnan Province, China, the Sherpas fled from Muya and moved to Xigaze and went over the Himalayan mountain pass of Nangpa La. They finally settled in Solu and Khumbu regions at the foot of Mount Everest. They prospered there and gradually formed the Sherpa ethnic group now living in Nepal. They wear Tibetan robes, aprons and loincloths, believe in Bön and Tibetan Buddhism and remain similar to Tibetans living in Tibet in terms of language, religion, culture and customs.

The Sherpas refer to their homeland of Solu at an altitude of 2,600-3,200 metres as 'Sho Rung', meaning 'land of milk and honey'. The area from eastern Jiri to the Dudh Kosi River features a pleasant climate, flourishing trees, vast pastures, a continuous expanse of farms where corn, wheat, barley and apples are grown, and where the silvery, verdant land mingles with the blue sky. Sherpa settlements are believed by some to be safeguarded by the monks and nuns who are followers of Nyingma.

Today, Hindus can be found across Nepal except in the alpine region of the Himalayas. Water from the sacred river is used for bathing and cleaning during Brahman ceremonies. Maybe the alpine water is too cold, and that is perhaps why Brahman has not reached Solu and Khumbu regions. It may also explain the fact that the style of Gompas in these areas is still that of their Tibetan ancestors.

Wherever they live, the Sherpas build their houses at higher locations than those of other ethnic groups. There's a Gompa, at least one Mani stone wall or a giant prayer wheel in each major village. Tibetan Buddhists refer to their religious buildings as 'Gompas' rather than 'temples' because temple is a word used by Hindus. The Gompas are dark red with a golden steeple on top. A square 'Kaani' gate is built in some villages and pictures of the Buddhist master Padmasambhava are painted on the inner walls and ceiling. During the Mani Rimdu festival in autumn, red-capped monks perform various dances. In spring, the azaleas and lily magnolias in Solu bloom more beautifully and splendidly than in other parts of Nepal.

Most trekkers passing through Solu advance along the road opened up by previous expedition teams. The dream of following in their footsteps motivated me to get up early each morning. Egor, who had climbed all the major mountains in Europe, encouraged me: "Pearl, be unique, be yourself. It's our lifestyle."

Indeed, at the start of our journey, going to Mount Everest was not about us finding a specific mountain but finding numerous possible ways of existence. 'Remoteness' is an emotional, appealing word to me. Going to distant places is not necessarily about tourism, business travel or visiting relatives, but in going somewhere that is remote.

Female knight in Shivalaya

It was already humid in Shivalaya in the early morning. The leaves had a fresh lustre in the dew.

The rising sun lit up the verdant courtyard of the Sherpa lodge and the petals of the pink and purple great bougainvillea were scattered on the ground. This was the first day of our trek, and I felt entirely peaceful. Tanned and thin, Pasang was shy and his English was poor. He went ahead with my bag on his back and I followed him carrying my camera bag. I trekked in a group of three for the first time, like the Monkey King, Monk Sha and Pigsy in *Journey to the West*. Clever 'Friday' Pasang acted as an advance soldier, while I, the Pigsy-like 'Pearl Sister', walked at the rear and loyal, honest, bald Egor walked in the middle looking like a real imperial guard. I called our three-member team the 'Three Monks'. Monk Xuanzang of the Tang dynasty represented the mountains that we climb each day and gave us encouragement to move on.

Walking out of Shivalaya, we climbed up, went over Sangbadanda (2,150 metres) and Khasrubas (2,500 metres) and came to Deurali Mountain Pass (2,705 metres). The ascent of up to 1,000 metres made both Egor and me sweat. The pass was marked by several long stone walls and a bodhi tree where colourful prayer flags were hanging. It seemed that we had left the realm of Hinduism far behind us and were gradually entering the domain of Tibetan Buddhism in the mountain area. Climbing over the pass, we relished the walk downhill to Bhandar. It was after 1pm and I pleaded that we continue walking after lunch.

There was a Gompa where the third eye of the Buddha was painted along with many lodges. If we made a short detour, we could go to Thodung (3,090 metres) where there was a cheese-processing plant built with the help of Swiss people in the 1950s.

It is my habit to relax, have a smoke or daydream after a meal. Or, if I decided to call it a day early, I would wander around taking photos. It was sunny in the courtyard. All sorts of beautiful flowers were blooming on the wooden window sills of the houses. The climate was subtropical and the scenery on the way was similar to that of Mutuo in Tibet, which I had once visited. The gurgling stream, the ripe bananas growing next to the path and the fog coiling up gracefully in the distance aroused sweet memories.

But Egor wanted to shorten our journey, walk more in low-altitude areas and allow more time to adapt to the high-altitude area in Khumbu region. I knew he was experienced and that his suggestions were right. But I felt constrained by the practicalities of travelling in company. I intended to ask him to go on ahead and we would follow. But I knew my slow pace would mean that we would surely part and then we would go our separate ways. Maybe it would take me a really long time to get to the base camp like the journey taken by the Monkey King.

In order to preserve the newly-formed Three Monks, show that I was a team player and, more important, stay with my handsome drummer of a knight, I gritted my teeth and persevered. Standing up and handing over my camera bag to Pasang, I kept on with the help of my trekking pole.

Frustratingly, the path ahead dropped away steeply. As the sun set behind the slope, we came down to the Likhu Khola at an altitude of 1,490 metres. Crossing a suspension bridge over the river, we walked along the valley. It got dark and I stumbled twice, the path being wet and slippery.

Egor stopped and reached out his hand to me. I found he had been sweating profusely, having to carry a twelve-kilogram bag on his back. Looking as if he had emerged from a sauna, he appeared more ashen and miserable than me. After all, I had been trekking for two months and was not carrying a backpack. It was his first day of carrying a backpack and the weight would prove a stern test of his stamina. It was already 7.30pm when we reached the beautiful small village of Kinja (1,570 metres) along the river. Registering our passports and mountaineering permits at the village checkpoint, Pasang showed us to Buddha Lodge.

Kinja is a small but bustling material distribution centre. Goods are carried there from Shivalaya and then to smaller surrounding villages. Jars of pickled peppers were stacked at the lodge gate. They are an important winter food in mountain areas. I ordered two *dal bhats* for supper.

Kinja is the starting point to Mount Lamjura, the peak in Solu. To keep pace with my handsome friend, I risked my life in walking fifteen kilometres on the first day. Thinking of more demanding slopes that lay in wait the next day and the prospect of scaling the dark, foggy mountains right in front of us, I felt tears welling up.

Junbesi, the village guarded by snow mountains

Since we would be climbing over Lamjura at an altitude of 3,530 metres, the highest point between Jiri and Namche Bazaar, Pasang suggested we get up early and set out at 6am.

I made a large pot of lapsang souchong tea sweetened with a spoon of honey. Adding honey and a slice of lemon to black tea was one of Kangaroo's secret recipes when we were at high altitude in Jomsom. The tea helped us replenish the lost water, energy and vitamins from our bodies during the trek. It is said that when a British tea trader gave black Darjeeling tea to Queen Victoria, the queen was full of praise for its amber colour and its sweet, mellow Oriental flavours. She referred to it as 'Oriental Beauty Tea'. Egor was flattered when I poured some into his flask.

I asked whether he should take out his cumbersome Cat's Meow sleeping bag and ask Pasang to help him carry it. His backpack was doubtlessly a burden, but he resolutely shook his head. On the journey, Egor refused to ask the much shorter Pasang to carry anything for him. Maybe it was something to do with being an independent mountaineer. He was self-reliant and hardened, someone who liked to test himself. I didn't have the physique or stamina of a European. I was thirty centimetres shorter than Egor and depended on Pasang's help to climb the mountains and ridges. But on the way I found my stamina increasing.

The path uphill was extremely steep at first. We went past Sete, a deserted temple, at 2,575 metres. From there, the villages on the way were almost all inhabited by Sherpas. Each village has two names, one in Nepali and the other Sherpa. The Sete Temple is a stopping point halfway up a hill. Some pedlars had brought up a few items and laid them along the roadside.

The mountain path from there to Mount Lamjura was long but not steep. The scenery along the way was beautiful. Tall azalea trees appeared now and then, their thick roots twisted and exposed, their canopies shielding us from the sun. The natural steps formed by the exposed tree roots helped us retain our grip as we walked, and it felt somewhat romantic to step on them.

When passing Goyom (3,300 metres), we could see remote Dukunda at the gate of a lodge. It was a good spot to have lunch and certainly an unusual place to answer nature's call. The wind chilled my exposed bottom and I looked up and saw the snow mountain. When I was thinking things were going well, I suddenly felt a 'male' leech clinging to my left buttock and I started bleeding profusely. Despite my shyness, I had to ask Pasang for help, and he started rummaging for some iodine and ointment in my bag and smear it on for me.

Before I had finished shrieking, a beautiful 'female' leach jumped onto the muscular leg of Egor. Everyone was exposed to these tiny leeches as soon as they stopped to relieve themselves. They were simply everywhere. We quickly finished our fried noodles and continued our climb.

A pure white pagoda erected on Mount Lamjura glittered in the afternoon sunshine. Standing there and looking at the rolling clouds and looming snow mountains, I suddenly felt the beauty of the soul's journey.

The wind was blowing hard on Mount Lamjura and fog was starting to settle. There looked to be plenty of rain on the other side of the mountain. Like fairies going to market, we followed the fog, descended the mountain and came to Thaktobhug (2,860 metres). We passed through a woodland of fir and azalea bushes before arriving in a lush meadow. The junction line of forest and meadow was as clear and smooth as an oil painting by the American realist artist Andrew Wyeth. Stag beetles crawled on the thick, soft fallen leaves. I asked Egor to catch a stag beetle like Bear Grylls on the TV show *Remote Survival* to make a hearty meal. But instead he threw a stone to knock down several pine cones and he picked up a specimen bigger than a grenade and gave it to me as a gift.

What am I? A squirrel? A golden pheasant? A black bear? I believed he must have thought he was gifting me a rose. We weren't to know that a surprise was waiting for us around the corner of the mountain pass.

The surprise was Junbesi (2,675 metres), a village guarded by three mountains: Mount Dukunda, Mount Number and Mount Himal. Feeling exhausted after climbing for more than ten hours nonstop, it was particularly moving to see a dreamlike village appear at the bend of the mountain pass.

The indigo stone path, the blue and pink roofs, the ancient stone walls, the bright yellow or red wooden window sills, the rows of attractive tables and chairs on the broad balconies, and evening prayers drifting from the red walls of the Gompa. The scene reminded me of Aden Scenic Area in Daocheng County, China, and a fairyland of the resting soul.

None of us wanted to leave this land of comfort and ease. In the absence of other trekkers, Junbesi was quiet. We each had a helping of apple pie that was so hot it burned our lips and a mug of nectar-like cider to warm us in the chilly wind and the setting autumn sun.

It was apple harvest time. The Sherpas sang songs in the yard and mashed apples in buckets to make cider. They also cut apples into slices and aired them on a board to make dried apples. Egor tapped the table and, with no pack on his back, looked more agile than a lynx. Bathed in the cool evening wind and in the rhythm of the working Sherpas, he sung James Blunt's *You're Beautiful*: "My life is brilliant. My love is pure. I saw an angel..."

I had listened to this song many times, on the city metro and in desolate taverns in foreign lands. But only when I heard the silky chanting in this quiet village did I realise that the autumn in the high mountains could also be so colourful and lively. Each unremarkable house had its own secrets and gracefulness, and each chance encounter on the way would trigger moments of beauty and affection.

Stopping at night on the river bank at Kharikhola

Small flowers bloomed in the dew as we stepped into the forest enveloped by the morning mist. The tranquillity was enchanting. The low-altitude path from Junbesi would lead to Phaplu, with its hospital and airstrip. We climbed up along the forest path to Khurtang, situated on a mountain ridge at an altitude of 2,980 metres. The landscape opened up and Mount Everest came into view.

"Almost there!" said Egor. "We'll arrive in Namche Bazaar in two days."

As I looked at the distant Mount Everest, Egor was like a giant towering over me. Afterwards, we came to Salung (2,980 metres) and went down to the Ringmo Khola and then up to Ringmo (2,570 metres), where apples and other fruit grew. Ringmo is a small village of no more than two hundred residents, along with a Bön temple. The villagers had inserted an ox skull in the cabbage fields to act as a sort of scarecrow.

. . .

I asked whether Egor knew about the Bön religion. He opened wide his gannet-like, blue eyes, shook his head and said he could not distinguish Bön from Tibetan Buddhism. I asked him to walk with me around the temple in an anticlockwise direction to pray for good luck. The Sherpas here walk on the right side of the temple and revolve the prayer wheel anticlockwise, the opposite to Buddhists who walk on the left side of the temple and revolve the prayer wheel clockwise.

Bön is a primitive Tibetan religion whose adherents believe in animism and worship natural objects such as the sky, the Earth, the sun, the moon, stars, thunder, lightning, hail, mountains, rivers, grass, trees, birds, sheep and cattle. Its rituals include performing dances to God, sacrifice, divination, execration and exorcism. Hence it is also called 'Shamanism'.

After Buddhism was introduced to Tibet in the early seventh century, Bön, the traditional religion that was formerly dominant, gave way to Buddhism and kept a low profile to conserve its forces. The thirty-nine tribes of Huoercuo in Dengqen County represented the thirty-nine Mongolian tribes, most of whom believed in Bön. However, Bön in some remote areas of Nepal is different from traditional Bön in Tibet. The sorcerer would wear a black robe decorated with colourful strips and peacock feathers, play a sheepskin drum to accompany the dance praying for good weather for the crops and chant an incantation for hours on end to demonstrate his amazing memory and gift for story-telling.

Unlike the red temples of Nyingma in Tibetan Buddhism, the temples of Bön are mostly white. When we were about to reach Trakshindu La Pass (3,071 metres), we saw a group of tall pagodas covered with moss. There were piles of exquisite Mani stone carvings and mounds of sheep and cattle skulls that seemed to have been here for years. They were awe-inspiring, as if warning people, irrespective of time and location, that they should hold nature in respect. Trakshindu La Pass is the junction of the Solu and Khumbu regions, where the views are panoramic. Warm laughter of Bön disciples burst from the tea houses.

Our journey now entered a new environment. After going downhill past a temple and crossing a suspension bridge over the Taibu Khola, we moved ahead to have lunch in Nunthala Town (2,250 metres). I felt slightly dizzy due to my exposure to the sun, and my favourite golden lentil soup tasted bitter. I seemed to be suffering from an electrolyte imbalance.

. . .

Continuing to walk downhill from Nunthala at 2pm, we came to the famous Dudh Kosi (1,480 metres). The river is affectionately known by the Nepalese as the 'Milk River'. The melted glacier water, as soft as milk, had flowed from Everest Base Camp.

The condition of the path was quite poor and stones were piled up on the suspension bridge following a landslide. After we gingerly crossed the Dudh Kosi, we marched along the east bank of the river and climbed to Jubing (1,680 metres).

Jubing was the only place around here, apart from Sete Temple, that was not inhabited by Sherpas. The residents came from the Rai ethnic group. Sherpas had once driven away the early Rais when they went over the Himalayas and into Solukhumbu district and conflicts broke out. Nevertheless they now get on harmoniously.

The Rais usually live in thatched houses on the valley floor at an altitude of 1,000-2,000 metres. The girls each carried a harmonica made of bamboo over their left shoulder and wore necklaces made of red glass beads and Indian coins, walking and singing cheerfully; the men are famous for their straightforward, irascible nature. Therefore, the Rais can either be your best friend or your worst enemy. They are followers of Shamanism and believe that all things have souls. They often decorate their houses and bridges with marigolds and plant assorted flowers around their houses.

In Nepali, large rivers are called '*kosi*' and streams or tributaries '*khola*'. Constant erosion by rivers has formed deep, precipitous valleys. We headed for the Khumbu having crossed a succession of valleys and suspension bridges. We climbed mountain after mountain. When we arrived at the village of Kharikhola (2,070 metres) in the evening, I was a spent force. What could be more welcoming than a lodge?

Many stores and lodges line the main street of Kharikhola, selling all sorts of daily necessities. It is an important material distribution centre and there is a checkpoint too. In the evening sunlight, several young monks in a Gompa were washing themselves under a simple tap diverted from the stream. Egor also took delight in washing himself. His naked torso had turned bronze, his face sunburned and his beard was now unkempt. He was quite different from the handsome young man I had met in the Peace Garden Bar.

I joked that he looked like a sexy Robinson Crusoe. The villagers were watching him from a distance. I followed directions for a hot bath, which I was yearning for. The beautiful windows decorated with dahlias and plants were exceedingly attractive. But in the end I didn't dare take a bath for fear of catching a cold and getting altitude sickness the next day.

Kharikhola is nestled between the mountain and the river. Maoist slogans and hammer and sickle symbols could still be seen on mud walls. I asked Pasang to add the tinned pork with brown sauce I had brought to the wild fungus soup we ordered. How fresh, invigorating and piping hot it was! For the first time, Egor talked about his motherland with me. It was only then that I understood the moving, tragic and horrifying past of the Balkans.

I recalled that, in my childhood, I watched the famous Yugoslavian films *Walter Defends Sarajevo* and *Bridge*. The song *Bella Ciao* sung by guerrillas in *Bridge* stirred the Chinese people and became as popular as Wang Feng's *Life in Full Bloom*. The vast wilderness, the sense of freedom and the distinctive heroism fascinated us young children. The Yugoslavs, headed by the Croatian Josip Broz Tito, led the Yugoslav communists in their resistance against the Axis occupation forces.

Decades later, Yugoslavia broke up and six countries declared independence in 1990, including Croatia, Slovenia and Serbia. Wars erupted in Croatia and Bosnia and Herzegovina in the first half of the 1990s. Before war broke out, the young women in Zagreb fed pigeons in the Basilica di San Marco, relaxed in coffee shops on the west bank of the Sava River, shared delicious cheese and bread from Dorak Market packed with fresh fruit and vegetables, and bought perfume made from lavender extracted from locally grown flowers, while the men loved to listen to the same band in the same bar, and tourists travelled on the old-fashioned trams in Tomićeva Street to visit the old and new city. The Croats, Serbs and Muslims who previously lived a refined and dignified life, were now suddenly becoming sworn enemies.

Everything collapsed in an instant. A popular European summer resort and land of peace whose winter scenes were printed on Christmas cards was reduced to a battlefield, the scene of the largest conflict in Europe since World War II.

. . .

Egor said he was only ten when war broke out. With a history of more than nine hundred years, Zagreb, originally meaning 'trench' or 'ditch', was a city built on two adjacent hills. This ancient city with colourful roofs had become a real 'trench'. At the age of thirteen, he began to learn drumming from a videotape, was performing at school a year later and was forced to hide in the basement to practise most of the time.

Croatia had a population of 4.29 million. After the war, the country implemented compulsory military service. Once Egor graduated from Zagreb University, he received military training, served in the army and became a member of the Special Forces. He continued drumming after he left the army aged twenty-six. Having walked with Egor for four days, I got to know his quiet and melancholic personality, typical of Slavs. Who could imagine this cool man had begun his musical career amid gunfire?

Those of us who have lived in peace cannot appreciate the sadness and chaos of war, and nor could we imagine the interethnic struggles in the pure land of Nepal, the anti-government guerrilla wars launched by 'Nepalese Communists' in the mountains that lasted ten years up to 2006. There are three major 'guerrilla warfare leaders' in world history: Josip Broz Tito of the former Yugoslavia, Mao Zedong of China and Che Guevara of Cuba. The history and culture of Croatia cultivated the great explorer Marco Polo, the statesman Tito and the Prince of Piano, Maksim Mrvica. When Maksim played *Croatian Rhapsody* in London, it was like a beautiful flower blooming on the ruins devastated by war.

In Nepal, whether they remembered the war or not, the people undergoing hardship and suffering on this land were eager for peace. When I met Egor, the Himalayas were like a quiet tunnel going through time and space. It connected Egor from the Adriatic Sea and me from the ancient Orient. It made me reach out and join hands with Egor.

A chance encounter is like reuniting with an old friend after a long separation. Smiling, I said to Egor: "I listened to the songs of your country in my childhood. Tomorrow, let's start off by singing *Bella Ciao*, the song of the guerrillas: 'And if I die on that mountain, then you must bury me up there and let the flower mark my grave.'"

The first physical limit in Phakding

A person, a drum and an era; a mountain, a road and a different life. From this point, I called Egor my 'comrade-in-arms'. I would surely travel to

Everest Base Camp in the company of a commando and drummer like the character in Günter Grasse's *The Tin Drum*.

Kharikhola was a turning point in our journey to Everest Base Camp. Up to this point we had been trekking eastward, but now we headed north. We moved against the flow of the limpid Dudh Kosi and rushed to the embrace of the village of Lukla.

We, the Three Monks, continued on our difficult journey with bags on our backs. The mountain road up to Bupsa Village (2,300 metres) was rather steep, and we spent quite a long time getting to half way up the mountain where there were several lodges. Climbing gradually from Bupsa, we now overlooked the Dudh Kosi flowing along the valley floor. The Dudh Kosi originates in the Himalayas, which is covered in snow all year round. The water was extraordinarily clear, and the river looked like milk due to the rushing currents and the white riverbed.

We continued climbing to the Khari La Pass (2,840 metres). In Nepali, fortress, pass and col are all called 'la'. It seemed whenever we climbed a mountain we would feel exhausted but happy. Standing on the Khari La Pass, we overlooked Puiyan, another of the Dudh Kosi valleys. On our way down to the Puiyan Valley, some places were too narrow for us to negotiate and we risked falling down to the valley floor. Afterwards, we dragged ourselves to Paiya La Pass at 2,805 metres and down to Surkhet District at 2,290 metres. Near to Surkhet, there is a path leading to Lukla. Many dragonfly-like airplanes flew overhead and landed on another mountainside over there. It was Lukla Airport, known as 'the runway on the roof of the world'.

Egor said the altitude of this section of path was only 800 metres on the map but was actually more than 1,200 metres. The mountain paths in Khumbu were all cut along the sides of mountains, quite different from our usual experience of climbing up and over ridges. Pasang said we should go on the ridge of a small hill. It was typical of Himalayan paths. The mountain was so steep that climbers would be left exhausted if they took the most direct route to the summit.

Instead, I saw them use a technique called switchbacking, in which they snaked from side to side instead of going directly up or down. They looked like experienced astronauts, gracefully walking in outer space. In stark contrast, the paths under our feet were zigzagging and would make me dizzy. Maybe the first Chinese character that Sherpas learned from their Tibetan ancestors was '之'. I walked as if I were scuttling like a crab, scurrying and staggering here and there, losing my breath as my chest burned the higher I climbed.

Sherpas refer to their homeland of Solu as 'Sho Rung'

In the afternoon, we continued our ascent after drinking some black tea. Passing through Mushe and Chaurikharka, we came to Cheplung Village (2,660) and met with a number of trekkers from Lukla who were climbing to the sacred Namche Bazaar.

The road leading to Namche Bazaar rose along the steep Duhakus Valley. The path winded through gorgeous firs, needle junipers, azaleas, oaks and white birches. Potatoes, barley, spinach, radishes and onions were planted on the long, narrow steps. Bustling villages were dotted amid golden fields. Birds chirped in the forest. All these presented a picture that was quite different to the bleak, barren scenery on the Tibetan side of Mount Everest above an altitude of 4,000 metres, covering an area of nearly a hundred square kilometres. The southern and northern sides of the mountain look like two different worlds. Sitting on a simple roadside bench made of stones in Cheplung, I waited for Pasang to register at the checkpoint, rummaged for two fist-sized apples, cut them into eight pieces with a Swiss Army knife and shared them with Egor and Pasang.

Those who had just got out of a plane from Lukla all looked cheerful and excited. Despite my tanned face, I appeared scruffy and exhausted, and I felt my spirits had sapped. Sitting on the stones, I said I couldn't go any further and wanted to return to Lukla and from there fly back to Kathmandu. This petrified my two 'guards'.

The clanging mules and horses were constantly delivering goods to Namche Bazaar and some were panting on the path nearby; a group of male porters aged fourteen or fifteen also walked by the stone terrace I was sitting on. The bags on their shoulders were too heavy for their thin frames, and they gritted their teeth with exertion as they rose to leave. A thirteen-year-old lad was wearing an orange T-shirt featuring the English word 'Quick'. We sat next to one another, taking a breather. The pack basket beside him was stuffed with all sorts of supplies transported by air from Lukla.

Unlike their counterparts in the Annapurna Peaks, the porters here carried bigger and heavier baskets. Two long sticks were bound on the pack baskets, a wide one on top and a narrow one underneath. Like small ladders, the sticks were bound with cases of items to carry, ranging from canned drinks, Pringles crisps and instant noodles, to toilet paper and kerosene tanks. The porters charge about two dollars a day for their services.

This lad wore a small piece of turquoise around his neck. On top of the stick hung his D&G baseball cap. I thought it might have been a gift from a trekker. He hadn't even brought any drinking water, and I cut up an apple and gave him two small slices. Having thanked me and stood up to leave, he placed the stick on his shoulder and used all his strength to pull himself upright. The items in the pack basket were stacked up to twice the height of the basket.

The young porters carry equipment for the mountaineering and camping teams. The stronger they are, the more they are able to carry and the more they earn. The porters hired by trekkers near the airport are little more than child labourers. The poor children are forced to grow up early. We trekked for enjoyment, and any hardships would last for only a few days; by contrast, they walked to make a living.

I thought it was human nature to crave a life of comfort. People would always prefer to take a bus, a car or plane, rather than risk their life walking with great exertion, let alone in an area at an altitude of 3,000 metres. At that time, I must have reached my physiological limit, my head was aching and I was suffering from a lack of oxygen, while the airplane flying overhead tested my resolve. Looking at the smile on Pasang's sweating face, I felt my cramped tendons were now restored and my idea to return to Kathmandu was scotched.

Egor comforted me by saying that he had heard there was a bar with live music in Namche Bazaar and he would play the drums especially for me. I followed him and hit the road again with tears in my eyes.

As it got dark, we reached the lively village of Phakding (2,800 metres). It is situated on flat ground close to a mountain slope, and when we arrived the wind was piercingly cold. More than thirty lodges were clustered there. White prayer flags hung on the long Mani stone walls. 'Please turn this wheel to purify your soul' was written in English besides the Mani stone wheel engraved with a six-word mantra. Sherpas believe that each walker can purify his soul by rotating a Mani stone wheel, and they should rotate the prayer wheel on millions of occasions during their lifetime to improve themselves. I reached out my sweaty hands, lightly spun the prayer wheel as if to soothe my fatigue, and felt an inner contentment.

Egor chose to stay in a primitive lodge near the Dudh Kosi. Melted snow water gurgled underfoot and wind blew in all directions. How cold it was! Observant and diligent Pasang helped me order coffee and lamb chops. He said my strength would recover after I ate sheep bone soup. A clump of Hylotelephium spectabile, medicinal herbs with pink-violet, umbrella-like petals that promote blood flow, bloomed delightfully in the courtyard. But he didn't know that his Sister Pearl was too exhausted to move on.

Fascinating Namche Bazaar

The morning sky was azure, the air was clear and hoar-frost glistened on the oval azalea leaves. Egor knocked on my door, cheerfully humming Nirvana's *Smells Like Teen Spirit*: "Load up on guns and bring your friends / it's fun to lose and to pretend." He was looking fresh and happy, maybe because we were due to arrive in Namche Bazaar later that day.

Yesterday, he coaxed me into walking seventeen kilometres and I felt I was going mad and even vomited. I resolutely pledged to proceed at my own pace.

Khumbu region, which suddenly came into view, was stunning. Trekkers slowed their pace to appreciate its beauty. There were white birches, Formosan juniper, flourishing Ghent azaleas, babbling streams, thundering waterfalls, a charming stone-strewn wilderness and mountains standing tall on the horizon, all of them familiar to me from my geography textbooks at school.

From Phakding, we walked across a long, pendulous bridge and clambered alongside the river to Benkar Township (2,700 metres), where the water cascading down a horsetail waterfall splashed in all directions and made it dangerous for trekkers to pass. We went across a floating bridge over the Dudh Kosi not far from Benkar, returned to the east bank, continued climbing to Chumoa Village and finally reached Monjo Village (2,880 metres) at noon when the sun was at its most dazzling.

The thrilling, graceful suspension bridges over the Himalayan rivers were built mostly with the assistance of foreign countries. For example, Shivalaya Rope Bridge was funded by the British, while Phakding Suspension Bridge was built with Swiss money. Throughout the journey, we felt we were on some kind of pilgrimage. It was more a stream of people than a path. It was a gathering place for trekkers and tourists from all over the world, from China, South Korea, Japan, Germany, Britain and the US. It felt like being in a mountainous version of the United Nations.

I met large numbers of Japanese and South Koreans who walked in groups with great strength and vigour. The Japanese travelled mostly in 'sunset glow' package tour groups for middle-aged and senior citizens. Wherever they went, they walked in the same order, at the same pace and close together, presenting a formidable sight. The South Korean trekkers were chiefly teenagers. It was really impressive to see them to travel so far to take part in a 'winter camp' at such a high altitude. Some Europeans asked their porters to carry their children aged three or four in bamboo baskets. What daring parents!

Other teams were professionally equipped, with yaks carrying complete sets of camping equipment. Some were total amateurs who simply wore sportswear and trainers. Different teams adopted different ways to relax. A guide was sitting on a roadside stone bench and romantically playing the long Nepalese flute. Sherpa porters streamed past, their heavy baskets tied to colourful woollen headbands wrapped tightly around their foreheads. We even saw porters carry a Haier washing machine and a full-sized mattress on their heads. They were luxury articles for a new home. I could not help tremble with fear and feel acute concern for the porters.

However, what pleasure it must be for the man you love being willing to carry the dowry over the Himalayas.

There were many good places to stay in Monjo. The village was the entrance to Sagarmatha National Park, and visitors were required to show their Trekkers' Information Management System card and entrance ticket. The entrance ticket for Mount Everest cost 3,000 rupees. According to information on the ticket, the money went towards protecting wild animals and removing litter. I thought it was inhuman to evade such fares.

The entire Khumbu region belonged to Sagarmatha National Park (also called the Everest National Park). It was established jointly with the assistance of the Himalayan Trust founded by the New Zealand government and Sir Edmund Hillary. To the north it bordered the Qomolangma Nature Reserve in Tibet. In 1979, Khumbu was nominated as a World Natural Heritage region, in recognition of the fact that the 150-kilometre-long trekking route with an altitude range of 2,800 metres to 5,400 metres is one of the most exciting and challenging high-altitude trekking routes in the world.

There was an army post at each stop on the way, comprising a basic wooden room, or perhaps a simple hut or a rain shelter made up of several bamboo poles. I rejoiced whenever I saw a brown-faced young soldier pop his head out of the window. For one thing, it meant I was getting closer to Everest Base Camp, and for another I could use the opportunity to have a rest, drink some tea and chat with the young men garrisoning in the mountains. They told incredible stories about red pandas, snow leopards, musk deer and impeyan pheasants that they had encountered on their patrols. The people who hunted, killed and traded these rare wild animals faced prison sentences of more than fifteen years and fines of more than 100,000 rupees. The Himalayas, this mountainous region covered with rocks and snow, are their last stronghold.

Each army post existed not only to check that trekkers had the right paperwork, but also to register their names, passport details and time of entering and leaving the mountain to help in any rescue efforts should trekkers become lost or get into difficulty. One such missing person was Tomas, whose details were printed on a poster. He was a trekker from Slovenia, and his photo showed him carrying a large backpack. Only twenty-five years old, he'd been missing in Dingboche Village for six months. The bulletin said anyone finding him would be entitled to a reward of 50,000 rupees. However, nobody had found him so far.

There were also shops, snooker halls and bars in the villages on the way. Nepalese and Tibetan songs, along with numbers by the Rolling Stones, U2 and Nirvana, lingered in the narrow lanes. There was also the Reggae Bar where a portrait of Bob Marley was hung on the wall, along with a sign saying 'The first and oldest bar in Phakding'. This bustling, noisy bazaar contrasted with the serenity and solitude of low-altitude Solu.

Egor said: "It's sad that you know nothing about Nirvana however much other rock'n'roll you listen to."

After six days' trekking, we finally arrive at Sagarmatha National Park

Many people go to Mount Everest to seek the mysterious indulgence of fleeing this noisy world, accompanied by the music of Nirvana. The band used to play to a lot of empty venues in the early years. Like Mount Everest, Nirvana, now known far and wide, not only represented glory, height and paradise but also a quiet, peaceful world without pain or desire.

After we went downhill from Monjo and crossed the Dudh Kosi, I slowly climbed to Jorsale Village (2,810 metres), walked across a high floating bridge, returned to the east bank of the river and trekked up a long slope that climbed 600 metres. There was accommodation available, and the temptation to stop was almost unbearable.

The air had thinned significantly after climbing more than 3,000 metres. We had reached an altitude that might cause acute mountain sickness for the first time. Yellow 'Slow down' warning signs could be seen at the roadsides now and then. Some trekkers were in danger of collapsing if they walked too fast. At least three trekkers die of acute mountain sickness in Khumbu region each year. Each step I took felt as heavy as lead. I walked at the back of our group and had to stop for breath every ten minutes or so. Many trekkers were heading for Namche Bazaar, and I was afraid they would take up all the accommodation by the time we got there. So I asked Egor to advance at his own tempo to help us book a quiet room. Pasang kept me company at a slower pace.

The fading evening sunlight looked magnificent and graceful. Although the snow mountain was in sight, it was actually still very remote. Mountains rolled upon mountains, endlessly. Thinking of scaling so many mountains, I felt the aches and pains well up.

When you pant heavily and want to climb no more but only hope to raise your head and look at the stars, you find that you have already been in Namche Bazaar. The light of the half-moon shone untruthfully in the starry night. More than a hundred houses were scattered on the rocky slope, linked by a labyrinth of footpaths. Songs and laughter came from numerous lodges. The brightest light I had seen during our six-day walk was up ahead.

I heard a loud call from a stone path: "Pearl!"

Egor was calling me! I saw his athletic figure.

The lodge was the most charming harbour in the night. What could be more welcoming than the sight of a comrade-in-arms and a warm fireplace!

Lives in bloom at the Hillary School

Gorgeous white snow smoke spiralled up into the blue sky in Namche Bazaar. Pushing the window open, I could see three glistening mountains.

Namche Bazaar, at an altitude of 3,480 metres, is a small, lively town, where the Dudh Kosi from the east and the Bhote Kosi from the west form a 'V-shaped' confluence. Namche Bazaar is seated at the foot of St. Ama Dablam (6,856 metres), containing more than a hundred households. Houses with white cliffs for walls were clustered against the horseshoe-shaped hillside. Sitting in the 'U-shaped' valley facing west, I could see Khumbila (5,761 metres) in the north, Thamserku (6,608 metres) in the east and Kongde Ri (6,187 metres) in the west. This was the economic hub of Khumbu region where Mount Everest is located, a large bazaar at the

Guide post to the Hillary School

world's highest altitude and the main base for climbing Everest.

The paths paved with all sorts of stone connected various shops, including supermarkets, banks, internet bars, a post office, police station, restaurants, bakeries, lodges with hot showers, swimming pools and bars. Rock bands, massage services and ATMs were all available, and GSM was accessible. The rivers supplied abundant hydroelectric power resources for Namche Bazaar and the surrounding villages for lighting, cooking and heating, and for running the shops and bars. Trekkers regard it as their own base camp, somewhere far removed from their mundane lives. It was like a Pandora's Box full of happiness, sadness, friendship, disaster and love, with infinite hope and ambition hidden at the bottom of the box. Looking out of the window at the city glistening at the foot of a mountain, I thought of the illusions and dreamland in *The City of Sky* by Miyazaki Hayao. But the beauty of Namche Bazaar actually existed before me!

Namche Bazaar is special in the eyes of Sherpas. It was originally just a village. Later, a bustling bazaar was held each Saturday, presenting a scene as spectacular as a Himalayan blockbuster. Known by the locals as Haat Bajaar, it is a market that has a special Nepal-Tibet flavour.

Solu and Khumbu trade with Tibet only in two seasons. The first is in May and June, when the ice and snow melt, the road to Nangpa La is open to vehicles and the unpredictable rainy season has yet to begin; the other season is during October and November when the weather is clear and dry, and Nangpa La has not yet been blocked off by ice and snow. During these two periods, the Sherpas export to Tibet materials such as grain, natural dye made from madder, purified butter, dried potatoes, raw sugar, fragrant coarse paper, buffalo hide and cotton cloth. Meanwhile it imports from Tibet materials including salt, wool, tea, tobacco, sheepskin, animal hair, dried meat, woollen fabrics, rugs, clothes, hats, boots, silk, silver ornaments, porcelain cups, woodcut books and all sorts of religious articles.

Yaks, known as ships of the Tibetan plateau, are the main means of transportation for Nepal-Tibet trade. Sherpas also use them to carry goods between villages and the summer pasture, and deliver mountaineering supplies and gear to the campsites. The service life of a yak is about eighteen to twenty years. It is easy to slip a rein on them and it only takes a couple of people to lead up to a dozen yaks through Nangpa La.

As a matter of fact, the Sherpas in Khumbu region monopolise cargo transportation from Gabra, the first border village, to Tingri County. On traditional trade routes where yaks have transported goods for more than five hundred years, only Sherpas who have great stamina and live above an altitude of 3,000 metres can carry loads along the endless glacier paths and pass through Nangpa La at a height of up to 5,500 metres. Even the Rais living on the hillsides cannot undertake such work. Thanks to the trade with Tibet, Sherpas are able to buy valuable jewellery, clothes, all kinds of household appliances and religious articles from Tibet. They travel in Tibet and keep frequent contact with China in terms of the arts and culture.

Early on Saturday morning, the Sherpas, Rais, Tibetans from Tingri County, porters and yak caravans swarm to Namche Bazaar from nearby villages. After trading is over, they flock to the local tea houses and highland barley wine bars to exchange gossip.

The Sherpas in Namche Bazaar usually live in two- or three-storey houses that can be used as residences or rooms for hire. The houses are built close together in wood and stone. Wooden pillars are used for the framework, stones are used to construct the walls, and the gaps between the stones are filled with a resin mixed with silt and cow dung, and the coarse stone walls are then whitewashed with lime. The carpenters are highly skilled. They do not use nails to construct buildings but instead use tenons to connect the wooden frame. The house fronts have three windows, each the shape of panda's eye. In the past, parchment covered the panes to withstand wind and cold. Now, with glass panes installed, the sunlight floods in.

The interior of Sherpa houses are very similar. A long row of cushions are placed by the window next to the wall in the sitting room, and next to them is a table featuring the Eight Auspicious Buddhist Symbols, and on which stands a pot of hot buttered tea and a butter lamp. The head of the family sits nearest to the fireplace while the guests sit leisurely on the cushions drinking tea or they relax in the sun. Most houses have prayer rooms for worshiping the Buddha, with colourful religious scroll paintings, known as Thang-gas, hung on the walls. Even the most frugal family will pay a handsome commission for a Thang-ga.

Tourists like to spend a while in Namche Bazaar in order to adapt to the environment because subsequent climbs would take them to an altitude in excess of 4,000-5,000 metres. Those afflicted with acute mountain sickness often think of themselves as among the most adaptable and healthy. Their problem lies in failing to adjust properly, doing too much and finally falling ill or even dying. Most trekkers spend their time drinking tea and basking in the sun in the sitting room with large glazed windows, climbing glacial drifts up to a hundred metres high for acclimatisation training and looking at the Mani stones and saffron Gompa that quietly protect the glaciers in Khumbu.

Egor was a sergeant, like Hermes, son of Zeus, with wings strapped to his sandals. His courage grew as we progressed. Like a soldier among trekkers, he asked me to pay a visit to the Hillary School in Khumjung Village and take a rest in Namche Bazaar in the afternoon. But I felt I was falling apart and only wanted to sleep in my soft Arc'teryx sleeping bag, have a good rest and sleep in the dark.

In the morning, after drinking my first bowl of buttered tea in Alpine Lodge, my spirits recovered. I could walk and climb, the swelling on my face had gone down and my acute mountain sickness disappeared. I asked Pasang to take a day off to visit his friends and relatives in his village. Egor headed north to Khumjung past the village of Zarok and alongside the Mani walls covered with fern and moss.

About two hours later, we saw a village where the hues and styles of the houses were similar, all set in a green land of idyllic beauty. Yaks were fighting on the hillside and children were shouting to try to part them. There was a small piece of open land around a two-storey, white-and-green building. The verdant roof seemed especially quiet and peaceful under the blue sky and white clouds. My instincts told me it was the Hillary School.

Sir Edmund Hillary had climbed Mount Everest nine times and had a deep affinity with Nepalese culture and its people. Despite all the adulation he received, he did not neglect the social problems of this small, poor country. It had few trained doctors and very little medicine, and the children lacked education and did not know how to plan their futures.

Namche Bazaar is the world's highest bazaar and the main base for climbing Everest

Sir Edmund set up the Himalayan Trust in 1960, returned to Nepal a year later and built his first school, comprising just three rooms. The school is located in Khumjung at an altitude of 3,780 metres. The funds he raised also went on constructing a hospital in neighbouring Khunde Village. In 1972, he built a small airport in Lukla with the purpose of transporting all kinds of materials and equipment to help build more schools and clinics in Khumbu.

Thanks to this airport, mountaineering teams and trekkers today can fly from Kathmandu to Lukla in around thirty minutes and walk to the base camp at an altitude of 5,300 metres a week later. But Nepal, Hillary's blessed land, gave him the greatest pain of his lifetime. In 1975, his wife Louise and his little daughter Belinda went to visit him at a time when he was helping Sherpas build the hospital. Their plane crashed and they both died. The Sherpas built a monument in Khumjung in honour of Louise and Belinda. Hillary could barely bring himself to look directly at it. On many evenings, tears rolled down his cheeks as he strolled on the hill in Khumjung in front of the Himalayas.

Hillary became depressed. But he knew that the best way to commemorate his wife and daughter was to live in Nepal and repay the help and kindness shown to him by the Sherpas. He dedicated the rest of his life to the Himalayas. In the fifty-five years after Hillary scaled Mount Everest, he built twenty-seven schools, two hospitals and thirteen clinics in Nepal, and teachers and doctors from New Zealand, Canada, the United States and Holland worked as faithful volunteers in this mountainous region. Hillary died in 2008, leaving behind the familiar rivers and ancient, serene mountains that had made his soul as deep as Mount Everest. The Sherpas built a monument for him out of their respect and gratitude to his family. Three holy white towers will forever nestle up to each other at the foot of the snow mountain.

Today, 350 students receive primary and secondary education in Hillary School. They can do their homework and learn Nepali, Sherpa and English at the long wooden desks in the playground in summer and plant saplings on the mountains in spring. When Hillary came to Khumjung for the first time in 1951, there were luxuriantly green trees everywhere, towering old trees and azaleas that grew at an altitude of 4,000-5,000 metres. Numerous caves were carved into the mountains for meditation and spiritual cultivation.

However, with the increase in tourism, Mount Everest was starting to resemble a rubbish tip. Hillary realised the destruction of the environment was caused by unrestricted mountain climbing. He began to spend more time on environmental protection and reforestation activities. He planted many saplings with local children and made Khumjung and Khunde twin green villages. Hillary dreamed that he could return the forest in Khumjung to how it had appeared to him so movingly fifty years previously.

When we climbed from the school to the top of a mountain at 4,100 metres in Khumjung, we saw in the distance three white towers glittering in the midday sunlight and at their base clusters of wild chrysanthemums and Mani stones. I thought of the saying: 'We should use the mental suffering we experience to live a fuller life.' During the journey of our lives, our bodies and minds are not there merely to remember suffering but more often to change and witness, that is to say, to change ourselves, our estrangement, our passiveness, and to witness growth and change, and usher in a vigorous life, an indomitable spirit and happiness.

. . .

Hand in hand with Egor at the foot of the snow mountain, I wished I could become one of the borderless volunteers in the Himalayas giving lessons to students and playing with them. White snow covers the area in winter and melts in spring, and streams flow into the blue sea. The sky above the Himalayas is always azure, possibly because of you and me.

DAY EIGHT - FIFTEEN

HIGH ALTITUDE: HIS LOVE IS FOR YOU

ONCE YOU SET OUT, you get close to the sky.

In Nepali, Mount Sagarmatha has many meanings, including 'Sky goddess', 'From the sea to the sky', 'Mountains towering to the forbidden kingdom' and 'The top of the world'. Once you arrive in Namche Bazaar, you will traverse a quiet land from the villages and mountain paths of blooming flowers to the top of the world covered with ice and snow at an altitude above 4,000 metres.

The majestic snow mountains on the trekking route to Everest Base Camp were the result of the crushing power generated during the collision of geologic structures that formed the Himalayas. As a result, eight of the ten highest mountains in the world came into being. These colossal mountains extended eastwards from Mount Dhaulagiri in the west and formed the natural boundary between Nepal and its neighbouring countries. Mount Sagarmatha (Mount Everest) and Mount Cho Oyu border China's Tibet, and the summits of Mount Kanchenjunga are shared by Nepal and the Indian state of Sikkim. A growing number of mountaineering teams have successfully climbed these awe-inspiring mountains above 8,000 metres. Climbing at this altitude tests the limits of human endurance.

Between the first attempt to climb Mount Everest in 1921 and the first successful ascent in 1953, the world witnessed two world wars, a steady rise in the mountain's height and ever greater publicity. Serving as a measurement of the achievements of humanity and those individuals who conquer adversity, the mountains in Nepal have become the ultimate sports ground of elite mountaineers.

Foreigners are unable to trek or climb these mountains without the help of Sherpas. When Nepal began to develop tourism, 'Sherpa' became synonymous with mountaineering and trekking. The Sherpas have always been famous for their cooperation, absolute sincerity and their rejection of cliques. By helping others climb mountains, they provide an important economic activity and a valuable source of income. It is a mystery to many foreigners how Sherpas are able to live in these high, imposing mountains.

Sherpas living at an altitude above 3,000 metres have adapted physiologically to the rigid cold at high altitudes. Due to the rarefied air, their vital capacity is astonishingly large, their blood pressure is quite low and their haemoglobin levels are higher than normal, which ensures sufficient blood supply to the brain. Metabolic adaptations allow their tissues to use oxygen more efficiently, while their physical flexibility and powerful muscles are well suited for climbing. The Sherpas also have extraordinary legs and feet. When I was resting on a cushion, I looked at Pasang's feet stretched out. His soles were wide, short and solid, quite different from our delicate, bony soles. This meant he could keep on walking quickly and stably, taking long strides. I thought it must have been his years spent in the mountains that made his legs and feet like that.

When a Sherpa climbs mountains, his legs are able to stretch flexibly. Like spiders crawling on a web, they will not be tripped up or injured by the loose stones that cover the mountains. Their lower legs and thighs become arc-shaped due to the stretching of their muscles since childhood.

Financially, it is the best option for the robust, poor and adventurous Sherpa youth to serve as guides and porters of mountaineering teams and trekkers. Traditionally, owning yaks is a source of prestige among Sherpas and a mark of their social status. Many Sherpas risk walking at high altitudes in order to save money to buy yaks in future. Pushing themselves forward in society, many dream of owning more yaks. Some better-off Sherpas feel it beneath their dignity to work the fields with sickles and hoes. They will feel especially satisfied so long as they can watch over their herds grazing on the pasture and wander between white clouds and meadows. This is it the most dignified job for men.

Pasang told me that he hoped to have enough cash to buy his first yak after the current peak season of trekking was over. He intended to cross the national boundary, go over the 5,500-metre Nangpa La and come to Tingri County in Tibet. He wanted to buy a Tibetan yak, which was without doubt the most valuable coming-of-age ceremony for an eighteen-year-old Sherpa boy.

Mountaineering is dangerous. When disaster occurs, the Sherpas will bravely charge forward to fight the challenge. When foreign explorers wait in their tents for next climb towards the peak, the Sherpas are busy carrying equipment to and fro. They are constantly exposed to danger, and many of them die in snow slides, crevices and falls. Some experienced travellers fear that tourism might destroy the Sherpas' way of life and extinguish the pure, unique and wild elements there. Today, you can see Sherpas wearing business suits, listening to rock'n'roll, surfing the internet, playing on their mobile phones, sending text messages and making friends on Facebook. But those trekkers who have walked with them all know that their natural instincts and intrinsic qualities are no different to their ancestors who so deeply impressed Western mountaineers.

A Frenchman called Fisher who would lead a group to Island Peak, also known as Imja Tse, today said smilingly: "Sherpas are brave, happy, straightforward and self-confident. They still retain their ardour and hospitality. They always wear a broad smile, laugh at everyone's jokes and sweep away your mountaineering pains. But they are susceptible to excessive drinking."

I imagined the braveness and heroic spirit of Sherpas drinking raksi and listening to the snow slide and ice crack nearby!

Being beloved by God

Having had breakfast and morning tea in Alpine Lodge, Egor, Pasang and I decided our route for the coming days along the high-altitude paths.

There are three trekking routes in Khumbu. There are villages along each of the eastern, northern and western routes that offer spectacular views: Chhukung (4,730 metres) on the eastern route, with Mount Chhukung Ri (5,546 metres) at the zenith, and Mount Lhotse (8,516 metres), the world's fourth highest peak, above you and Mount Makalu (8,463 metres), the world's fifth highest peak, within reach; Gorak Shep Village (5,160 metres) is on the northern route, near Mount Kala Pattar (5,545 metres), and which gives the best views of Mount Everest (8,848 metres) and Mount Nuptse (7,861 metres), leading to Everest Base Camp (5,340 metres); Gokyo Village (4,750 metres) is on the western route, on the side of Mount Gokyo Ri (5,360 metres), and is the best place to view the world's sixth highest peak, Mount Cho Oyu (8,201 metres).

The three routes are closely linked and have a total length of 130 kilometres. Nevertheless, most trekkers choose the northern route because it is the quickest way to get to Everest Base Camp, or go over Cho La Pass (5,420 metres) from the northern route after trekking to Everest Base Camp, switch to the western route and continue from east to west more easily.

Egor and I both decided to walk from the western route to the eastern route. I smilingly said we would be travelling in an anticlockwise direction like Bön disciples. This route also meant avoiding the swarming throngs climbing to Everest Base Camp and gave us a chance to quietly enjoy the changing scenery of the awe-inspiring snow mountains. I had once agreed with the notion that men are from Mars and women from Venus, that men and women are like two hedgehogs from two different planets that are drawn close to each other because of their different ways of thinking but can also get hurt for the same reason. I didn't expect that Egor and I, who had met each other on the way to Mount Everest, would have such tacit understanding.

I said alpine trekking for 130 kilometres sounded a horrible idea and I might give up halfway or collapse to the ground, dead. Egor said with a smile: "Pearl, you must at least try so as to discover whether you are beloved by God. You can make it with your faith."

Maybe that's why we choose to climb mountains. To seek a secret treasure slumbering at the bottom of one's heart and to release the secret power of a wild animal lying in the depth of one's body. When Hillary stood at the peak of the world, he said what we conquer is not mountains but ourselves. Only through willpower can we pursue our goals and make improvements.

After spinning the prayer wheels in Namche Gompa at 7am, Egor and I set out amid the undulant chants of scriptures and walked into the beautiful, passionate snow smoke, the realm of gods beyond the human world.

Yak's secrets revealed by Pasang at Dole

As usual, Egor carried his fifty-litre, silver-grey Mammut backpack, with his trekking poles and water bag hanging outside. He hadn't shaved for a week, and he looked like a weather-beaten, middle-aged man. The mountains had aged him by more than ten years. He said he would shave and assume a new look after finishing the journey and returning to Kathmandu. I looked at him as if he were an ascetic monk, a Baba, walking from morning till night. Luckily, there was no need for him to kiss anyone on our journey. He liked to eat *dal bhat* with water, and then kiss the stones and the prayer flags with his dirty, messy beard. During these days, Pasang had become more outgoing and I sensed I knew the reason.

After we climbed the slope behind the house and turned right to the Mani stones engraved with scriptures, we left the alpine-like resort town in just a few minutes. The view before us was quite different to what we had experienced over the previous seven days. Snow-capped Mount Everest and

Mount Lhotse came into sight, and the '山-shaped' Mount Ama Dablam (6,856 metres) standing in front of the mountain path looked even more imposing and majestic than Mount Everest. The Sherpas venerate Mount Ama Dablam as their god of the mountains. It means 'mother's necklace' in Nepali, and it marks the entrance to Mount Everest.

The doctor in the Himalayan Rescue Association said that, at an altitude above 3,500 metres, it's best to keep ascending at a rate of 500 metres a day. So we decided to spend our first night at a campsite in Dole (4,090 metres).

The noisy village of Sanasa (3,600 metres) is at the junction of the eastern and western routes. Sherpa women had laid out on the ground hand-knitted woollen scarves and socks, and woollen hats with two long plaits, with a piece of paper reading: '100% yak wool'. I stopped at the stall of a rosy-cheeked girl and spent 400 rupees on a military green scarf for Egor. The scarf could be wound twice around his neck, keeping out the wind and making him look experienced and full of courage. I bought a plaited hat woven with pink and grey yarn, with a picture of Mount Everest embroidered on it and the words: 'Everest Base Camp 5,340 metres'. This was my destination and I dreamed of finally arriving there.

Some trekkers bought practical woollen mountain products just to help out the Sherpa women and enable them to buy their children some school supplies. The frostbitten girl saw me buy two items, grinned to reveal a missing tooth and smiled brilliantly. I held her up, and was surprised to find that I could actually do so at an altitude of 3,600 metres. I felt the exercise over the previous seven days had made me powerful and I was no longer a home-bound, effeminate woman.

We had separated from most of the people starting off in the early morning, followed the glistening light of the Dudh Kosi and slowly climbed to Mong La (3,975 metres), the first col of Khumbila (5,761 metres).

There were three tea houses in the tiny settlement of Mong La, where golden eagles hovered on the barren massif and a cold wind blew strongly. The village was the birthplace of the fifth reincarnated lama of Rongbuk Monastery in Tibet, called Sange Dorje. It is said that he flew over the Himalayas with supernatural power and introduced Tibetan Buddhism to Khumbu in the sixteenth century.

We went down to Phortse Thenga Village (3,680 metres) near the Dudh Kosi. There were several red-roofed lodges by the river. We ate fried noodles, refilled our bottles with hot water and continued to climb along the valley to Tongba (3,950 metres).

We crossed bridges, climbed slopes and walked on a meandering path through a forest of azaleas and white birches. Smooth birch bark was strewn on the path. Shrubs covered the valley and the splash of a waterfall could be heard nearby. Pasang said musk deer often appeared there. The children of Khumjung Village School had used lime powder to paint a deep green musk deer on a big mossy stone, with the words: 'Save the musk deer'.

Timid and alert, musk deer, also known as white-belly musk and Himalayan musk, live independently. They have lovely spots on their fur, a pair of large, straight ears, a short tail and big, sabre-shaped teeth, though no antlers. Like the deer painted by the children, they look like adorable babies from another planet. Pasang said softly that, during the day, musk deer sit quietly in dark, secluded places under a bush or on rocks, while before dawn or after nightfall they come out to seek the twigs and leaves on pine trees, the lichen and moss on cliffs or on their favourite firs.

The musk gland of stags, situated between their abdomen and genitals, gives off a strong but pleasant smell. It is irresistible to female musk deer and perfumers alike. Musk is also precious in traditional Chinese medicine. It seems to be a commodity like gold or silver that can always be traded for cash, and it has become one of the most expensive animal products in the world.

We walked softly out of the forest for fear of disturbing the treasures protected by the Himalayas. We also saw Himalayan Tahrs at low altitudes. With their long, golden brown hair they gazed at the distant, narrow mountain ridges. The mountains on both sides were the last areas to be moistened by warm, wet air.

Egor was wearing his cobalt blue windcheater as usual, but I was in the habit of changing my clothing according to the altitude and weather; I was scared of getting cold because of my sweat-soaked underwear. In this sense, I admired Egor's physique and stamina. He had been walking at a constant speed like a soldier marching to a drumbeat, neither too quickly nor too slowly, neither accelerating nor slowing down, and keeping a calm temperament, neither too happy nor too sad. It seemed that his body could adjust to heat and altitude differences, just like Pasang, a Sherpa, and he could move, stay still and survive like the fittest musk deer. A signpost indicated that it would take seven hours to get to Gokyo from Namche Bazaar. But that was based on the speed of professional mountaineers. If you got carried away by the scenery and walked too fast, acute mountain sickness could drive you back home ahead of schedule.

Yaks can climb to an altitude of up to 6,000 metres

At 3pm, we safely arrived in Dole, set off in a dense forest. Dole is divided by two clear streams, one of which is the source of the Phule Khola. There were six lodges. Most teams preferred Yeti Lodge in the north but we chose to stay in the more secluded Namaste Lodge on the southern side. It was the earliest we had reached our destination in seven days of trekking. Two snow mountains above 5,700 metres, Khumbila and Taboche, loomed over the village to the south and north respectively. A herd of yaks were grazing and taking a rest there. The hair surrounding their eyes was black and shaped like a beautiful water drop.

Pasang said yaks could climb to an altitude above 6,000 metres. Their udders are extraordinarily strong and their windpipes are thick and short, similar to that of dogs. This means they can adapt to quick breathing necessary in the mountains and ice fields at high altitudes, where the air pressure and oxygen levels are low.

I knew Pasang's secret wish was to own a herd of yaks that could graze on the high mountains, transport materials over the ice floes and snow fields, then have children and grandchildren and become head of a Sherpa family of some prestige and social status. I held a glass of hot yak milk and shouted "Yak!" to a 'tall, rich and handsome' yak with long hair like black satin, only for two suckling baby yaks to glare at me disdainfully because I had disturbed their 'afternoon tea' and 'dessert'.

To my great joy, I wasn't suffering from the dreaded acute mountain sickness, probably because I had a short and thick trachea like the yaks. That night, I slept deeply with the sound of melted snow water gurgling all around.

Lost in the arms of Gokyo

In the icy wind at 7am, we left Dole in high spirits. The scenery along the way began to change drastically, and we came to the alpine pasture of the Sherpas.

The Sherpas live in two types of residence: fixed residences in the village proper and summer residences that amounted to sheds. The village proper, inhabited throughout the year, is where the main houses are built and where most family property and all valuables are stored. It is also the gathering place to celebrate religious festivals. The sheds are mostly located in small clusters on alpine pastures above the treeline. They are small and shabbily furnished, chiefly used when the yaks are grazing in summer. When the mountains are closed with ice and snow, the Sherpas lead their flocks and herds back to the village proper.

Pasang reminded me that the small villages above Dole were all dotted with summer houses often inhabited by only a few households and also accommodating trekkers. We filled our flasks with tea when we started off in case we were unable to refill them with hot water along the way.

We climbed along a steep, barren hill, with a few sparse shrubs dotted on a belt of frozen earth. We were all alone in the pristine high mountains and cold alpine desert, apart from some enormous, yet placid brown-black yaks. The yaks primarily feed on psychrophytes such as Formosan juniper with purple and red berries, feather grass, sedge and nutgrass flatsedge. The yaks are used for almost everything. The Sherpas drink yak milk, eat yak meat, burn yak dung, wear yak hair clothes and live in tents made of yak skin. They also make good guides, like old horses. They can avert pitfalls and choose the right path, hence their reputation as 'ships of the plateau'. They also often serve as guides for trekkers.

In Machhermo Village (4,330 metres), where we decided to take a rest, we saw five pine log cabins built by Sherpas and a rescue post of the International Porter Protection Group situated within a stone wall. The mini rescue post provides emergency treatment for trekkers and porters afflicted with acute mountain sickness. Pasang told us the legend of a yeti killing three yaks and a Sherpa shepherdess in 1974. He asked me to open my eyes wide because the snow monster liked to appear in dim light.

The legendary Himalayan yeti is the most fascinating of all the world's mysterious creatures. Strong evidence exists. In 1951, Eric Shipton shot a photo of a yeti on the Menlung Glacier; in 1986, Reinhold Messner, the first person to conquer the world's fourteen highest mountains, claimed to have seen a yeti in Tibet. He said it was as powerful as a Tibetan brown bear and he wrote a book entitled *The Six Mountains Travel Books*. For Sherpas, the name 'yeti' means monster living on rocks. They firmly believe in yetis, which stirred my imagination of the elusive snow monster.

After climbing for more than two hours, we came to Pangka Village (4,390 metres) and Mount Cho Oyu (8,201 metres), the world's sixth highest peak, came into view for the first time. Mount Cho Oyu, situated thirty-two kilometres west of Everest, is known as the 'Turquoise Goddess'. In 1954, Austria's Herbert Tichy was the first person to climb the mountain without supplementary oxygen, albeit with the help of six Sherpas. The achievement thrilled him. He said he experienced complete harmony, an unearthly joy he hadn't known before, and regarded the loss of several fingers to frostbite as a price worth paying. Cho Oyu is also known as 'Peak of Joy'. Graceful as a peacock spreading its feathers, it has attracted many mountaineers to climb its summit and admire its gorgeous folds.

Tiny Pangka is nestled at the end of the rolling Ngozumpa Glacier which flows from the north of Mount Cho Oyu for a distance of twenty kilometres, making it the longest continental glacier in the Himalayas. When a trekking team took shelter from the wind in Pangka in 1995, a sudden snow slide killed all the team members. We panted as we walked for more than three hours along the right side of the Ngozumpa Glacier and came to Gokyo (4,750 metres) on the icy lakeside at sunset. I was exhausted and found it hard to breathe. Falling onto my small bed in Cho Oyu View Lodge, I didn't have the slightest desire to move.

Seven lodges in Gokyo were perched against the Ngozumpa Glacier

Seven seasonal lodges in Gokyo were perched against the Ngozumpa Glacier and faced the crystal snow mountains and azure lakes, offering the most scenic board and lodging. As someone who lives in an oppressively hot valley at low-altitude, being transported to this chilly, remote glacier, I could feel the realm of my mind being purified the higher we climbed.

People who live in complex conditions have different lifestyles. The owners of our lodge were considerate to both trekkers and yaks. The shaggy 'giants' walked along a narrow stone path by the river to return home at dusk. The male and female owners repeated the same melody, ground yak dung into powder, kneaded it into dung paste shaped like walnut cakes, and stuck the paste onto the walls of the log cabin for airing. It served as cooking and heating fuel for trekkers. When winter came, yaks carrying bags of dung paste would be driven to the village proper where it serves as a superb natural fertiliser for the growing of tomatoes and highland barley.

A French couple we met in the lodge had stayed one day in Gokyo. They invited us to join them in climbing Gokyo Ri to take photos of the sunrise. In reality, since Everest Base Camp has become overcrowded, commercialised and short of accommodation, veteran trekkers and photographers prefer to trek and take photos on the west route of Gokyo Ri at the bend of Mount Everest.

The west route is characterised by numerous lakes. Gokyo became a Ramsar site in 2003, meaning it had gained recognition as a wetland of international importance. I initially thought the deep lake water was salty. Without realising it, I had come to the world's highest freshwater lake system. Gokyo is seated next to Dudh Pokhari, the third of five lakes in the vicinity of Gokyo. Alpine ice lakes sitting between icy snow mountains under a blue sky appeared almost too beautiful for this planet.

As the sun set on the southern slope of the Himalayas, Dudh Pokhari glittered a bizarre blue, a soft mist rose slowly, ice blocks in the lake started to fade from view, cloud and mist filled the Ngozumpa Glacier, then rose and dispersed between water and sky, quietly taking care of the village like an elf or a prince, and the white snow glinted on the mountains. There were no footprints on this pristine land and everything had the warm, original appearance as described in Genesis.

Egor said he was in pursuit of Shangri-La, where, together with the girl he loved, he would go herding some day, listen to the sound of the lake water lapping the shore, make love in the quiet night, give birth to children and bathe in the moonlight. He said the scenery there was different from any mountain he had climbed in Europe. It was barren, remote, primitive, uninhabited and unadorned, like the Garden of Eden. I sat silently beside him, looked at the glacier in the distance and imagined spring when flowers bloom and ice and snow melt, and pictured myself carving a statue of the Buddha in the decorative design of pineapples and disseminating prayer flags in the wind on a strip of land between hills...

It was an overwhelmingly beautiful image of the mortal world. However, as long as you love and embrace the secluded land, you'll forget time, and your thoughts will turn to non-earthly things.

Thrilling travel across the Ngozumpa Glacier

There is no transcendence or resplendence without imagination and instinct.

We tied our hoods and kneepads at 5am to march towards the top of Gokyo Ri (5,360 metres) at dawn, where we could see a sight we had been looking forward to for ten days: the sunrise over the four world-class snow mountains.

Starting off in a northerly direction from Gokyo, we had to climb 610 metres on loose stones to reach the peak. Walking into an icy wind, we mingled with other foreign trekkers and wormed our way step by step towards the bald, black summit.

Although I had been trekking for more than two months in Nepal, this was the first time I had climbed a mountain at such a high altitude. The thin air at daybreak made it difficult to breathe and I had to stop every dozen steps, inching up like a frozen snake and taking small steps of no more than ten centimetres.

Maybe due to the lack of oxygen, I seemed to be floating in zero gravity, my brain empty and my innermost being quite clear. I beamed with joy and sensed an indescribable wonder, with the shadows of my pet dog Xiaoban, my mother and my husband floating before my eyes. I thought it was the realm of samadhi to sit quietly, meditate and enter nirvana. Long-forgotten, sweet memories surged into my mind one after another in the wind.

When I was about to reach the peak after a ninety-minute climb, the sky had turned red by the sunlight. The formerly gloomy mountains glittered brightly, and the rose-coloured clouds started to rise slowly. Awestruck by a view beyond imagination, I stopped to lean against a stone near the French lovers. Most of the trekkers were watching quietly. It seemed that time had ceased to exist and had extended from an unending past to a boundless future.

The view of Mount Everest from Gokyo Ri is even better than that at Everest Base Camp. The four mountains over eight thousand metres – Mount Makalu (8,463 metres), Mount Lhotse (8,516 metres), Everest (8,848 metres) and Mount Cho Oyu (8,201 metres) – stood majestically. The Ngozumpa Glacier, like a glittering and translucent tear, reclined between two imposing snow mountains. Dudh Pokhari Lake stretched before us like a shimmering magic mirror reflecting the two snow mountains in the distance, Pharilapche (6,017 metres) and Taboche (5,700 metres). It was like the most realistic and fabulous movie in the sky. I seemed to both hear and smell the snow. I felt my body was as light as a feather.

It was a wonderful scene and experience that even the finest camera could not capture. Just as the Prince song goes: "Nothing compares to you." Only when you stand there in person can you understand that everything in the universe is full of spirit and the great beauty of nature is beyond description.

Walking into an icy wind, we worm our way towards the bald, black summit

Pasang was so thoughtful that he continued to carry my camera bag after we had watched the sunrise. Egor was unencumbered with bags and advanced lithely and swiftly like Nezha, a deity in Chinese mythology. His figure was as robust as the soul of a mountain. Following behind him, I couldn't help wondering why he had previously insisted on carrying a heavy bag. The soul will feel lithe and pleasant only when the body is unburdened.

Adult Hindu men will take a holy bath in the Sacred Lake or Sacred River

We melted into the warming sunlight and would arrive at base camp on Mount Cho Oyu if we pressed on seven kilometres north from Gokyo and then past the fourth and fifth lakes for more than three hours. When it is full moon each August, each adult male Dvija of the Hindu social system celebrates Janai Purnima. They will take a holy bath in the Sacred Lake or Sacred River and exchange holy red threads around their necks or wrists. Hindus living on low-lying land will trudge for days in groups to pilgrimage in Gokyo's five sacred lakes. It is the habitat of Nag Devata, god of the snakes, and a place of shelter for rare birds such as ruddy shelduck, grouse and common pochards. Devotees blow graceful ox horns and bathe in the freezing snow water.

Since the base camp on Mount Cho Oyu was only open to mountaineering teams, most trekkers returned from Gokyo and we got ready to set off again to traverse the four-kilometre-wide Ngozumpa Glacier and switched from the western route to the middle route.

We walked down from Gokyo and came to the second lake, Taboche Tsho (4,710 metres), about an hour later. A large flock of rare ruddy shelducks gather at the side of the lake all year round. After walking on a dirt track, we began to experience the most exciting moment of trekking – going over a pristine snowfield.

Ice and snow cover the Ngozumpa Glacier all year round. The path on the glacier changes with the seasons and the moving snow and melted ice. The yak pack trains cannot get through in some seasons and trekkers run the risk of falling. The only signs on this dangerous path are the stone tombs and footprints left by previous walkers.

The French lovers parted from us there. The girl was starting to get acute mountain sickness and they decided to take the former route to Pangka (4,390 metres), go across two alpine pastures near Nha (4,400 metres), trek down along the Dudh Kosi to Phortse (3,810 metres) and from there turn to Pangboche (3,860 metres) on the middle route. It was a comparatively low-altitude route and was therefore less stressful on the body. But we had to detour for two more days. It is important to trust your companions while trekking. An accidental slip, a loose rock, a selfish action or a failure to understand a situation might have severe consequences. Without Egor backing me up and giving me strength and confidence, I couldn't have chosen the more dangerous shortcut.

Traversing the Ngozumpa snowline like insects together with Egor and Pasang

Writing the code of love in the snow

No more than ten trekkers crossed the snowfield each day and the temperature had dropped to below zero. The ice layer creaked when we stepped on it, and the white snow groaned gently. We took great care, moving step by step, like tiny bugs crawling inside the glacier.

I asked Egor whether he'd ever watched *Ice Age*. I told him that we were walking on the same glacier that covered the Earth more than 20,000 years ago and that we were risking our lives. Jokingly referring the characters in *Ice Age*, Egor said: "You're the quick-tongued sloth Sid and I'm the moody woolly mammoth Manfred. But I trek together with you willingly."

As we advanced, we found a trekker had slipped no more than ten metres away from us, which frightened me rigid. The cold weather made our limbs numb and our bodies stiff and inflexible. But the ice was quick and slippery, and the ice caverns hidden beneath were treacherous. Any careless slip might lead to a fall into the frozen caverns.

The guide of that small team managed to pull him out with a climbing rope. It was scary, but he was not injured. Noticing us standing nearby, they asked us to go first. Egor warned me repeatedly: "Pearl, hold me tight!"

I held him firmly as if holding the hand of God. I hadn't had the opportunity to ask what Egor had done when he served as a commando. A scene from *Ice Age* flashed into my mind. I first watched the film while I was at school but the sentiment now resonated with my feelings on the ice. "I don't want us to be together because we have to. I want us to be together because we want to." I had just started to learn English and didn't understand what the three weird animal heroes were saying. My English teacher encouraged me to listen to the dialogue repeatedly because it was particularly challenging. I remembered that Egor and I had bumped into each other twice on the same day and the coincidence made us fail to notice the name of the coffee bar, 'Ever'. In coming up with that name, maybe the bar owner wanted his coffee to remind customers of their 'past lives'.

People meet and then fall in love with each other. Love can arise at unexpected times and it can be both a happy and tragic journey. It is aesthetics, imagination and resonance between two lovers. True love is not the preserve of lovers but also exists between siblings, between friends and between man and animals. For instance, *Frozen*, a Disney animation, overturns the convention of 'true love' between males and females. The little yeti Olaf is distraught at seeing the princess Anna lying on the floor so it lights the fire so that Anna will not freeze to death. Anna tells Olaf to get away from the fire but Olaf disregards the warning. The yeti begins to melt but still manages to groan: "Some people are worth melting for."

The difference between sex and true love is that sex can be like flowers that bloom with vigour and vitality but then fade with relative ease, whereas true love is like a cup of hot coffee that people want to hold for a long time.

If you haven't walked across a glacier at an altitude of 4,700 metres, you cannot imagine how dangerous it is. After trekking for about an hour, we were relieved to see two adventurers from the middle route. Their presence showed that the snow route was safe and unimpeded.

Cold and hungry, we spent three hours crossing the Ngozumpa Glacier. My tears fell when I caught sight of Tagnag (4,700 metres), the first village beside the glacier.

There were only three lodges and a few beds in Tagnag. It was desolate and imbued with a sense of beautiful loneliness. A vast meadow stretched away from the bank of an ice river, the mountain slope was covered in a carpet of grass and the snow water nourished the withered grass for the flocks and herds, similar to scenes in the film *Dances With Wolves*.

We stayed in the Tashi Friendship Lodge. After checking in, I ordered three bowls of lentil soup. We each held a bowl of the hot soup to warm our frozen hands. The lodge owner gave us several small pieces of cheese, which Sherpas eat to replenish energy. The cheese can keep for a long time and the Sherpas often take several pieces with them on their journeys. Egor and Pasang exerted great strength to chew the cheese. Egor said that Croatia boasts more than fifty different kinds of cheese, and the country is also famous for its barbecues, Dalmatian smoked ham, goat's cheese and salty cheesecake. When he talked about food in this way, I started to feel dizzy due to low blood sugar, and I almost started to drool.

Trekkers believe that the depletion of energy reserves through inadequate food consumption is more dangerous than acute mountain sickness. In dire hunger, all they can eat is *dal bhat*, lentil soup, pickles and beans; fresh vegetables, fruit, meat and fish are all unattainable luxuries.

That night we three stayed in a dorm room. Even though I was in a down-filled sleeping bag, I still felt cold. The temperature at midnight dropped below minus 8 degrees Celsius and I was wakened by the cold. Perhaps I had consumed too much fat during sleep, a good way to lose weight!

The ox dung burning in the fireplace created a lot of smoke and made it difficult to breathe. Ox dung can barely burn efficiently in ideal conditions, let alone in a small room with depleted oxygen at an altitude of 4,700 metres. Egor poked his head out of his sleeping bag, changed beds with me and suggested I sleep near the window so that I could be closer to the fresh air near the door. The wind whimpering in the wilderness reminded me of Lieutenant Dunbar in *Dances With Wolves* who is stationed alone in a remote border sentry post, seeks a new lifestyle and rides a horse to the campsite of native Americans in the west. Dunbar is isolated and lonely and he befriends wolves and other animals, observes them and sometimes dances with them.

The prolonged loneliness gives Dunbar plenty of time to write a diary. It is the magnificence of the wilderness and a native American woman called Stands With A Fist that attract him most.

I had trouble breathing and could not fall asleep. Becoming lost in wild, fanciful thoughts, I suddenly felt that Sherpas were the only indigenous people in this world who lived a peaceful, monotonous and aloof life in the remote Himalayas. I, together with Egor who behaved like a sergeant safeguarding a border town, trudged there during a long, tiring journey. But all we heard was the echo of the valley and our beating hearts. Our souls became increasingly lonely. What we desired might be the serene paradise granted by the borderless wilderness.

Crossing Cho La Pass to Lobuche

When we woke up in the morning, the attractive 'frost flowers' pasted on the window sills and the towels hanging on ropes were frozen into ice slices and the boots that we had taken off before we went to sleep were now stiff and made a clanging sound when you gave them a tap. The lodge owner asked Pasang to add more honey to our black tea before preparing three additional pieces of Tibetan bread for us to eat on the way.

Today we would go over one of the world's highest mountain passes for trekking, standing at 5,420 metres. The Sherpas call it 'Cho La Pass', meaning 'flying fairy'. There are no human settlements on the desolate, six-kilometre-long path.

Leaving Tagnag, we entered a huge valley that looked like it was the scene of an explosion, with dark stones piled up randomly here and there. It was exceedingly difficult to make out any paths. We might have become lost and died in this labyrinth without our veteran guide and porter Pasang leading the way or the help provided by the Mani stones.

In addition to its high altitude, the mountain is extremely rugged and difficult to negotiate. Pasang struggled ahead with a bag on his back. Porters are also human and are not immune to acute mountain sickness and fatigue, being burdened with heavy loads at extremely high altitudes. The broad valley was totally silent save for our occasional panting and slow footsteps. The sounds made by the growling ice river, grunting yaks and the rusting of poplar leaves in the wind were all consumed by the vast space.

When we removed our backpacks, sat down on a boulder and looked back down the valley, Egor took out his iPhone and shot a video. It was the first time that I heard him speak Croatian. He was whispering something and panting with excitement. I couldn't understand what he was saying. He turned round and recited a sentence from *The Bible*: "You are a marvellous and powerful creature."

Walking on the road, Egor introduced to me his motherland: God discovered that he had forgotten the Croatians when he allocated land and had no alternative but to give them the land that he had originally left for himself. Egor said the country's natural resources, history and culture were all gifts from God. They enjoyed an exceptional landscape of mountains, rivers and seas and also gratefully regarded them as the gifts of God. Looking at this man lying beside me, who combined the ebullience of East Europeans with the delicateness of South Europeans, I admired him because of his high praise for me. I soon forgot about my physical pain and difficulty in breathing and was fascinated by the beautiful scenery.

Actually, the valley, with mushroom-shaped clouds overhead, looked extraordinarily beautiful, albeit somewhat post-apocalyptic like those NASA photographs that appeared to show lizard-like creatures on Mars. Back in 2012, the now-defunct Mars One project based in the Netherlands aimed to establish a permanent human colony on the planet. It is believed that the technology does not exist for volunteers to return to Earth from Mars, so all those volunteers heading for Mars had all bought a one-way ticket. I was afraid we wouldn't get out of this valley that seemed to be scarred by nuclear explosion. I forced a smile and asked Egor what he had done as a commando, saving people or killing them? Providing disaster relief, countering terrorism or fighting?

Egor smiled and rubbed his frozen nose, replying with honesty that he only took part in extreme training, such as rock climbing, diving, hand-to-hand combat, practising Wing Chun martial arts, performing emergency rescue, testing stamina and resolve when on the verge of collapse, and keeping calm in the face of punishing tests. I said we didn't need to move to Mars at a distance of four hundred light seconds and instead we could stroll in the valley like a pair of lovely 'pre-historic animals'.

After we left the post-nuclear valley, we came to a long slope that rose 400 metres to the dazzling Cho La Pass. Although an altitude difference of 400 metres might not appear much to climb, I found it the most depressing and frustrating experience, and there was no going back. I regretted not following the French lovers who took the low-altitude route but instead went on the high-altitude route with Egor who was not even my lover. What gave me this misplaced confidence? I was captivated by the mountains and this man as tall as a mountain! It was a risky decision.

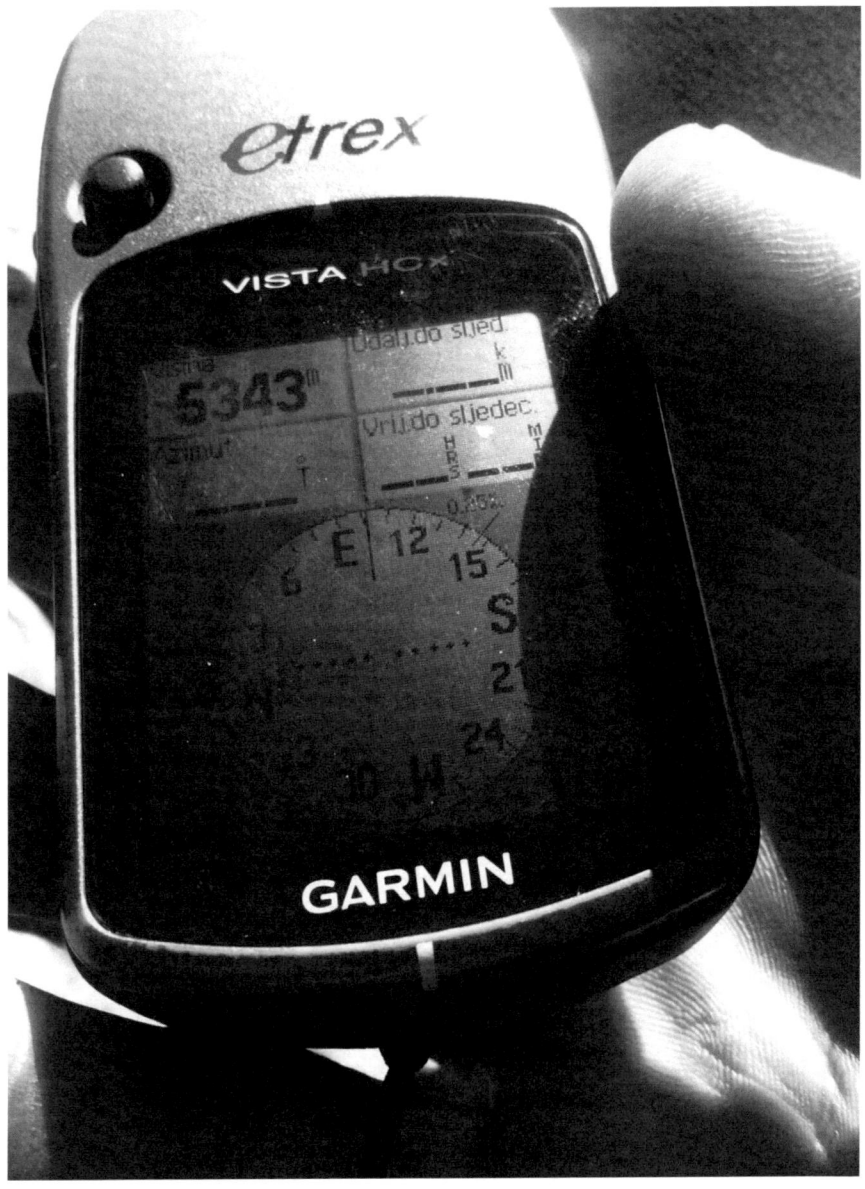

A string of figures plot our journey on the barometric altimeter: 5,343 metres

The mountain pass was covered with snow all year round at an altitude of 5,343 to 5,420 metres. My head seemed to burst, my heartbeat raced, my body was out of control, and I slipped and struggled with each step. Pasang took the heavy trekking pole from my hand in an attempt to alleviate my burden. Egor used his hands and feet to pull and push me, saying: "Pearl, grit your teeth and keep your eyes looking forward." His power could be felt in the air and in the ground beneath our feet. We had no alternative. We could not retreat. There were mountains and gullies everywhere we turned. There was only one thing that gave us energy and supported us during this physical torture. That was willpower.

At the top of the slope in the rigid wind was the 'Fair Lady' with prayer flags fluttering in the air, namely, Cho La Pass. We had set off at 7am and reached the top after climbing for three-and-a-half hours. There was a crowd of people taking photos on the blade-like mountain top and I, like an octopus plucked from the sea, was feeling feeble all over. Sitting on a nearby boulder, I couldn't help crying out of joy. 'Superman' Egor was feeling rather more deflated. His bag like an iron block followed him all the way, and there was no one to help him out. Sitting weakly beside me, he lovingly patted my blue, swollen cheeks. I saw a string of figures that plotted our journey on his barometric altimeter: 5,343 metres, 5,400 metres and 5,420 metres! My God! What kind of power have you endowed us with? We consecrate everything we have to you!

From Cho La Pass, we looked into the distance at Mount Cholatse (6,443 metres) and Mount Ama Dablam (6,856 metres) in the southeast and the Gokyo Glacier, Mount Pharilapche (6,017 metres) and Mount Kyajo Ri (6,186 metres) in the west. They presented a wild and magnificent scene that compelled admiration. Human beings were so small in comparison, but so tough and tenacious all the same. Climbing to the peak was not about conquering but transcending our inherent cowardice and breaking through the potential in the depth of our bodies.

There was a long snow slope to negotiate when we went downhill from Cho La Pass, which would seriously stress my knees. Egor helped support me. I didn't know what magical stuff was in his backpack besides his GPS and sleeping bag. The crampons he took out helped prevent me from slipping and saved energy. Actually, when he set out from the Adriatic Sea, he brought mountaineering kit with him in his determination to finish all the trekking routes to Everest Base Camp. If he had not met me, he might have hurled himself into a new challenge at a height much greater than that of Mont Blanc, Europe's highest mountain at 4,810 metres.

We trekked for more than two hours and came to Dzonglha Village

(4,830 metres) at the foot of Cho La Pass. Going uphill and downhill on both sides of the pass was tiring. There were only two lodges in Dzonglha with a small number of rooms, all in poor condition. Just like those in Tagnag, they were also halfway lodges from the middle route to western route. We ordered three cups of strong milky tea and had a simple meal comprising Tibetan bread and the Sichuan pickles I had brought with me. We decided to trek another two hours and more to Lobuche Village (4,930 metres), reputed as a mountain resort. It used to serve as a summer hut for Sherpa shepherds and is now a commercial campsite on the way to Everest Base Camp. With comparatively better conditions than in Dzonglha, more trekkers stopped there.

On the mountain path afterwards, I began to get symptoms of acute mountain sickness. Extreme tiredness and a lack of oxygen made me feel like I was walking on clouds. I could see vapour when I breathed. The temperature was below zero and I couldn't tell whether I was human or some kind of celestial being.

Lovely Lobuche was near Lobuche Glacier where there were eight or nine large wooden lodges. Trekkers from all countries gathered there, along with herds of yak. Compressed yak dung covered the ground, bamboo baskets containing various items were scattered here and there, and the whole environment was cold and in a state of disorder. Pasang took us to a cosy eco lodge at the top of the village. While all the other lodges were built of wood, this one was a traditional Sherpa structure made of stone. A Tibetan carpet was laid out in the room and ox dung was burning in the sitting room fire pit. Lifting my head, I could see two blade-sharp snow mountains, Mount Nuptse (7,861 metres) and Mount Lhotse (8,516 metres), glitter through the window. I suddenly realised that the logo of our North Face down coats looked like the white Mount Nuptse before our eyes. The company's two founders were trekking fans. Mount Everest, like the Queen of Heaven, stood majestically between these two mountains without any trace of conspicuousness.

Most trekkers walking the middle route rest for a day in Lobuche. Some excitedly walked along the Khumbu Glacier in the east to adapt to the altitude, while one emotional fellow had hung a red banner on the message wall beside the fire pit. The white Chinese characters read: "Girl, I love you!" It moved the women on their way to Everest Base Camp.

Native Americans are often named to reflect the scene where they were born. For instance, wise men are named 'Kick a Bird', tribal chiefs 'Big Bear', the women 'Black Shawl', the children 'Many Smiles', macho men 'Hair in the Wind', widows 'Stand With a Fist' and wolves 'Two White Socks'. Each name has its own special meaning. I asked whether Pasang understood the words on the banner. He nodded his head and smiled. He had passed through puberty. He crossed the snow mountains on the Sino-Nepal border together with the strong adult men in his village. He certainly knew the meaning of the most common adult words in both Tibetan and Chinese.

We drank Everest Beer and *chhaang*, the alcoholic drink made by Sherpas. Pasang secretly told me that if a Sherpa man fell in love with a girl, he would ask the matchmaker to take a bottle of *chhaang* to the girl's house. If the girl's family did not approve of the match, they would refuse to accept it. If they agreed, they would drink the *chhaang* together. I asked Pasang whether he had sent any rice beer in this manner. He replied shyly that he would invite a matchmaker to send *chhaang* after this trek.

I burst into laughter and applauded the romantic custom. Although Himalayan Rescue Association doctors warn trekkers not to drink at high altitudes, I gladly ordered a small cup of *chhaang* for each of the two knights. After all, we three had climbed over the snow line and the ice mountains.

All the crevices, glacier tongues and granite on the snow mountain had accumulated with the passage of time. It allowed others to avoid taking the more difficult route via the isolated Gokyo Lake. They thought it too troublesome to find their way across that Mars-like, post-nuclear valley. So few people visited the area and discovered its beauty. Meanwhile, the bright sun penetrated our wild souls and the most beautiful part of my heart was lit.

Time loses meaning in Gorak Shep

It can difficult to sleep well at an altitude of 5,000 metres. When we started off at 7am, I felt top-heavy, as if I were walking on cotton, and stumbled along like a toddler learning to walk. Today, we would sprint to Everest Base Camp.

It is not far from Lobuche to Gorak Shep (5,160 metres), about six kilometres north. But it is an undulating and difficult route along the narrow ravine between Khumbu Glacier and the mountain cliffs. Pasang told me a well-known Sherpa proverb: "No trees above four thousand metres and no grass above five thousand metres." The ground was devoid of vegetation, bare rocks and dry, sandy soil were everywhere, and it was slippery and rough underfoot, which increased the difficulty of trekking at high altitude. The lack of vegetation also reduced the oxygen content in the air, which exacerbated trekking conditions.

We snaked along for half an hour, turned left and paid a visit to the 'Italian pyramid' several minutes later. The research station built in 1990 by the eminent Italian mountaineer Agostino Da Polenza and geologist Ardito Desio was initially used to measure the precise height of Mount Everest and K2. Agostino had climbed the world's second highest peak, Mount Chogori (K2), for the first time in 1954. Now the station primarily serves to carry out research on Mount Everest environmental protection, atmospheric change, mountaineering technology and the influence of altitude on human bodies. The scientists live at the 8000 Inn near the pyramid, where the guarding Tibetan dogs bark at passers-by. The research station is open to trekkers during the day, but don't count on any eccentric scientist to be your guide.

The attractive glass pyramid like an artefact from outer space stands erects in the thin air and made me think it might be the launch pad for the Ark on which mankind could escape to outer space when Armageddon comes or the place where the heroine of *Gravity* pilots the spaceship out of the Earth's atmosphere.

Returning to the main road, we continued to climb and then descend. We saw the slope crests in the distance. The view of Mount Everest was blocked by Mount Lhotse and Gorak Shep was far away and not within easy reach.

Gorak Shep was the last campsite on the middle route, and all the materials were carried there by yaks. In the peak mountaineering months of April and May, expeditions heading towards the southern slope of Mount Everest are replenished at Gorak Shep. A Swiss mountaineering team once built Everest Base Camp there in 1952 but they didn't succeed in reaching the peak.

There are only six lodges in the village and it is famous for the limited supply of beds and scarce materials. When we reached Gorak Shep surrounded by mountains, Pasang had already arrived and ordered a room with walls as thin as paperboard in the 'yeti resort'. There were large gaps between the walls through which light and wind entered. But we were lucky to secure a room. Throughout the afternoon and night, other trekkers had to sleep in sleeping bags on a mat in the dining hall or on the floor of the sitting room. However, wherever they slept, everyone would reach the peak of their dreams.

Usually, trekkers choose to go to Everest Base Camp at noon carrying only light packs, trek for about four hours, return to rest in Gorak Shep and climb mountains for ninety minutes the following morning to Mount Kala Pattar (5,545 metres) to see the sunrise at Mount Everest.

We unloaded our backpacks, took only water and chocolate on our slow walk along the loose stone path at the side of the Khumbu Glacier towards Everest Base Camp and met with a tour group of middle-aged and senior citizens from Britain. The silver-haired group walked with an easy gait, one of whom had brought a traditional black British umbrella. They had walked more than ten days from Lukla Airport. Filled with admiration, I didn't think I would have the courage to trek to Everest Base Camp at their age.

A healthy trekker who has already adapted to high altitudes can finish the whole journey from Lukla to the Everest Base Camp in three or four days. I once saw a porter carry a shining aluminium casket for senior citizens. I was very curious about what it was. An oxygenator? Surgical dressings? A video camera? A paraglider?

Everest Base Camp lies at the northern tip of the Khumbu Glacier. I could see a belt of white ice in the far distance. It is quite difficult to walk on the path to Everest Base Camp even when carrying only a light pack. Most of the ice surface is covered in grey dust, coarse stones and granite. The occasional piece of translucent ice stuck out of the surface like glossy jade, under which were ice holes with melted snow water. We constantly passed mounds of glacial boulders. Tall, fat Tibetan snowcocks and pikas sometimes appeared, cast their lovely, innocent eyes on us and then they disappeared in the messy scree. At first, I thought I was still walking on the stone path before suddenly realising that we had unconsciously turned east and were now walking on the Khumbu Glacier itself.

According to a report by the Italian Pyramid research centre that we had just passed by, about ninety-five per cent of Himalayan glaciers are in retreat and the Khumbu Glacier is a good indicator to measure changes in all the Himalayan glaciers. Since 1953, the glacier had receded by up to five kilometres, largely as a result of global warming. For every one hundred climbing accidents on the southern slope of Mount Everest, about thirty per cent occurred on the Khumbu Glacier. Snow slides, avalanches and crevices might take the life of a mountaineer at any time. The melting and seasonal movement of the glacier made the Khumbu Glacier unpredictable and dangerous. When trekkers pass, they move and slide, and the sound of loose ice and snow can be heard faintly overhead in the distance. Once a snow slide occurs, people have no more than ten seconds to escape danger.

When we came to the last section of the journey to Everest Base Camp, we crossed another snow line. The melted snow water poured along a multitude of river channels, both overground and underground. I breathed heavily all the way and did not have the strength to take any photos. Pasang held my hand and loudly encouraged me to move on. The closer I got to base camp, the lonelier I felt. I hallucinated that I was alone on a desolate exoplanet.

When several nylon dome tents finally appeared, I was on the brink of collapsing. My tears gushed. The Tissot altimeter watch on Egor's wrist showed we were at about 5,340 metres. I hadn't expected to reach my destination crying. My tears froze quickly in the air.

In fact, Everest Base Camp is only a small, flat area of ground close to the mountain and there were columns of seracs and glacier tongues formed by the freezing water pouring along the sides of Mount Everest. Unlike the base camp on the northern slope of Mount Everest that I had visited before, this base camp was built at the end of the Khumbu Glacier, which extends nineteen kilometres. A decade ago, the ice cascades at Lho La Pass and Mount Everest were contiguous. However, with the serious erosion of the Khumbu Glacier, Everest Base Camp had moved backward, at different positions each year, even in spring and autumn of the same year, but in nearly every case at a higher altitude. But what puzzled me was that the place was so small and inconspicuous. Without the signs that were carved on some rocks, no one would know where it was!

Reaching my destination in tears

It was unimaginable to think that tens of teams gathered here in the peak mountaineering seasons. The flags of teams from different countries and the colourful prayer flags fluttering over the Mani stones danced in the wind. Team members from different countries played poker, gambled, strummed guitars, read books, ate delicious food and sunbathed, idling away the hours until the weather improved. Under the leadership of John Hunter in April 1953, a British mountaineering team learned from the experience of a Swiss team encamped in Gorak Shep and chose the route of the Khumbu Glacier. In total they took thirteen tons of materials, employed hundreds of Sherpa porters and up to a hundred yaks, and they all travelled to the base camp.

From there they climbed up to Camp 1, Camp 2... Altogether, they built nine 'Z-shaped' campsites along the ice walls. Finally, Edmund Hillary and Sherpa Tenzing climbed to the peak via the southern slope at 11.30am on 29 May 1953. Hillary buried the cross given to him by team leader Hunter at the summit and Tenzing buried several sweets as a gift to the gods. They stood at the top of the world and huddled together with safety ropes around their waists.

"It's so good to be here," Hillary said.

"I think of the gods and the gods' creations," Tenzing said.

The two heroes stayed on the peak for only fifteen minutes before descending.

. . .

The oxygen content in your breath at base camp is only half of that at sea level, and that on the top of Mount Everest is just a third of that at sea level. At an altitude of 5,340 metres, base camp is the destination for trekkers but the starting point for mountaineers aiming to conquer the summit. Those humans who live at sea level have the physical potential to adapt to this altitude. But if you are flown by helicopter to the peak of Mount Everest without time spent on acclimatisation and without supplementary oxygen, the oxygen in your body will quickly leak from your lungs and you'll lose consciousness in several minutes and die in a couple of hours. But your body will be well frozen in time like Mallory, whose eyes are still dark blue seventy-six years later.

It is a genetic miracle for a person who has been climbing and taken time to make the necessary adaptations to be able to carry out normal activities at high altitude. The peak of Mount Everest is probably the limit for human survival without supplementary oxygen. In other words, Earth's highest peak is the zenith for human survival. This discovery attracts more people to go to base camp and attempt the infinite miracle of climbing to the peak.

Each of us who arrived at base camp was panting and feeling excited. But it turned out that the peak of Mount Everest was not visible from this position. Nevertheless, we still rushed to take photos in front of the colossal peak. A trekker wrote his name and feelings on his bandana and tied it to a prayer flag dancing in the wind. It looked awesome! But the moment he left, a guide took the headband down and put it under a stone. We all laughed. Yes, how could he think of using a place for holy prayer flags as a message board?

The British have a reputation for being reserved, but British climbers are not so reserved on Mount Everest. The mountain is a great source of the pride to the British. Although Sir Edmund Hillary was a New Zealander, he was part of a British mountaineering team. The elderly group we encountered before opened a small box, in which there was a Santa Claus costume and a Union Jack flag. Then they started singing like angels. It was the most soulful anthem dedicated to the Sky Goddess.

Some other trekkers climbed to the Khumbu Icefall (5,800 metres) at the head of the Khumbu Glacier to experience first-hand the cold on the Himalayas. The serac is a rare and treasured sight that can only be seen on continental glaciers. The crystal clear chunks standing at a height of ten to twenty metres are worked slowly and carved carefully by nature. Like giant shark teeth sticking out in the ice and snow, they glitter dark blue at different layers in all directions in the scorching sun, presenting a pure and beautiful view.

Mountaineers who have climbed Mount Everest know that the weather usually changes in the afternoon, often from a breeze to a gale and even a blizzard two or three hours later. Therefore, Sherpa guides repeatedly emphasise the time restriction to their clients so that they can climb down safely before the weather changes. The yaks carrying materials to the base camp also need to go downhill on the same day too because there is nothing for them to eat at base camp and they would quickly lose strength.

At 4pm we braved the strong winds and trudged back to Gorak Shep at the foot of Mount Kala Pattar. Gorak Shep was like a silent, dull bowl with a flat base, where the lodges were packed. Just like at base camp, it was impossible to see Mount Everest from Gorak Shep. By then, most trekkers had set out to Mount Kala Patthar to see the sun rise over Mount Everest.

'Kala Patthar' means 'black stone'. It is the best place on the middle route to view Mount Everest and Mount Lhotse. As a matter of fact, most trekkers do not go to base camp but directly to the peak of Mount Kala Patthar which is 205 metres higher than that of base camp. Besides, the scenery there is stunning. Mount Everest rewards trekkers every step of the way with a glorious image of this unique black triangular mountain. I felt incomparably weary and had to give up. Egor joked that it was his task to become James Bond and take photos before nightfall. Then he patted me on the shoulder, asked Pasang to take good care of me and left by himself.

Gorak Shep was very quiet at dusk. Smoke curled up from kitchen chimneys into the serene sky. Several monuments to mountain accident victims are erected on nearby slopes. On 10 May 1996, four mountaineering teams climbing Mount Everest were caught in an unexpected hurricane and snowstorm in late afternoon, and twelve people died. The most famous victim was the New Zealand mountaineer Rob Hall, who had scaled Everest for the first time in May 1990. His crazy plan to 'conquer the seven highest mountains in seven continents in seven months' caused a sensation in mountaineering circles, and he completed the task in December 1990.

Afterwards he set up Adventure Consultants, a company that helps teams climb the world's highest peaks and which sent thirty-nine mountaineers to scale Everest between 1990 and 1995, three more than the total number in the twenty years following Hillary's historic achievement. However, it remains a cruel fact that mountaineers will not always succeed in conquering every high-altitude mountain.

The temperature dropped below freezing after the sun set. We circled around the iron stove in the sitting room to warm ourselves and patiently waited for Egor to return. The dirty shoes and smelly socks of trekkers were drying out around the stove. I put a stainless steel folding cup of black tea on the stove lid to keep it warm for Egor. Those trekkers who had failed to book rooms huddled together with the guides and porters and slept on Tibetan cushions, as excited as a big family celebrating the Spring Festival. The lodge owner told Pasang that two Frenchmen had serious acute mountain sickness when climbing Mount Kala Pattar and were taken away on an Aérospatiale SA315B Lama helicopter, which I too might need if I were to attempt to climb the mountain.

It's not uncommon for a person to die from acute mountain sickness at an altitude above 5,000 metres. At such a height, your body may fail to adapt, your thinking may slow down, your nerves may get damaged and you will inevitably lose weight and suffer muscular injury. Breathing rapidly at high altitude, you will become dehydrated and lose strength and awareness. So in a certain sense, the victims all 'vanish' in the rarefied air.

When the lodge owner made steamed buns for us in a pressurised paraffin stove, I dipped a few smelling slightly of paraffin into the thick chilli sauce and swallowed them with difficulty. Then I began to feel worried about Egor. I wasn't sure if he had the stamina to return safe and sound. I could only picture the scene of the sun setting over Everest and the rays shining like golden threads on Egor's face. There is nothing above Mount Everest. No icicle or serac but only the sky in which the gods prowl. It is the end point of the world, above which is the starry cosmos.

At about 7.30pm, I looked out of the window and saw a light at the foot of the mountain in the distance. I shouted hysterically: "Egor!" I finally saw him wearing an LED head lamp, stumbling along with other two trekkers on this windy evening and returning to the lodge filled with pungent paraffin smells and warm light.

That night I got a serious headache, felt suffocated as if my head was covered by a plastic bag and vomited the paraffin-flavoured steamed buns onto the floor like an expectant mother. Egor helped me up and I leaned against a wall panting. Pasang asked me to drink some honey water. A small bottle of hot water cost 800 rupees, more than the rent for a night of 600 rupees. Pasang poured some hot water into a small basin to warm my hands and feet. But when I moved a little, I vomited again. I once had serious acute mountain sickness two years previously when I was in Rongbuk Monastery on Mount Everest's northern slope at an altitude of 5,100 metres. At that time my husband created oxygen on three occasions using mineral water and a handy oxygenator. I sucked in the bubbling, life-saving gas and sat throughout the night facing the glory and holy countenance of the Goddess Mother of the World.

When I felt ill and gradually lost my willpower, the warm phantom of my husband appeared before my eyes once again and gave me strength. I thought that suffering could be conquered in all tough situations so long as your lover is there to share good and bad times with you, even in spirit only.

It seems that acute mountain sickness varies with each individual and their physical condition. When you walk in the daytime with your eyes open, you will subconsciously quicken your breath so that the haemoglobin in your blood can take in more oxygen and maintain your physical health and improve your ability to adapt. Even on Cho La Pass at an altitude of 5,420 metres, you can only stay there a short time, perhaps several minutes; when you sleep at night, your breathing rate slows down and the amount of oxygen held by the haemoglobin will be lessened. At that time, you'll feel severe oxygen deficit and the pain will be exacerbated if you remain outside at high altitude for a long time. It happened to me in Gorak Shep at an altitude of 5,160 metres. I didn't ask Pasang about the meaning of 'Gorak Shep' in Sherpa. I felt sure it must mean the highest point, limit or stop.

That night I woke up after having continuous nightmares. A girl next door also afflicted with acute mountain sickness was coughing constantly, and together we performed a kind of duet. Egor was woken in the night and kept me company for a while. To distract me, he spoke about his two ex-girlfriends. One was an interior designer and the other had been the singer in a band. He also told me why he liked playing the drums and go mountaineering, and why he didn't want to get married. Then he massaged my forehead and hands, and he hummed these words from *The Bible*:

"Glory to God in the highest, and peace to his people on Earth." The singing soothed my mind and alleviated my suffering due to oxygen deficit.

At dawn, the biting wind outside started to abate. The piercing pain started to relent and my breathing quietened. It was at that moment that I felt the meaningless existence of time at the foot of Mount Everest, and only the Holy Virgin Peak could prove the eternal, real existence and at the same time bear the brilliant glory and prolonged loneliness.

Pheriche, the highest rescue post

Footsteps could be heard in the lodge at 5.30am as trekkers set out to see the sunrise at Mount Kala Pattar. Pasang came into my room and asked whether I wanted to go too. I hesitatingly nodded. The sky had suddenly turned calm and pale pink. I carried a basin of cold water mixed with some hot water to wash my face and freshen up. I found the water in the basin as pale pink as the sky. The influence of height on the brain is similar to that on the body. Before I could work out what was happening, Pasang noticed my nose was bleeding.

Putting on thermal clothes, I stuffed a glob of tissue paper up my nose, which by now was looking like a radish. I wore a big pink scarf around my pink plaited hat, leaving a gap just for my eyes. My head and body looked like a big *zongzi*, the traditional Chinese rice pudding eaten during the Dragon Boat Festival. Could a *zongzi* made of sticky rice climb Mount Kala Pattar at an altitude of 5,545 metres?

Time and tide wait for no man. My ability to think failed me and I had to mechanically follow Egor and Pasang out of the lodge gate. I discovered many black shadows and stiff *zongzi* inching along the stone-covered Khumbu Glacier and climbing towards a black hill at the back of the lodge.

I was moving like an ant and felt heavy in the legs. Pain was shooting through my head, I was panting heavily and my body was frozen and numb. Pumori (7,165 metres), nicknamed 'the unmarried daughter of Everest', is the snow mountain closest to Mount Kala Pattar. With a huge flag-shaped cloud above the summit, it seemed to be wearing a garland bathed in sacred light and it drew me up about 150 metres. I felt as if I could touch its snowy skin but I failed to get close. I wanted to lean against a frozen rock to take a rest, but ended up sitting on the snow-covered ground. Too exhausted, I could not stand up again.

Trekkers set out to see the sunrise at Kala Pattar

A man with a brown teddy bear draped over his shoulder walked slowly towards us. His girlfriend had acute mountain sickness and had suffered in the lodge the night before. They had set out from Seattle and came to the foot of Mount Everest with the toy bear. Unable to make the final leg of their quest, his girlfriend asked him to see the sunrise at Mount Everest with the teddy bear as if she were going with him. He breathlessly told Egor: "Take your girlfriend downhill. This little teddy bear will see the sunrise on her behalf." He wiped away the sweat from his forehead, smiled, turned around and climbed on ahead. I smiled feebly and nodded in tacit understanding.

It was devastating to give up climbing Mount Kala Pattar. Returning to the lodge and finishing packing, Egor insisted that I should get treatment in Pheriche Village (4,240 metres) as soon as possible. He said he would go alone to Mount Chhukung (4,730 metres) on the eastern route, draw me a route map and take photos for me as if he were a soldier on a mission. If my condition was not serious, we could meet in Dingboche Village the next evening and return to Namche Bazaar together; if not, I should return directly to Namche Bazaar with Pasang and wait for him there.

I was dejected to part from him. At that time, Mount Nuptse on the right of Gorak Shep looked golden. Mount Everest was like a large lotus flower in bloom, a colossal, pyramid-shaped mountain up to 3,000 metres higher than the bottom of the cirque. At its northern latitude of 28°, the last rays of evening light and the first rays of morning sun disperse and rise again between the summits every day. I looked back in the direction of Everest and heard a rumbling in the sky. The sound came from a jet carrying passengers to see the sunrise at Mount Everest and witness the brilliant origin of life at a cost of 140 dollars. But I had chosen to walk to the place of my dreams, step by step. Even though I might suffer nosebleeds and burst my lungs over a myriad of high mountains, I would go there personally to view the great mountain.

It was a round trip. The views on the return leg were different. I didn't have to climb with endless pain. I could breathe more easily and my headache gradually got better as the altitude fell by each metre. Passing by trekkers advancing towards Everest Base Camp in the morning, we would greet each other and give a knowing smile. As we walked downhill in the light breeze, I could not help encouraging the suffering trekkers clambering uphill with their trekking poles: "Keep going, up, up!"

I thought they must be encouraged to see me, the straggler with a bleeding nose and a blue face, and hear my clarion call. In the peak mountaineering season, there is the miraculous sight of hundreds of trekkers from all walks of life walking in a line in the valley of Everest Base Camp dressed like beggars, *zongzi* and Santa Claus, all heading for a once-in-a-lifetime experience on the snow mountain.

Egor told me an incredible thing that happens once every two years at Everest Base Camp. The world's highest marathon is organised by the UK-based Bufo Ventures trekking company to raise funds for the development of Khumbu. An elite athlete can finish the whole forty-two kilometre distance from Gorak Shep to Namche Bazaar on the middle route in just four hours. But the participants must have received training for two weeks in advance. Another endurance event, the Royal Penguin ultramarathon, has been held on the western route since 2014, from Namche Bazaar at 3,440 metres to Dole at 4,200 metres, Gokyo at 4,700 metres, Renjo Pass at 5,340 metres, Marlung at 4,260 metres, Thame at 3,800 metres and finally back to Namche Bazaar. Some participants can complete the forty-two-kilometre-long mountain route uphill and downhill in eight hours.

I felt more relaxed with Egor's encouragement. I imagined the fearless participants charging downhill from an altitude of 5,000 metres. We had walked for twelve days and might dash downhill as fast as antelopes. To the brave, scaling the highest mountains is the peak of their ambitions.

We had to part with Egor after walking down into the sun along the U-shaped valley on the northern side of Khumbu Glacier to Lobuche. He would traverse the Khumbu Glacier and Kongma La Pass (5,535 metres), the highest point on the whole trekking route, and walk to Mount Chhukung on the eastern route.

Mount Chhukung is a really isolated, serene village. It is surrounded by the Nuptse, Lhotse Nup and Ama Dablam glaciers, as well as several snow mountains, including Mount Lhotse (8,516 metres), Mount Makalu (8,463 metres) and Island Peak (6,189 metres). Island Peak is the most popular mountain for trekking, the most beautiful of the various peaks that mountaineering teams conquer before their ascent of Mount Everest.

Due to the high altitude and the fact that there is no village to act as supply point along the ten kilometre route from Lobuche to Mount Chhukung, few trekkers dare to tackle the eastern route. I thought it was a journey that Egor would prefer to take alone.

Watching his dark blue shadow with a pack on his back gradually disappear in the snow slope of the glacier, I felt him light a flame inside me. I was drawn to men who were relentless in their pursuit of a goal, for instance Xuanzang on his Western Journey, Marco Polo's travels to the Far East and Columbus's arduous voyage to discover the New World. The scenery of Mount Chhukung Ri was different from that of Mount Kala Pattar on the middle route and Gokyo Ri on the western route. I thought of the demoiselle cranes that can fly over the Himalayas. Each November, about 160,000 demoiselle cranes fly from Central Asia and the highlands, grasslands, marshes and deserts in northeastern and northwestern China, over the summit of Mount Everest and to India to spend winter on the southern slopes of the Himalayas. They are the world's smallest cranes and their slender bodies only measure sixty to seventy centimetres long. They also undertake one of the most difficult and impressive migrations. The bodies of these pretty, elegant cranes contain enormous energy. In flight, they get close to one other and communicate between themselves. Some of them drop through exhaustion and others are caught by golden eagles. But they cannot turn back and help their fallen comrades. Instead, they soar even higher thanks to the rising warm air flow until they have flown over the natural screen of the Himalayas.

The demoiselle cranes have no idea that these are the world's highest mountains. They fly for survival, for the call of life and to pursue their dreams. They demonstrate the splendour of life. Why not be a demoiselle crane in my life? I thought I would surely meet Egor who had climbed Mount Chhukung Ri in Dingboche.

Heading down from Lobuche and crossing the stone hill at the end of the Khumbu Glacier, we came to the 4,800-metre-high Duglha Mountain Pass. On a high stone slope, eroded by the movement of the glacier, are more than twenty traditional stone monuments in honour of those who have died. The Chukpilhara Commemoration Area surrounded by mountains commemorates those fearless mountaineers who have perished in the mountains, most of whom were Sherpas. One of the monuments is in the name of Babu Chiru Sherpa, who is held in high esteem by mountaineers.

More than two hundred mountaineers have lost their lives climbing Mount Everest since 1922, more than sixty per cent of whom were Nepalese helpers. Mountaineering teams from different countries and Nepalese helpers risked their lives to fasten ropes with ice pitons and make a 7,000-8,000-metre safety rope to facilitate logistics, provide directions, help with climbing and guarantee safety for the mountaineering teams. They risked their lives helping mountaineers realise their dreams. Pasang said each Mani stone tells a story about the Sherpas and the Himalayas, and they mark the resting place for the souls of mountaineers who perished climbing Mount Everest. So far, about 2,000 mountaineers have reached the peak, along with some 1,500 Sherpas. Few mountaineers could have made it by themselves, without the help of Sherpas.

Many of the finest mountaineers are Sherpas. Babu Chiri Sherpa, born in 1965, began to climb mountains at thirteen, creating and keeping the record for scaling the peak. Most Western mountaineers can reach the peak in three or four days, but he made it in only sixteen hours and fifty-six minutes without the help of an oxygen bottle. He was the first to scale the peak twice within two weeks at the age of thirty in 1995; he stayed twenty-one hours on the peak in 1999 to raise funds for the education of Sherpa children. Tragically, in April 2001 at the age of thirty-six, coming down after conquering Everest for the eleventh time, he fell down an ice crevice and died. He was taking photos of the fantastic scenery in the fading light of the setting sun at the foot of the snow mountain outside his tent. The undoubted king of mountaineering had departed the mountains.

Pasang would walk around every monument or huge stone that he went past. He touched the stone lightly with his forehead and put his palms together devoutly to show respect to the god of mountains and to each mountaineer that he held in such high regard. When he lowered his head and prayed, colourful prayer flags fluttered above his head in the blue sky, dancing to the peak of Mount Nuptse in the distance and finally to the farthest peak of Mount Everest. This simple worshiping ceremony deeply moved me and made me re-evaluate reticent Pasang and all the ordinary porters passing by. I seemed to see their unyielding mind too. The mountains are the main part of their lives and the place they call home.

Together with Pasang, I picked up a small stone, chanted 'Om mani padme hum' in a low voice and placed it lightly on a Mani stone. I sensed I had become one of so many stones and part of the mountains too.

The Chukpilhara Commemoration Area at Duglha Mountain Pass

Although it is a place of permanent sorrow, the journey to Everest Base Camp is the most awe-inspiring and unforgettable experience. Carefully observed, the inscriptions on the tombs belonging to Italians, Bulgarians, Japanese and South Koreans all read 'To our beloved and remembered friend'. I could picture them, with unswerving determination, making their way between the crevasses and rocks. Their eyes still looked directly into the remote mountains penetrating the clouds. Nothing is more glorious, eternal and immortal than to die in the embrace of the god of mountains and at the highest and most gorgeous place on Earth at the most wonderful moment of life. A gust of wind moistened my eyes. Come climb, brave mountaineer, just to see the higher sky above the mountains!

With my eyes misty, I turned around, continued to walk downhill and came to Dughla (4,620 metres), a small village next to the Khumbu Glacier. Torrential floods washed away half of the village in 2007. There were only two lodges left, both in poor condition. A round solar cooker donated by international aid agencies was situated on empty ground at the back. A tea kettle was placed on iron rings in the middle of the cooker. At the back of the cooker were the words in Sherpa and English: 'Bread and energy for all people on Earth.' The cooker, like an all-embracing big-bellied arhat, collected solar energy in the rarefied air. Its silvery sheet metal reflected the snow mountains, sky, huts, yaks, kitchen, food and people. I felt reinvigorated, my body was no longer heavy, my headache and panting alleviated, and I even had the energy to care about others.

I saw a young Chinese man wearing a thick down jacket, snow cap and snow goggles. He was sitting on a plastic chair on the empty ground with his head drooping in dead silence. I knew he must be afflicted with acute mountain sickness. I went over and gave him two paracetamol tablets. The Chinese know that this medicine can alleviate neuropathic and muscular pains. Holding the tablets, he nodded to me. I couldn't see his eyes behind the huge snow goggles that reflected light and shadow like the solar cooker. I knew that he could move on upward to the new altitude he desired in a couple of hours despite going through extreme suffering.

Having a simple meal with Pasang in quiet Duglha, I looked back at Mount Pumori, known as 'the unmarried daughter of Everest', which was fifteen kilometres northwest of the world's highest mountain. The snow on Mount Pumori always gave off beautiful vapour that never dissipated. I missed climbing the passes with Egor, his vigour, vitality, agility, humour and eyes as azure as the limpid Adriatic Sea when he looked at the mountains far into the distance. I didn't know whether he had climbed over Kongma La Pass at an altitude of 5,535 metres without any supplies. He went alone. Did he regard me as clumsy and ugly as a *zongzi*? My heart and my insides were instantly touched; I'd never explored his soul as deeply as that.

A close friend on a journey is like a mirror reflecting the truest and most elegant part of our natural instincts. Unless they travel together, people will never understand the sadness and grandeur of the snow mountain or experience the profundity of trekking.

Going downhill and fording the streams of snow water in the valley, we came to Phulaji Kala (4,343 metres), a small Sherpa village. Trekkers, porters and yaks climbing uphill had created a smooth and muddy path. As the ground opened up and levelled out, we arrived in Pheriche at the bottom of the Khumbu Valley at 4pm. I felt as if I had returned to paradise, somewhere I could breathe easily and where my headache and dry coughing disappeared.

There were more than ten lodges in Pheriche at an altitude of 4,240 metres. We stayed in White Yak Mountain Hut, with constant water, a flush toilet, snooker table and satellite phone all available. I looked up and saw a photo of Sir Edmund Hillary on the sitting room wall. A cream coloured *khata*, a ceremonial scarf given used as a greeting gift, was draped over the black frame. I was shocked by his eyes.

It was the first time I had seen a large picture of him. In the picture, he is standing in Duglha Village with a coil of climbing rope on his shoulder, his nut-brown curly hair blowing in the icy wind from Mount Nuptse behind him. His long, thin hands are clutching trekking poles, and he has a resolute look on his lean face as he stares far into the distance. Handsome, he stands there like an immovable mountain. Since he was a young man, he had trekked on the same paths and mountains that we had just covered. Many trekkers passing by Pheriche took off their T-shirts, wrote down the date along with their name and nationality with marker pens and hung them close to his photo. They were pinned all over the wall and even on the ceiling, all watched over by Hillary.

Embrace! Embraced by Hillary and a multitude of snow mountains, I felt exceedingly content. What unparalleled happiness and blessing!

There is an aid station sponsored by the Himalayan Rescue Association in Pheriche, a place of legend, romance, love and dedication. The aid post has four rooms and six volunteer doctors who pay for their own round-trip tickets to Nepal. Young people from across the world travel to the Himalayas to work as volunteers in order to help the mountaineers. In 1973, four members of a Japanese tour group died of acute mountain sickness nearby and the aid post was set up soon afterwards to treat the condition, equipped with portable hyperbaric cabins and a room with oxygen machines. It also provides free medical treatment for local Sherpas and spreads information about the dangers of excessively fast and vigorous climbing.

Before the establishment of the aid post, one or two out of every 500 trekkers traversing Pheriche died of acute mountain sickness. This astonishingly high mortality rate excluded those who died as a result of accidents on the mountains. Most victims were ordinary trekkers observing all the rules and regulations. But now the mortality has dropped to no more than one person out of every 30,000 trekkers. When I was there, an aid post doctor discovered that the oxygen content in the blood of the Chinese man was inadequate and suggested that he should climb no more than 300-400 metres and take a rest every two days. He followed the doctor's advice and stayed in Duglha to adapt to the upcoming altitude above 5,000 metres. Many trekkers have benefited from the advice and first aid given by the volunteer doctors.

In 1990, thirty-year-old Rob Hall climbed Mount Everest for the first time. When he reached Pheriche, he met Doctor Jan Arnold in charge of the aid post. Self-confident and highly competent, Jan attracted the young New Zealand mountaineer. Before leaving the village and carrying on upwards, he asked: "Would you be happy to leave with me after I come down Mount Everest?"

Without embellishment or rhetoric, the world-famous mountaineer had made a simple marriage proposal. Jan nodded and said to the man she'd just met: "OK, I'll wait for you here, so long as you come back safe and sound."

Rob Hall not only reached the peak together with Sir Edmund Hillary's son but also made a live radio broadcast on the peak of the world. Obstinate and unconventional, Hall took Jan away from the aid post when he returned. Their first date was to climb Mount McKinley (6,194 metres) in Alaska, the highest peak in North America, and they jointly climbed Mount Everest when they got married in 1993. In another crazily tantalising mountaineering season in May 1995, Hall died and his pregnant wife would never see her handsome, robust husband again.

. . .

Pheriche, where the wind blows hard, is the world's highest seasonal aid post. It is a place where surplus food and sweatshirts donated by previous mountaineers can be found, but more than that it is a place of warmth and laughter. When I walked alone to visit the aid post in the evening, I saw a stainless steel monument at the gate erected in 2003 to celebrate the fiftieth anniversary of the first ascent of Everest. The tapered monument, split down the middle, symbolises Mount Everest. The names of the climbers who have lost their lives in the embrace of the 'Sky Goddess' are carved on the surface of the monument. Each year six doctors from across the world take turns to work here as volunteers. I bent down to place one of my books at the bottom of the monument.

The wind would blow the characters and the snow would kiss the pictures. It was my act of respect to the climbers and volunteers working on the mountain.

I panted, stood up and walked slowly into a warm room in the aid post. On a wall reflecting the lingering light of the setting sun hung a row of T-shirts and fleece coats printed with snow mountains and the red cross logo. The trekkers and mountaineers passing through Pheriche could buy a T-shirt for 800 rupees or a fleece coat for 1,500 rupees, with the money going towards the non-profit aid post. I took out a coil of rupees from my pocket, put it into a donation box and chose a thermal cobalt blue fleece coat for Egor.

A strong American man named Leach was lying on a stretcher in the aid post. He had wolfed down his meal and walked too fast, which led him to showing the painful symptoms of pulmonary edema, a condition caused by excess fluid in the lungs. It can be caused by acute mountain sickness, which is still the top 'killer' haunting Khumbu. A female doctor called Jennifer was looking after him. She came from Nevada, famed as 'the mountain of light', and was serving as a volunteer in Pheriche for three months. Weather permitting, she said, a helicopter would send him to the hospital in Kathmandu at sunrise the next day. The alternative would be to walk 120 kilometres to the nearest highway. I knew it was Shivalaya where Egor and I started off. I prayed good luck for Leach.

The huge peak of Mount Ama Dablam, 2,616 metres above where I stood, flickered dark blue rays and overlooked the whole valley. The ice looked like the garland symbolising beautiful love worn by Sherpa women.

Although the 6,856-metre-high Mount Ama Dablam looks inconspicuous on the road to Everest Base Camp, it is an eternally sacred mountain in the mind of Sherpas. It is the way to get to Mount Everest, the place where trekkers and mountaineers must go through and the celestial realm of the gods. I thought each mountain and each climber there had a soul that was unrelated to its height, difficulty and size. Mount Everest is synonymous with grandeur, Mount Lhotse with its sharpness, Mount Makalu with its strangeness and Mount Cho Oyu with its vastness. Mountaineers who persist in keeping going believe in a life with no regrets and their eternal love for the mountains is pure and as endless as the sky.

A thing becomes more beautiful when it is pursued. Trekkers will meet unexpectedly at the most opportune moment. I will continue to trek to sublimate my life. Like Jan, I hope to meet my ideal man, as strong as a mountain…

Dingboch as brilliant as a bonfire

Mount Ama Dablam displays a different beauty at different times of the day: imposing late at night and resplendent at daybreak.

It was clear, cloudless and relatively still. The yellow rescue helicopter approached Pheriche and landed on an area of sandy soil marked with small yellow-black stones. The striking 'H' in the centre of the stone circle refers to 'help' and 'hope'. We looked out and prayed for the safety of the strong American man named Leach as well as the aviator.

The rarefied air made it difficult to land and take off. Superb piloting skills are also required to steer the helicopter through the valleys, turbulent air flows, and the clouds and mist. So flying by helicopter also involves inherent risk as well as bringing hope of survival to trekkers and mountaineers. Since 1990, more than forty high-altitude helicopter accidents in Nepal have added to the number of deaths and alpine rescue attempts. Staying in Everest Base Camp for days, we lived a chaotic existence. Then the long-expected helicopter appeared in the clear, boundless sky and the trekkers got ready to take a flight to their desired height. In good physical and psychological shape, we were the last to leave Pheriche, crossing the bridge over the Khumbu River at a steady pace and heading for Dingboche (4,360 metres) on Mount Ama Dablam.

The mountain rescue helicopter landing point

We spent little more than two hours walking from Pheriche to Dingboche. Mount Ama Dablam is the snow mountain that accompanies trekkers for the longest time during their journey. Uniquely shaped and penetrating the sky, it displays different colours and postures from different positions, from different angles and at different times of day. The snow-capped mountain towered ahead of us, looking majestic however it was photographed.

Dingboche lies at the confluence of the middle and eastern routes. We met many other trekkers on the way. A Swedish girl named Laura joined us for a small section of the path. She wore an inexpensive down jacket, purified stream water with a pocket-sized ultraviolet germicidal lamp and drank the purified icy water from the Imja Khola, which aroused my admiration. She didn't hire a porter but walked slowly alone to Everest Base Camp via the eastern route with a small thirty-litre bag on her back. A porter said to her: "Don't think about Everest Base Camp, just think about tomorrow."

It seemed that this advice could benefit all trekkers who had just started off. She walked step by step, made plans for the following day's route, especially where to have a rest and where to have tea, and placed importance on the route taken and how to conserve energy rather than just walk to the base camp as fast as possible.

It was exciting to walk on the footpaths and see the world-class landscapes! We were as lithe and free as butterflies. Seeing her self-confidence, toughness and bright disposition as she walked alone through the rocky landscape with two trekking poles, I joined her in walking slowly to appreciate the landscape and enjoy the serenity of the wilderness. The strong wind buffeted my body and the prayer flags all around. I stretched up into the fairy blue sky, thrusting my head, shoulders and even entire body in the sky. I only wanted to stay where my heart belonged, be together with the wind, the sky and light, to let it go and be encircled by the surrounding beauty.

We breezily arrived in Dingboche at 11am. I took a liking to this serene Sherpa village. Whether going uphill or downhill, most trekkers prefer to stay in Pheriche or Tengboche because they have a wider range of tourist facilities and more people. But Dingboche was comfortable, clean and beautiful because of its independence and distance from the noisy world. Its solar generator enabled more power to be generated here than in other villages in the valley. It was pleasantly warm and relatively still. There was also an internet cafe with superb network speed. How was that possible? An internet cafe at an altitude of 4,360 metres?

There was also a bakery with French windows. What a luxury to sit in a sunny room with floral curtains, drinking a cup of hot chocolate and eating apple pie or a piece of carrot cake!

The red, blue, green, yellow and white prayer flags were hanging on strings all over the slope and were swaying in the wind. The ancient pagoda is the divine burial place of lamas and where the ashes of eminent monks are kept. Mani stones carved with exquisite inscriptions stand on the highest mountain pass like sentinels. I had my first hot bath after seven days of high-altitude trekking in a warm, sunny house. Praise the Lord! Then I sat beside a yak pen piled up with rings of stones, with the snow mountains at an altitude of some 6,000 metres framed against the sky. I clicked the mouse lightly to read an email from another world, experienced strong heartbeats, bathed in the sunshine and forgot the existence of time and the mortal world. It seemed as if I were an alien from outer space.

We ate lunch punctually at noon for the first time since we arrived in the Snow Lion Lodge. Sherpas do not like vinegar with their MoMo (dumplings). Tomato sauce or curry sauce is served on a saucer and the sheep entrails and garlic soup tasted strong. Pasang said it was good to have soup on the high mountains. Unexpectedly, as we ate the soup to warm our stomachs, we witnessed our first a blood ritual in the yard.

Sherpas never kill animals themselves but they eat the meat of those that have died by accident or have been killed by others. Professional butchers mostly come from other areas. One of the Sherpas' strangest customs is to drink the blood of live yaks in order to promote the health of the yaks or cure them of infertility. They bind the legs of the yak, tie its horns to a tree trunk in the yard and restrain its neck with a rope. A sharp awl is inserted into the yak's blood vessel and the blood flows along the awl into a basin. Generally, just over half a litre of blood is taken. When the awl is pulled out, the wound automatically seals and the yak appears unaffected. Afterwards, they add salt and water to the blood, place it in the open air so that it starts to freeze and then it is stewed or fried.

A pound for a pint of yak's blood. That's quite expensive. The whole blood-extraction process looks simple but really requires skill. With the sounds of the monks swishing their sleeves and chanting sutras, the heart-stopping 'revival of the dead' scene stunned us city dwellers accustomed to eating supermarket food.

As a feminist, I was curious about the Sherpas' marriage system. I wondered whether it was still a 'kingdom of females' in which women were the heads of households just like the Musuo people in China's Yunnan province. In the past, to prevent the dispersion of wealth and consolidate fraternity, the Sherpas universally adopted polyandry. But now, the people have shifted their attention from traditional yak business to tourism in order to make more cash. Traditional efforts to maintain their property and herds gradually waned and the change directly affected the Sherpas' marriage system. In fact, Sherpa men can now support their wives and children by working as guides or porters, running lodges and becoming involved in tourism. The established practice of maintaining the integrity of family property is less important and the tradition of polyandry has lost its economic foundation. The Snow Lion Lodge owner said polyandry disappeared in about 1970 in Khumbu region but still existed in some desolate, backward areas, such as Polzer Village in the west.

Most mountaineering teams going to Island Peak (6,189 metres) take up quarters in Dingboche. Many keen outdoor photographers also head for Island Peak. This mountain is the least difficult for amateur climbers and can be reached with limited ice-climbing skills and the assistance of guides. Therefore, it has become the most popular mountain for hiking. Situated between the Lhotse and Lhotse Shar glaciers, it faces the Chhukung Valley. In 1952, an expedition led by Eric Shipton was the first to arrive here. They called this most beautiful mountain 'an island in a sea of ice'. Island Peak, composed of ice, snow and rocks, can be seen clearly from Dingboche, towering overhead and offering many beautiful views.

A camping group arrived at Island Peak in the afternoon. Their helpers began to deftly pitch tents and set up cooking facilities on the grass. Pasang told me that so many guides, cooks, porters and yaks were needed to carry the materials for accommodation, food and fuel to last more than ten days on the mountain. Pitching a tent is no cheaper than staying in a lodge. In fact, just the opposite. In Khumbu, those people sleeping in tents were all wealthy and they each spent at least a hundred dollars every day. Poorer trekkers stayed in lodges. The lodge we stayed in cost 500 rupees, about six dollars. The mountaineering teams would climb Mount Nangkartshang (5,090 metres) nearby to physically adapt before going to Island Peak. I could not help thinking that Egor, who reached the peak of Mount Chhukung on the eastern route, must have been on the way to Dingboche.

There was Nangkartshang Gompa (4,760 metres) on the hill behind Dingboche. It is the highest monastery in Khumbu and also the best position to overlook the fifth highest peak Mount Makalu (8,463 metres), Island Peak and Mount Ama Dablam. The monks in the monastery begin to burn incense at nightfall. The vigorous sutra chanting and the playing of drums and small cymbals drift from afar in the chilly air. Seeing the highland barley flour blown into the sky by the wind so soon, leaving only the azure sky permeated with the smell of temple juniper, I felt the word 'god' repeatedly spring to my mind. The snow-capped mountains remained cold and sober, and we moved from the ground above sea level to the world of the god of snow mountains in the sky.

I was sitting with a group of trekkers on rocks outside the monastery looking at the mountains and the ice river and discussing whether we might learn snow climbing there one day, when I saw Egor and two other trekkers strolling into the village with bags on their backs. The warm, brilliant twilight rays penetrated the clouds and fell on the smoky eaves of the lodge. The snow mountain in the distance was so magnificent that my heart throbbed when it came into view. There were scratches on Egor's face, his beard looked like messy straw and his facial expression resembled a gambler taking a train to Las Vegas. When he saw that I was waiting for him in the village, he rushed forward to give me a bearhug.

When we went upstairs to have supper, along with two French trekkers staying in the same lodge, Egor took out a nautilus fossil wrapped in Nepalese newspaper from his backpack and gave it to me. It was a fist-sized, heavy black stone they had picked up when walking through the rock bed of Lhotse Nup Glacier. Mount Lhotse, three kilometres south of Everest, had previously been mistaken for the 'South Peak of Mount Everest'. In Sherpa, it has another beautiful name, 'Cyan Beautiful Fairy'.

Egor said morning climbing was particularly exciting because there were few trekkers around and the glaciers were quite steep. Even though he had set out from Chhukung, the altitude difference was 700 metres, the limit for one day's climbing. The Nuptse and Lhotse Nup glaciers situated respectively in the east and the west, flank the mountain. They were the only three to reach the peak of Mount Chhukung Ri at an altitude of 5,546 metres, as if it were a feast granted by the mountain god and exclusively enjoyed by the soul. At sunrise, the three snow mountains – Mount Lhotse, Mount Makalu and Island Peak – towered and glistened brightly. The distant, boundless sky reflected the lofty peaks covered with snow, looking pure and perfect.

Egor ate his sheep entrails and garlic soup and said to me: "Pearl, what you see and experience at any moment will not occur again." In coming years, he might change his job, become an alpine guide and climb Island Peak 6,189 metres high, followed by Mount Nuptse, 7,861 metres high and Mount Lhotse, 8,516 metres high.

I asked whether he would give up playing the drums. He said he wouldn't and that he would play the drums for six months and climb mountains for the next six. When he was a soldier, the British musician James Blunt tied his guitar to a tank and fought while composing songs. In the daytime, he was a military officer serving among 30,000 peace-keeping troops in Kosovo. In the evening, he composed *Bonfire Heart* in a tank, which went on to win the hearts of millions of British people. Hearing what Egor had said, I burst into laughter. It was my ideal existence, travelling half the time and writing articles in the study the other. I said: "OK, let's climb a mountain together each year. I already knew you to be an excellent alpine guide when I set out from Shivalaya."

The first day we stepped out on the path to Everest Base Camp, I believed that mountaineering summoned the bodies and souls of trekkers. It gave significance to our formerly meaningless lives. Our distracting thoughts disappeared gradually with the rise in altitude. Not merely our souls, but also our bodies seemed to have been bleached by the wind and even our intestines were dyed the colour of the sky. We had been filled with admiration for the rays and glamour of the Himalayas.

I took off my gloves and, touching the pretty cross grains on the nautilus fossil, I suddenly understood why Egor picked it up for me. The highest place on earth used to be part of the Neo-Tethys Sea, an ancient Mediterranean that was home to multitudes of prehistoric lives including the pearly nautilus fossil in my hand. What power could possibly push the sea floor to the sky and become the Himalayas? What willpower and energy was needed to move a life to such a height? In his *Travel Instructions*, Fei Yong said: "The fossils and the starry sky, one under our feet and the other above our heads, point to an infinite secret." I thought that only people living above a certain altitude enjoy rarefied air and clean snow and ice rather than the urban noise and distractions of films, bars and social media. There is only advancement towards the sky and a pure life.

I returned the fossil to my backpack with heartfelt delight. It sparked a bonfire in my mind. When Egor and I went downstairs, through the yard and back to the room, I raised my head and saw the Milky Way flash from the rear of Mount Ama Dablam; countless stars twinkled and glistened in the extraordinarily chilly sky as if guiding us to part from the worldly desires of lovesickness. We seemed not to be standing on earth but were suddenly thrust into the cosmos. It was a real epic story of the cosmos. By the crystal stars and snow light, we could even make out the grains of rocks and the cracks on the ice peaks. I guessed it must look like the scene confronting the characters in *Gravity* as they looked out of the window of their space capsule. The two surviving lovers trust each other, confidently find each other and spare no effort in advancing towards their native land of gravitational force...

Starlight twinkled in my heart. I turned round and asked Egor whether the cosmos had a frontier. He lowered his head, looked at the starlight reflected in my eyes and said the nebulas we saw were at least eight billion light years away from Earth, and it was the farthest place of the cosmos already known to mankind.

At that time I felt we belonged to the nebulas and crossed the Earth to meet at the speed of light of 300,000 kilometres per second. Our love for the mountains was as loyal as that between soldiers, and our fascination for the starry sky was as firm as the fossils. The mountains in the distance always enhanced us, led us into a reverie and filled us with lofty aspirations. On the snow peak at the world's highest point, Egor and I got close to the starlit sky in the cosmos and embraced each other.

Music and bodies under the starlit sky in Namche Bazaar

You will encounter unique surprises during your trek to Everest Base Camp. When you climb a certain mountain pass or peak, you may find a splendid, breathtaking view before your eyes.

Like a blue ribbon, the Imja Khola gradually woke up in the glistening morning rays. Through a small window of the Snow Lion Lodge, I saw fairyland-like snow mountains in the distance. The bleak, smooth glaciers shone beautiful rays of light and showed the unruffled beauty of this white world. The light clouds around the mountainside seemed to mark the boundary between sky and earth, aiming to separate heaven from the mortal world and making the morning magic, dynamic and charming. A flock of wild pigeons flitted by the white Gompa on the mountain and the dancing white prayer flags. Their wings were covered with dew and the glory of freedom.

I could not help taking photos of birds in the sky each time I saw them. They reminded me of the legend about birds whose bones were hollow and spent their entire lives in the air. Maybe because I didn't know much about these birds, I yearned to have their ability to fly. And the new aspiration for freedom also inspired and encouraged us that our bodies could recover after a night's rest. Egor and I seemed like soulmates who had met on a remote journey. Carrying backpacks, we walked downhill and entered a magnificent, primitive mountain pass with the purpose of returning to Namche Bazaar and becoming 'bandit kings' once again.

Setting out from Dingboche, we were surprised to enter a meadow covered with exotic flowers and rare herbs. A crystal ice frost covered the tiny flowers, which looked extraordinarily refined and fell into the reclusive domain of celestial beings. At first I didn't know the fairy-like flowers growing along the path were the same rare medicinal herbs used to make the pills in my backpack. The gentian, as secret as a gem, the vibrant rhodiola coccinea, the Chinese wormwood with dense grey, short soft down and fresh blue comastoma pulmonarium. All the plants and flowers were Tibetan remedies to cure acute mountain sickness and activate cells. The flowers nestled up to each other like friends, bloomed romantically on the 4,000-metre snow line and magically guarded the path we walked on.

For the first time I saw plants and flowers growing and blooming indomitably and beautifully on the ice-covered mountain and the snowfield. It made me cherish the reunion of the Three Monks after a short parting. Pasang put a blue gentiana veitchiorum in my hat rim and I put a thick rhodiola coccinea leaf in Egor's hand. The Three Monks continued downhill even more harmoniously and with greater energy.

Traversing the valley along the Imja Khola and passing by several gorgeous Mani stones, we came to Pangboche (3,860 metres). Here is the oldest Gompa in Khumbu, supposedly containing the skull and hand bones of the legendary yeti. White pagodas accompanied me all the way, including one on which the footsteps of Sange Dorje Rinpoche, who introduced Tibetan Buddhism to Khumbu, could still be seen. But I found that the colour of the 'Buddha-eyes' of Bodhnath Stupa in Kathmandu was different from that in other places in Nepal.

White pagodas accompany us all the way

Both the Buddha-eyes of Bodhnath Stupa in Kathmandu and the 'Swayambhunath' religious monument also known as the 'Four-eyed Skyshrine' were an imposing presence amid the sutra chanting of the people. I guessed that they must have seen the ups and downs of the mortal world which is why they looked exceedingly solemn, graceful, poised, reserved and silent. The Buddha-eyes were almost azure, as good-looking and innocent as cartoon images. At the entrance to the village, at a bend in the mountain pass and the highest point on the mountain ridge, I could see those cordial, sincere and intrepid eyes as I looked up. With the change of seasons and the ice and snow melting, the mortal world seemed to be just a blink, a fallen leaf, a flower, a drop of water and a meeting on the path. It seemed to ask us to convey thanks to those who deserve our gratitude and informing them that they are important to us.

Some virtues and love are revealed in adversity. I hadn't expected that the affectionate Buddha-eyes, together with the azure sky, would present such wonderful scenery and arouse so many sentiments. It prevented Egor and me from becoming lonely or doleful.

At noon, we went through Debuche Forest where Chinese monals and musk deer appeared and then disappeared. Passing by a nunnery set among ancient trees reaching into the skies, we went downhill to Tengboche Village (3,870 metres), the soul of Khumbu region surrounded by trees.

Sherpas are followers of the Nyingma school of Tibetan Buddhism. There were altogether more than thirty Gompas in the Solu-Khumbu regions, among which Tengboche is home to the most famous, important and charming one. The Rinpoche here is the leader of all the Nepalese lamas. There is no such term as 'living Buddha' in Tibetan; the equivalent is called 'sprul-sku', 'lama' or 'Rinpoche', meaning 'treasure of people' and 'most valuable'. Among them, 'Rinpoche' is the only appellation universally used.

In the peak climbing season each spring, the Rinpoche, dressed in a raspberry wine-coloured robe, hangs a white *khata* around the neck of each mountaineer for their blessing. In 1953, the gaunt New Zealand mountaineer Edmund Hillary met the energetic young Tenzing driving yaks in Tengboche. The mountaineering team stayed there for three weeks to adapt to the local climate and environment. Before setting out with the team as its guide, Tenzing took a precious photo of his mother Kinzom, hoping for the blessings of the Rinpoche. Kinzom returned home, reassured after confirming that her son's health permitted him to climb Mount Everest. Afterwards, Hillary and Tenzing jointly climbed Everest, becoming the first humans to make footprints on the summit.

For generations, Sherpas living in the Solu and Khumbu regions have been an especially proud and confident people. Thanks to their diligence, braveness, reliability and wisdom, they have forged a unique and irreplaceable position in Himalayan mountaineering and trekking, and are highly popular with foreign travellers in Nepal. It was their professionalism that kept them independent of other castes or ethnic groups that had greater political power.

In Solu and Khumbu, the Gompa is the centre of all cultural and religious activity. All the village ceremonies are held there according to tradition. The Sherpas have two important festivals. One is a new year festival called Losar, equivalent to the Chinese Spring Festival, for which Sherpas from far away must return home for reunion. The other is Dumje, which lasts six days in late July to celebrate the eminent monk Padmasambhava, who introduced Esoteric Buddhism to Tibet in the eight century, laid the foundation for Tibetan Buddhism and is therefore worshiped as the founding father of Esoteric Buddhism and the Nyingma tradition. When the festival arrives, the farm work has been finished, the peak mountaineering seasons have ended and the livestock have been driven to graze on the alpine pastures. During festivals, everyone gathers in the local Gompa to listen to the lamas chant sutras, drive away ghosts, pray to the gods for blessing and then dine together, drink wine, sing and dance. They believe that observing these rituals can bring prosperity, good health and beauty to the village and even the whole country.

We climbed up along the steep mountain road to Tengboche Gompa. The famous temple that overlooks ravines, the entire valley and numerous rivers was destroyed by fire in 1989, yet it became even more imposing and stylish after reconstruction. Behind it stand Ama Dablam, Everest, Nuptse, Lhotse and other mountains. It is set amid wild azalea shrubs, while yak herds grazed on the slopes or wandered in the temple as if there was no one else around. Few temples anywhere can offer a panoramic view of two mountains above 8,000 metres at the same time. Yaks were wandering about in this temple with white walls and a golden ceiling. There is a busy campsite and many lodges there. During the full moon in October or November, Sherpas celebrate the three-day Mani Rimdu festival there. Sutra chanting to music takes place in the Gompa at this time, and Buddhists wearing silk clothes and coloured masks perform sacrificial dances. Pasang warned that many Sherpas and foreign trekkers would swarm to Tengboche, so the scores of lodges around would be packed and we would probably be in the company of yaks, counting the stars at a campsite if we failed to book a room.

Fortunately, we managed to get hold of some newly baked Tibetan bread and drink a pot of warm buttered tea in Tengboche Lodge with its back to Mount Ama Dablam. The scripture hall in the Gompa kept thousands of volumes of Tengyur and Kangyur Buddhist scriptures in Tibetan, with Thang-Ga pictures of the Buddha dating back to the sixteenth century hanging on the wall. The Buddha was sitting serenely under the *bodhi* with the clouds rising around him. We walked in the Gompa with overwhelming warmth. In the Buddha's awakening, the light of the snow mountain reflected on the wall of scriptures through the window lattice in the pattern of the Eight Auspicious Symbols of Buddhism. Egor and I stopped at a 1.5-metre-high statue of Mandkesvara who looked angry and had the frenzied appearance of a man in sexual congress. It made me catch my breath.

Mandkesvara, also known as father-mother and only worshiped in Tibetan Buddhist temples, is a statue comprising two bodies: Vidyā-rāja and his consort hugging each other and becoming one. Most people regard Mandkesvara as a Buddhist statue of a man and woman making love face to face. Egor asked me who was the woman being hugged by Mandkesvara and whether she was Avalokitesvara that admonished the vile creature.

I could not help laughing. I thought this was not just how a Westerner would think but what anyone would feel on first seeing the statue.

Actually, the appearance of Mandkesvara was just a symbol. Vidyā-rāja was sitting in the lotus position and his consort was holding a dharma vessel in one hand and with the other embracing his neck, with her legs around his waist. They were hugging, their chests close to each other, completely naked in sexual intercourse. Esoteric Buddhism advocates 'becoming Buddha through physical practice', that is to say, disciples can become Buddha when they practise with their bodies. In the view of disciples, their bodies seem to be ships or bridges crossing a river. The man's body represents the masculine gender, reason and mercy, while the woman's body represents the feminine gender, the womb and wisdom. The embrace of man and woman symbolises the combination of *dharma* and wisdom and the unity of the two features hidden in the innermost being. 'Joy' in the appellation of 'Mandkesvara' refers not just to the sexual love between men and women but also to a three-dimensional Buddhist fable, flying against the wind, witnessing the blissful realm of nirvana where body and soul unite, and generating sensational and spiritual astonishment in the form of imaginary sexual intercourse between men and women in the real gestures of yoga.

Thang-Gas of Mandkesvara are often hung in alcoves in the homes of Sherpas, Gurungs and the Marga people. 'Joy' is also part of the belief of 'the God of Sex' originating from the integration and pleasure of heaven and earth, yin and yang, man and woman, body and soul, up and down, left and right, water and soil, and wind and cloud.

When we encountered Mandkesvara in Tengboche, our 200-kilometre trek was coming to an end. I didn't think that a Christian would be able to really understand the 'God of Sex'. Unexpectedly, Egor turned his head towards the mountains outside the Gompa. Facing the sunlight, he pointed to the mountains in the distance and said: "God is with us forever. We were created by Him, and He will grant everything to us because He always loves us." I saw his deep green sunglasses reflect the perfect kiss of the cuspidal edge of the snow mountain and the azure sky. The two resonant souls of the mountains and the sky were the paradise of each other.

Maybe this is the religion and philosophy the Himalayas want to tell us and the optimistic life we should experience in person. The gods and the Buddha are living in a mortal world and travel between heaven and earth together with human beings, animals, flowers, rocks, paths, temples, mountains and the sky, filling our bodies, mind and soul with inborn pleasure and joy.

After leaving Tengboche, we walked along a path to a water-powered prayer wheel near the Imja Khola. Going downhill, I was full of spirit and energy, cheerful and carefree. Pasang asked why I was so happy and wasn't complaining about the toils of travel. I said the sooner I came to Namche Bazaar, the sooner I would start enjoying myself. I could take a hot bath, drink hot *chhaang* rice wine and eat spicy curried mutton. Egor was speechless, with the melancholy of parting hidden in his light blue eyes. I knew it was because our trek would come to an end in Namche Bazaar and that we would go back in the next two days.

We returned to Namche Bazaar having walked in the high-altitude holy mountains for eight days. Namche Bazaar was still lively and bustling, where trekkers came and went, the shops sold climbing gear and delicious food, and the air permeated with the strong smells of freshly-made German bread, Swiss chocolate, French pies, Russian sardines and Italian sausages. Shops renting anti-slip climbing shoes, climbing boots and sleeping bags were still crowded. Large and small shops sold everything you would expect to find, such as oxygen tanks, second-hand travel books, novels and Tibetan jewellery. After we confirmed our tickets back to Kathmandu for the day after the next with the aviation office in Lukla, we went to the Club Paradise near the Everest Bakery. It was the liveliest nightclub in Namche Bazaar. We hugged each other, drank beer, played snooker, sang loudly and line-danced to celebrate our successful journey.

Fearing that I might be knocked over in the revelry, Egor held me up and let me stand and dance on his feet. He smelled like the snow mountains. During the trek, he had lost four kilograms. Dancing on his climbing boots, I found he was no longer as tall as a giant. He was gentle, lithe and as innocent as a teenager. A local band member rushed over to push Egor before a shabby drum kit. He waved the wooden drumsticks and played along to *Come As You Are* by Nirvana and my favourite *Bonfire Heart* by James Blunt.

I knew he was fulfilling his promise to play them for me, for the great mountains and for every mountaineer present. I hadn't expected that a mountain climber could play drums so well! Before my eyes was a thirteen-year-old Croatian playing the drums in his basement with the surrounding gunfire licking the heavens. Everything was like that Kurt Cobain song: "Come as you are, as you were, / As I want you to be, / As a friend, as an old enemy, / Take your time, hurry up, / The choice is yours, don't be late, / Take a rest, as a friend, / As an old memoria, memoria, / Memoria, memoria." He controlled his tone, his strength, his speed, my breath when we climbed mountains and my heartbeat flaming like a bonfire.

. . .

The music in the night sky in Namche Bazaar seemed to come from the moonlight and the body, the lightning strokes after the meeting of the eyes of Salammbô and Mathomet, the collision of two identical stones and the extreme temptations of mermaids for sailors, filling our hearts. Our mutual affection when we were caught in wind, rain and snow, the heartthrobs and headaches when we struggled in the blue-green sky, the experience of traversing the snowline like two insects, my endless loneliness, romance and yearning for him when he went to Mount Chhukung, my pursuit of stories about previous mountaineers, the lips facing the sky, the stars we watched, our shoulders leaning against each other, the flame burning when we embraced each other, the tightly clasped hands and the faith and affections blooming all the way flooded our fingertips and toes like the snow mountains and as my permanent memory.

Only music can go beyond time, space and soul, only music can make time stop. Let's live in the masculine drumbeats of the Himalayas, never open our eyes and never bid farewell.

DAY SIXTEEN-SEVENTEEN

BEING AT HOME: COME AS YOU ARE

"Learning the world through fear." The man reached the peak of the world's ninth highest mountain, Nanga Parbat (8,125 metres) for the first time at the age of twenty-six in 1970, and sixteen years later he became the first to conquer all the world's fourteen highest mountains. He continued: "I am Sisyphus in Greek mythology, and it is my fate to push the rock unceasingly to the mountain top." The person in question was the Italian mountaineer Reinhold Messner.

Walking on the same path as Mr Mountain, who was devoted to mountaineering and expedition, we felt the blood coursing through our bodies. There were snow mountains to the front, to the rear and to the sides. Each mountain was surrounded and surpassed by other mountains, which made it unbearable for us. Looking up each time, I held respect and devotion in my eyes. Trekking is like a gorgeous, adventurous journey and it is our task in life to firmly push forward the mysterious rolling stone.

When we trekked back from Namche Bazaar, the road was long and mostly downhill. The scenery was the same but our mental state was totally different. Our bodies seemed to have thoroughly remoulded themselves and become lithe. Egor said the step-counter in the soles of his Nike shoes calculated that we would take about 20,000 paces in a journey of fifteen kilometres in each of the following days. Our brains were also stimulated. Exercise, like morphine, releases endorphins, which trigger a positive feeling in the body.

"Definitely," Egor continued, "sex is also appealing because that too generates endorphins. So sex is a topic people take delight in talking about. When we do yoga, sit in meditation, eat spicy food, travel, listen to music and entertain ourselves, the concentration of endorphins in our brain increases. Anything exciting or interesting can stimulate endorphin secretion."

He talked as he walked, looking back at me now and then, filled with a trekker's elation. For the previous sixteen days, Egor had been carrying his Mammoth backpack and did not leave it even for a single moment. Even when he climbed the toughest Cho La Pass, he didn't ask Pasang to carry it for him. For my part, I was more skilled travelling when we went downhill. I walked much faster than fifteen days before and was able to keep up with Egor. The silver grey backpack clinging to his body and swaying before my eyes seemed to be his endorphins and his whole person in microcosm. I called out to him: "Hey, tall man, Superman, Spiderman, you're two days behind your original schedule of fifteen days. Was it because of a woman? Is she your endorphin?"

We, men and women, trudging distances of up to three hundred kilometres, are as addicted to trekking as some people are to morphine. We rejoice in the happiness of every cell in our bodies. Trekking has existed since mankind first learned to walk upright. People still choose to trek in the era of industry, wheels, engines, computers and satellites just because of its irresistible charm.

Egor was wearing quick-dry shorts, and the song *You Are Beautiful* was playing from the side pocket of his backpack. Feeling elated, he had taken off his shoes and socks and was walking on the stony ground in his bare feet. The distance we walked on the mountain path in one hour was more than that covered by the average American in a whole day.

In his book *A Walk in the Woods*, the author Bill Bryson said that whatever distance modern Americans travel in a week, they cover ninety-three per cent of it in their cars, and walk the rest of the way, totalling an average of only 6.6 kilometres. "It's ridiculous to walk only nine hundred and forty yards a day!" said an emotional Bill. As a matter of fact, when we carry everything we need on the mountain path rather than speed by in a car, our minds and endorphins are more agile and faster than vehicles. When our bodies enjoy the love endowed by the cosmos, our inborn energy will really exceed our imagination.

Turn your back against the sun

There was a checkpoint at the entrance to Namche Bazaar, where we got a yellow-green trekking certificate that listed the altitudes of the six landmarks: Mount Gokyo Ri (5,360 metres), Cho La Pass (5,420 metres), Everest Base Camp (5,340 metres), Mount Kala Pattar (5,545 metres), Kongma La Pass (5,535 metres) and Mount Chhukung Ri (5,546 metres).

Egor, a sergeant and drummer, put a tick against each landmark higher than 5,000 metres. I couldn't believe that I, an indoorsy, fragile woman, a shadow, a 'mangy dog' walking and deliberately making a scene, a slug inching along while crying, a poor fellow with a splitting headache and a nosebleeding 'terrorist' surprisingly followed him and marked three ticks in succession.

The ladykiller said: "Hey, Pearl, you should change your name. You should no longer be named after a jewel. You've already been a boulder on a five thousand-metre-high mountain."

Why didn't he give me a better name? For instance, Rolling Stone, Goddess or Trekking Queen?

The route down from Namche Bazaar became steadily easier, which gave me more strength to joke with this handsome man.

The path to Lukla forked at the villages of Phakding and Cheplung. Turning right and trekking for three or four days, we would come to Shivalaya Village. The group formerly known as the Three Monks puffed all the way. Turning left and entering Dudh Valley, we would walk to Lukla in no more than a day and return home by plane.

The magic land was still picturesque, the magnificent sink-shaped ice peak reached to the sky at a vertical height of more than 3,000 metres, and the pine forests permeated with fragrance. It was no longer the savage, wild land of five hundred years ago. All kinds of crops were planted on the narrow, long and stepped land, where potatoes and yaks provided a source of living. The Sherpas planted potatoes, wheat and corn in low-altitude Solu for their own consumption and supplied the residents of other regions with the surplus produce. But the high-altitude Khumbu region was only suitable for growing buckwheat, radishes and potatoes. The potatoes did not grow there originally but were brought in by European explorers. The small potatoes on the barren land at an altitude above 3,000 metres were nurtured in the sun, ice and snow. Bright yellow inside, seasoned with rock salt, the potatoes tasted like chestnuts and were the richest and most delicious food we ate on our journey. The crop is usually harvested in September or October. Digging potatoes is an onerous job and Sherpa men disdain all farm work. The harvesting women were in high spirits, labouring and singing, with the cheerful songs lingering in the valley.

On the way to Namche Bazaar, we encountered a great many porters who hurried on, carrying wood felled from low-altitude areas. Each log measuring about two metres weighed at least forty kilograms. I felt extremely concerned at the sight of them walking skilfully on the cliffs as if on a tightrope. The porters sweated and laboured for just two dollars a day.

A variety of trekkers, yaks, pack animals, monks in red robes and barefoot Sherpas whose waists were bent by the weight of kerosene tanks and drinks cans came up and down the path. Mr Mountain, Reinhold Messner, once said with emotion that Namche Bazaar was like a highway, crowded with so many tourists that it resembled a London traffic jam.

For better or worse, Khumbu's economy and culture depends on about 18,000 trekkers and mountaineers who pass through in different seasons of the year. To satisfy the increasing demands of foreign mountaineers and trekkers, a variety of lodges, tea houses and dining halls have been established. Most of the trees in the valley have been felled for firewood or used to build multi-storey houses. The number of trees in the mountain areas along the trekking route has dropped drastically. Experts on environmental conservation and culture who have visited Khumbu are worried about the changes brought by the travelling craze and the increasing number of Western mountaineers drawn to this land of idyllic beauty. The forests and the mountains of Nepal are the pillars of its tourism industry as well as being a natural resource in their own right. Nonetheless, with a rising number of tourists, more and more trees are being felled. Nepal is endangered by a vicious circle caused by poverty. Mountaineering expeditions and tourism have affected natural resources and local society.

Most of the local trees were chopped down before Nepal's national park system was established, which specified that no trees should be felled for energy or building materials purposes. It takes sixty years for new trees to grow fully at such high altitudes. Now, all teams entering the mountains are required to take their own fuel, such as paraffin, diesel oil or gas cookers. The lodges along the way are ordered to replace wood with kerosene for their heating and cooking, and small-sized power stations and solar stations are now more common, chiefly for lighting. The Sherpas in Khumbu are becoming increasingly wealthy from rising tourism, but contact with foreigners, especially Westerners, has accelerated change in the local culture, even in the deepest part of small villages. Young people gathering in the Namche snooker hall and the shuffleboard parlour wear American jeans and Chicago Bulls T-shirts and AC Milan tops rather than traditional, elegant Tibetan robes. Indian songs and the latest Hollywood blockbusters are played in video halls. People living on the high mountains do not want to be isolated from modern society. The wise, brave Sherpas do not want to become museum specimens like the Mayas or Native Americans.

. . .

"Nepal is a country of mountains, and their presence provides a natural boundary. The rivers originating in those mountains water South Asia and Southeast Asia. To live with those mountains is to know the gods and all the challenges that the gods throw at humans.

To walk in those mountains is to know our limitations. Nepal has suffered from many of those human limitations and yet its mountains remain and continue to teach us. Now they tell us about the crisis of climate change and what will happen if we don't take care of our environment."

In Namche Bazaar, like an alpine holiday resort, I happened to receive an email from a French writer. She had once served as a cultural ambassador in Nepal and China. We formed a friendship in China through literature. Although unable trek to Everest Base Camp in person, she passed on her sincerest wishes to Nepal, where we once lived and where we are trekking!

Clouds drifted above my head and rotated in the light autumn rays. The Three Monks walking towards the sun trekked step by step through the recovering Khumbu Forest and came to Lukla situated above the Dudh Valley.

Lukla is a small, bustling village of only one street situated on a hill at an altitude of 2,866 metres. More than thirty lodges, dining halls, cafes and bars are built alongside the 'L-shaped' runway, extending from its memorial arch to the airport no bigger than a rural bus station. In the afterglow of the setting sun, I took a deep breath, relieved at having endured the pressure of sixteen days of travel. Breathing the light wind rich in oxygen ions, I took pleasure in the joy of low-altitude walking. It was so good and I shouted: "Amazing!"

Egor asked me whether I'd had enough of walking.

"Is that all?" I responded.

"Let's do it all again," he said.

I was moved to tears. The next morning, we would return to our respective motherlands. I felt the melancholy of parting. At that time, I only saw the setting sun cast the last warm rays in the boundless blue sky like the soft blond hair of Venus.

Parting at one of the world's most dangerous airports

I was frightened about flying from Lukla, ranked as the riskiest airport in the world.

Lukla Airport is situated on a cliff over a 700-metre-high abyss, down to the Dudh Valley. Usually, the standard length of an international airport runway is around 2,500 metres. But the L-shaped runway of Lukla Airport is only twenty metres wide and 475 metres long. The runway has a gradient of 12 degrees, which helps planes to slow down when landing and gathering speed during take-off. Since the plane needs to drop by about 2,760 metres before landing on the runway, a miscalculation of one or two metres might cause the plane to break through the perimeter railing and into the mountain. Once committed to descending the plane, the pilot must go through with the landing; there is no possibility of aborting the manoeuvre and having another go. If the plane fails to gather enough speed at the end of the runway for take-off, it will plunge into the abyss. Therefore, Lukla does not just have one of the world's shortest runways with one of the steepest slopes, it is also recognised as one of the most dangerous airports worldwide.

Most planes flying to Lukla are the nineteen-seater Twin Otter and Dornier Do 228 twin-engine aircraft. Since Hillary built the airport in the 1970s, many crashes have occurred due to the complex terrain and weather conditions. But to those eager to trek in the Himalayas and climb to the peak of the world, the thirty-five-minute flight to Kathmandu is an unforgettable experience and Lukla is just the beginning of numerous challenging expeditions.

Forty-two years ago, serene Lukla, as its Tibetan name suggests, was a 'shy' place hidden in the valley. But now it has become the most bustling village in Khumbu, where more than ten flights land and take off every day in peak seasons. The planes bring in trekkers, guides and all sorts of goods. Every Friday, hundreds of barefoot traders and porters line the roads in Lukla, carrying goods to places as far and remote as Namche Bazaar. Every morning, the dining halls and cafes near the airport are crowded with trekkers like Egor and me waiting for early flights. The changing wind direction often causes flights to be delayed or cancelled.

Flights are not as romantic as some might imagine, the blue sky is not as beautiful as that in one's dream and there's no paradise above the clouds. Danger occupies the thoughts of everyone around, and all we could do was drink coffee, eat cinnamon rolls and silently wait for the wind to die down and the clouds to thin in the high sky. Once a small plane lands on the runway safe and sound, the relieved passengers inside and outside the silver waiting lounge burst out into applause, while the local Sherpas quietly wait to receive their new customers.

With the sun emitting diamond-like rays of light on the frozen massif, the Tara Air plane I was due to board landed successfully. I hugged Pasang goodbye and choked back sobs. He was my porter when we started off and had only made a meagre income, but he was my brother by the time the trip ended. On the way, he was always willing and always smiling. I listened to his strange stories and his rendition of *Resham Firiri*, the traditional Nepali song. He had told me that he would ask a matchmaker to take a bottle of *chhaang* to the house of the girl he liked. I tasted the delicious potatoes he coated in chilli sauce for me. I drank the intoxicating *chhaang* and danced strange 'devil-expelling' dances with him in a shabby bar. I watched him carry a ten-kilogram backpack over mountain passes above 5,000 metres and staunch my bleeding nose with his coarse fingers. Without him, I would have been half dead and exposed to great difficulty. For all this, all I paid him was the equivalent of one tenth of the yak of his dreams.

Amid the noisy, crowded security checkpoint with a bag on my back, I didn't know how to bid farewell to Egor. There is only a narrow metal gate to Lukla Airport through which arriving and departing travellers can squeeze through. My nerves were shot at the prospect of parting for ever. Egor held my hands in his big, warm hands and said: "Pearl, I'll catch you in China. That's my mission."

I was heart-broken. Only missionaries, sergeants, mountaineers, James Bond, knights, drummers and volunteers would use the word 'mission' to describe his steadfast loyalty and determination to keep on travelling.

The plane took off. I saw Pasang put his palms together devoutly outside the runway and make a standard, formal Hindu greeting '*Namaste*'. Both he and Egor would soon be out of sight, but Pasang's devout and kind feelings and his courtesy deeply impressed me.

Maintain your way of life

I returned to Chongqing two days later. The first email I received was from Egor's iPhone. He said he had landed safe and sound and had returned to his city, Zagreb. I asked him about the distance and time that separated our two cities. He replied that there was a difference of 6,900 kilometres and six hours, and that a vast ocean lay between us.

For the subsequent six months, we communicated in this manner. We wrote an email every two weeks as if we were greeting each other face to face. We didn't make phone calls. We didn't send lots of texts, we didn't use Facebook or Twitter. During this period, I accompanied my mother until the end of her life. On the morning of 14 January 2013, I received ten sample books by express delivery from the publishing house. I placed a copy of one of these thick books, completed with my blood and tears, at the head of her bed and said it was dedicated to her.

She smiled feebly like an innocent child. She said she would buy five books for her five favourite students. I said she didn't need to buy them because the books were dedicated to her and the students who had helped her. In the small hours before dawn, on a cold, wet and windy night, she said to my husband who was attending to her: "Go and sleep. I'll sleep too." Then she quietly slept and her life ended. My mother passed away after a painful one-year struggle against cancer. She gallantly donated her body to Chongqing Medical University and asked us to scatter her ashes in the sea.

I dressed her in her favourite white coat, rose red scarf and tawny glasses. With my tears flowing like a river, we silently waited for the Chongqing Medical University staff to take her away. We could not hold a farewell ceremony for her because the donated body must be removed without delay. I could only kneel before her body, touch her face and pledge: "Mum, I'll donate my body as you have done to help more people in need."

Seeing the receivers come in with a shabby stretcher made from an old plank, I didn't want them to take my mother away. After all, my mother painted flowers, birds, mountains and rivers and transcribed Buddhist scriptures all her life. How clean, simple yet elegant her innermost being was and how she loved beauty, life and other people. I didn't expect that the plank used by Chongqing Medical University to take away bodies would be so thin and stiff, without even a plain flower on it.

In anguish and unable to do anything, I hesitated before my mother's body. I seemed to see the Buddha in the painting *Flowers for the Buddha* that she reproduced walk over to me. It was a world of no more than twenty square centimetres. The Deity of Cloud in the seventh century was ready to present some flowers to the Dipamkara Buddha who was walking and begging for alms. Fearing that the Buddha's feet might get dirty on the way, the Deity of Cloud loosened his long hair and spread it on the muddy road so that the Buddha and others could walk on it. Later, the Dipamkara Buddha predicted that the devout Deity of Cloud would become a Buddha too after going through myriad disasters. The Deity of Cloud was Buddha Sakyamuni in a former life.

Profoundly touched at that moment, I thought that although 1,400 years had elapsed, we should never lose faith in kindness and sincerity, and we should firmly believe that the power of kindness and the warmth of love are a shelter for our tired souls no matter whether we held religious beliefs, or whether we were followers of Buddhism or not. I thought my mother's state of mind was broad and selfless. How would she mind the trivial crudity and bleakness?

In the small, narrow lift, I held my mother's cold hand and said to the stretcher carriers: "My mother liked painting and quietness. Please move her gently." A white ambulance took her away in the rain. I thought it might change direction at the turning ahead. My husband helped me cross the road in the hope of having one last look at her. But the vehicle didn't change direction and it disappeared into the rain…

I didn't dare think of where my mother was being taken because my heart would hurt. Her ashes had not been sent to me before Mother's Day so all I could do was put a bunch of lilies in front of the small red certificate of donation and commemorate her in the sun and the dust. There is a story of an American couple who took their son on holiday to Italy where the son was tragically shot. The mother agreed to donate his organs and they were used to save the lives of seven people. American driving licences are printed with the word 'Donor' and a red heart. Annually, about 10,000 donors donate their organs but about 100,000 patients still wait for life-saving donations. About five million Chinese have lost their sight. Although those fortunate patients receiving organ transplantations are not permitted to know the names, home towns or ethnicity of their benefactors, they will convey their sincerest thanks to the unknown good-natured people from the bottom of their hearts.

My mother was the 903rd person to donate her organs in Chongqing, which has a population of thirty million. The donors are ordinary people, mothers, fathers, sons and daughters, cancer patients, leukaemia patients and cardiac patients. Their medical donation will help other ordinary people.

I cry whenever I watch *Todo Sobre mi Madre (All About My Mother)* directed by Pedro Almodovar. It always reminds me of my mother. Dear Mum, if we were to be mother and daughter in the afterlife, our roles should change. I would be the mother and you the daughter. I would give birth to you, take care of you, attend to you, love you, help you, support you, embrace you, shelter you from the wind and rain, heal your pain... Mum, thank you for endowing me with my talent and the quality of mercy and for embracing the world, which will be my wealth for life. When we were together, it was like one drop of water or one beam of light merging with another.

Like the Buddhist sculpture she copied and the nirvana depicted in the Buddhist paintings she painted every day, my mother disappeared from this world. The person who loved me most had left me, and everything was now different. I felt incomparably sad. Egor had been constantly writing to me, telling me that he had thought he had lost me in the crowd before we met for the second time in the Peace Garden, but the merciful God gave him a secret power to find me again in this chaotic world.

He said that his heart beat the fastest on sunny afternoons, at a rate of 180 per minute, much faster than when he reached the highest peaks in Europe. However, the winged horses that could hear the sound of God and find the source of spirituality were immortal. He told me that he'd placed the White Tara I had given him one dark night in Namche Bazaar on his drum kit and the extraordinary 'Buddha's head' was inspected several times at Customs because it looked like a cultural relic. The White Tara wore its black hair in a coil, eyes slightly closed, looking pure white and always smiling gently at him, as peaceful, quiet and clean as the moonlight and like a white eight-petal lotus.

When I knew that Egor had formed a new band, I unhesitatingly named it Shiva, the God of Destruction and Salvation and the symbol of sex, strength and love in Hinduism! I joked that an American pop singer was called 'Lady Gaga'. In Chinese, the character '婆' pronounced 'po' in 'Shiva' does not refer to 'wife' or womanishly fussy Lady Gaga. It refers to the lithe and graceful universe and the 'ephemerality', 'human society' and 'the mortal world' we live in. I would search his band on YouTube because music can be appreciated beyond national boundaries and beyond language.

Even when not climbing mountains, I will raise my head high

In today's highly connected world dominated by social media, I prefer to communicate by email. 'Speed is soon forgotten while slowness stays in the memory!' I can imagine the mountains where Egor walks for a thousand kilometres, with my hand in his. How romantic it is to tramp over hills and dales to see one's lover, staying together and watching the clouds and stars! Similarly, when we trekked on our journey, I got to know other lifestyles in this world. To be brave and pure! To listen to the call of the heart! To have faith, unaffected by the outside environment! To be true to oneself! Those who live the most meaningful lives must derive the most inspiration from life and dedicate the most to life.

I've finally returned to an ordinary, trivial life among the crowds. Even though I was no longer climbing mountains, when I was on the subway or just feeling sad, I would raise my head, search for the green mountains, cast my eye to the sky and look in the direction of the mountain top. It meant that I would leave the land of skyscrapers, follow my innermost desires, get close to the Himalayas and fly to its scenic spots.

The world of ice and snow was a garden belonging to Egor and me. Even though we were far apart once we had finished trekking, our mutual affection was preserved.

Some people are destined to belong to the wilderness and mountains.

ITINERARY

Bus route
Kathmandu to Jiri to Shivalaya (200km, 14.5hr)

Low altitude Trekking route
Shivalaya (1,767 metres) to Bhandar (2,190 metres) to Kinja (1,570 metres) to Sete Temple (2,575 metres) to Junbesi (2,675 metres) to Nunthala (2,250 metres) to Kharikhola (2,070 metres) to Bupsa (2,300 metres) to Cheplung (2,660 metres) to Phakding (2,800 metres) to Monjo (2,880 metres) to Jorsale (2,810 metres) to Namche Bazaar (3,480 metres)

Distance/Duration
71 kilometres/6 days

High altitude Trekking route
Namche Bazaar (3,480 metres) to Sanasa (3,600 metres) to Phortse Thenga (3,680 metres) to Tongba (3,950 metres) to Dole (4,090 metres) to Machhermo (4,330 metres) to Pangka (4,390 metres) to Gokyo (4,750 metres) to Gokyo Ri (5,360 metres) to Gokyo (4,750 metres) to Tagnag (4,700 metres) to Cho La Pass (5,420 metres) to Dzonglha (4,830 metres) to Lobuche (4,930 metres) to Gorak Shep (5,160 metres) to Everest Base Camp (5,340 metres) to Gorak Shep (5,160 metres) to Mount Kala Pattar (5,545 metres) to Gorak Shep (5,160 metres) to Lobuche (4,930 metres) to Duglha (4,620 metres) to Pheriche (4,240 metres) to Dingboche (4,360 metres) to Pangboche (3,860 metres) to Tengboche (3,870 metres) to Sanasa (3,600 metres) to Namche Bazaar (3,480 metres)

Distance/Duration
130 kilometres/8 days

Return route
Namche Bazaar (3,480 metres) to Monjo (2,880 metres) to Phakding (2,800 metres) to Cheplung (2,660 metres) to Lukla (2,866 metres) to Kathmandu (1,337 metres)

Distance/Duration
25 kilometres/1 day

POSTSCRIPT

WE LIVE TO MEET EACH OTHER

I always hold the view that travelling has two purposes. First, it is an indispensable process, like education in childhood. Second, it gives us spiritual wealth, helping us identify qualities such as elegance, leniency, sympathy, tenacity, erudition and courage.

I spent two years writing on my travels in the Himalayas. Before finishing, I went back to Nepal three times and experienced a period when my mother was very sick and then passed away from cancer. It was the porters and guides on the mountains, my relatives, my husband, random strangers and fellow travellers who held my hand, sent me to the top of the world and enabled me to meet myself, and give me love and enlightenment. Chance encounters and departures are part of life.

When you read this book, I imagine your heart, as wild as mine, is freely riding in the moonlight and trampling on ice and snow, with your eyes following the Himalayas. I think your body will finally get there one day. Everything in the world will appear and then disappear. The lovers will find love. But as the Buddha in Nirvana says, the world is great and life is sweet.

Here, I'd like to convey thanks to my fellow mountaineers for their friendly assistance. They include: writing camp owners: Li Yili, Lai Hong; hand illustrations and maps: Su Nan, Hu Hong, Long Shengjie and Wang Jing; photos: Thomas, Scott, Basanta and Egor.

There is one person in my life who gives me indescribable love and kindness. He is my husband, Hu Hong, an oil painter. I met him in college at sixteen when he was twenty. Since then, I've called him 'Elder Brother'. We've accompanied each other ever since. He's my lover, elder brother, closest friend, companion, knight, psychologist, spiritual mentor and greatest supporter in my travel, life and writing. He gives me his love for life, and he is the one sent by God to take care of me.

My thanks should also go to the authors of the following books: *Trekking in the Nepal Himalaya* published by Lonely Planet; *Into Thin Air* by the American writer Jon Krakauer; *La Marche Dans Le Ciel* by the French authors Alexandre Poussin and Sylvain Tesson. Their trekking and experience in the Himalayas offered significant guidance and help to me, and their stories have been a source of warmth and encouragement during my long, solitary life of writing.

In April 2015, ninety-two years after Mallory set out for Mount Everest, an 8.1 magnitude earthquake struck Nepal, causing more than twenty thousand deaths and injuries, affecting more than eight million people. Twelve world cultural heritage sites were destroyed. In Nepal, the land of the Buddha and a place of idyllic beauty, about one million foreign travellers visit each year for trekking, mountaineering and travel. It has some of the world's most picturesque scenery, important world cultural heritage sites and a strong atmosphere of religion. Yet it is also one of the poorest countries. Local residents, guides and porters carry the equipment, backpacks and luggage for multitudes of travellers and help them complete their journeys in the Himalayas. Without Nepal, without the kind and friendly Nepalese people, no one could go to the Himalayas or reach the highest peaks.

After the earthquake, I was disappointed not to be able to visit Nepal once more. Having travelled there, I was able to learn more about myself and the world around me. Together with China Translation & Publishing House, I diverted funds from the sale of *Himalayan Quest* to support the people of Nepal. Readers and I have donated about 5,000 yuan from book sales through the Tencent Earthquake Aid Package. The money went on supplying water to the region. I believe that the world cannot be changed by the great efforts of the few but by the small endeavours of the many.

. . .

In 2016, I was finally in a position to pack my map for a long journey, travel across one tenth of the earth and arrive in Nepal for the fourth time. Much of the country was in ruins after the earthquake, but amid the grief there was also rebirth and opportunity. I trekked for ten days to Upper Mustang District with my guide Bishnu, then served as an international volunteer in Pokhara Municipality, helped the locals learn Chinese, and thereby in a small way helped this small country dependent on tourism recover from the disaster.

We should not merely enjoy the gorgeous scenery and religious culture of Nepal but also see its backwardness, suffering and educational shortcomings. Some journeys are about material enjoyment but this time it was about spiritual fulfilment. Imbued with a sense of responsibility and gratitude, this travel was more like another kind of education, after which my life and orientation would change.

Lastly, I should give special thanks to my chief editor, Mr Zhang Gaoli, my editor in chief, Guo Yujia, and copyright editor, Fan Wei of China Translation & Publishing House. In the four years following the publication of the Chinese edition of this book in 2014, they did a lot of work, raised funds for its translation, finally won a translation subsidy from the Fine Contemporary Chinese Literature Translation Project sponsored by the Chinese Writers' Association, and enabled an English version of my stories about the Himalayas to be published.

Before the translation of this book, I spent two months polishing, modifying and adding new content to the original Chinese version. I've been trekking and modifying the manuscript as an act of spiritual self-transcendence. We all need to know ourselves, the world and everything around us through the act of trekking.

I have been to Nepal four times in the last nine years. Whenever I am there, I seem to feature in the tales told in *One Thousand and One Nights*, seemingly returning to my previous stay, especially on nights illuminated by the moon and stars. 'Himalaya', an eight-letter word, is like a small silhouette of the splendid skyline of the eight mountains above 8,000 metres. Whatever happens to Nepal, home of the Himalayan Valley, the Buddhist sound enshrouding and curling up in the brown temple would make me intoxicated in its composed, serene atmosphere.

The Nepalese advocate keeping composed under all circumstances. This land of unrivalled serenity is the abode of deities in this mortal world, and the land of ideals and dreams of all mortals.

ACKNOWLEDGMENTS
PHOTO CREDITS

Thomas
Pages 26, 41, 74, 251

Scott
Pages 97, 98, 99

Igor
Pages 101, 256, 261, 271, 274, 277, 278, 279, 287

All other photos by Pearl Hong Chen

ABOUT THE AUTHOR

Pearl Hong Chen is a Chinese travel writer and founder of the Hong Chen International Writing Camp. She pursues what she regards as an ideal lifestyle – spending half her time travelling and the other half writing in her study.

Previously, she was a magazine editor for ten years and a senior visiting scholar for one year at St. Cloud State University in Minnesota. Currently, she is professor for Journalism and Mass Communication at Chongqing Technology and Business University.

Pearl Hong Chen has published a series of books under the category of 'travel literature', based on her own personal experiences on the road.

Her books include: *On the Road: Stories in American Universities*; *Fragrance of Nepal*; *Yoga Code in the Holy Land of India*; *Across Paradisal Tibet*; *Across Paradisal Xinjiang*; *Himalayan Quest*; and *Incense for Buddha*.

Across Paradisal Tibet is highly popular among travellers, while *Himalayan Quest* was listed as one of China's Top 100 Lifestyle Good Reads in 2014. *Incense for Buddha* received the accolade 'Excellent Book' at the 2018 Beijing International Book Fair.

WeChat: reddust66
Public Account: hongchenguoji
E-mail: reddust66@qq.com